LIMITED E____

MAXTREME QUALITY X

BOGANOMICS

THE SCIENCE OF
THINGS BOGANS LIKE

E. CHAS McSWEEN, ENRON HUBBARD,
FLASH JOHNSON, HUNTER McKENZIE-SMYTHE,
INTRAVENUS DE MILO and special guest contributor
MICHAEL JAYFOX

hachette
AUSTRALIA

hachette
AUSTRALIA

Published in Australia and New Zealand in 2011
by Hachette Australia
(an imprint of Hachette Australia Pty Limited)
Level 17, 207 Kent Street, Sydney NSW 2000
www.hachette.com.au

10 9 8 7 6 5 4 3 2 1

National Library of Australia
Cataloguing-in-Publication data:

Boganomics / E. Chas McSween … [et al.]

978 0 7336 2670 8 (pbk.)

Contributors: Enron Hubbard, Flash Johnson,
Hunter McKenzie-Smythe, Intravenus De Milo,
and Michael Jayfox

Personality and culture.
Australian wit and humor.
Australia – Social life and customs – Humor.

McSween, E. Chas.
Hubbard, Enron.
Johnson, Flash.
De Milo, Intravenus.
Jayfox, Michael.

305.50994

Cover design by Design by Committee
Cover photograph courtesy of istockphoto.com
Text design by Kirby Jones
Typeset in Officiana Serif by Kirby Jones
Printed in Australia by Griffin Press, Adelaide, an Accredited ISO AS/NZS 4001:2004 Environmental Management Systems printer

CONTENTS

INTRODUCTION

Thursday, 22 June 2006
Location: QV retail complex in central Melbourne
A queue hundreds of bogans long snakes its way up and down the walkways of the complex, doubling back on itself in open spaces wide enough to allow the bogans to do so. A Krispy Kreme doughnut store has just opened in the building, and the bogan is queuing for up to three hours to take advantage of the free introductory doughnut promotion that the store is running. Three hours in a queue, for a $3 doughnut.

Wednesday, 30 September 2009, 8.30 p.m.
Location: Lounge rooms the nation over
Over two million bogans tune their televisions to Channel Nine to watch *Hey Hey It's Saturday* – a show that was cancelled twelve years earlier because not enough bogans were watching. And it's Wednesday.

Thursday, 3 December 2009
Location: QV retail complex in central Melbourne. Again.
Ed Hardy opens its own Vodka Bar and Rockstar Bowling. Bogans queue around the corner to get in and listen to loud thumping noises and dress in garish colours.

Early April, 2006
Location: Chapel Street, Prahran
Lucky Coq opens. A bar, built on the site of the venerable rock venue The Duke of Windsor, dedicated to large biceps, short skirts, overpriced alcohol and underpriced pizzas.

Saturday, 27 November 2010
Location: Channel Nine programming department
Hey Hey, It's Saturday having completed its run of ten Wednesday screenings and ten Saturday screenings, is cancelled, as bogans realise that it was never any good in the first place.

Wednesday, 30 July 2008
Location: Everywhere
Coca-Cola, tired of being absent or a bit-playing failure in the booming energy drinks market, re-releases its Mother energy drink. The flavour is slightly altered. The packaging contains words like 'double the hit™' and 'heaps of energy™'. And it is twice the size of its former self and its competitors. Three year later, Mother controls 24% of the $120 million energy drink market.

Sometime in early 2010
Location: QV retail complex in central Melbourne
Ed Hardy Vodka Bar and Rockstar Bowling renames itself. To Rockstar Bowling.

Thursday, 12 August 2010
Location: Shopping malls everywhere
Ed Hardy Australia, having clad one too many bogans in demure attire featuring horned, sabre-toothed animals, has become passé, and collapses into administration.

Monday, 1 November 2010
Location: Krispy Kreme boardroom
Having successfully killed at least 370 000 bogans through induced cardiac arrest, Krispy Kreme begins to run out of clientele and collapses into administration.

Welcome to *Boganomics*

Boganomics is not a sequel to *Things Bogans Like,* the inexplicably popular misadventure in amateur sociology that launched a million boats, caused a million dinner-party discussions and likely resulted in a million violent interactions. This is far more profound, educational and important a tome.

It is not about purple suits, large energy drinks, Coldplay or cheap petrol, yet it is, contradictorily, about all of those things. It is quite simply, as the subtitle suggests, a textbook – the science of all things bogan. Having spent over two years rigorously indexing and logging incidences of the national bogan footprint, we at the Boganomics Institute decided that we needed to look deeper. We had to stop discussing the 'what?', and consider the 'why?'. Although *'what the?'* seemed to be the inevitable conclusion to much of our more detailed research.

And so began the journey that became the book you now hold in your hands. What began as an analysis of bogan spending habits – hence the title – rapidly metamorphosed into an uncontainable behemoth, as it became apparent that the bogan scourge had infiltrated almost every facet of Australian life. So while we can categorically state that this book will offer an explanation of the appeal of all things 'limited edition' and/or 'platinum' to the bogan, we also attempt to deconstruct how the bogan manages to convince itself that it is Doing It Tough while simultaneously purchasing a 60" LCD screen on 48-month interest-free terms from Harvey Norman. Why it considers gambling to be the apotheosis of all money-making strategies. Why it is that the bogan feels entitled to negatively gear its third investment property while happily complaining about refugees being flown to Sydney for a funeral.

Inevitably, when exploring the evolution of anything you have to start at the beginning. It is just logical. And we are all for logic so we look at where the bogan came from, who its progenitors were, and where our shared ancestry begins. The answers may shock and surprise. But answers are hopefully what you will find, and when you look out your window to see people queuing to access tickets to a stage show 'telling the story' of a dead musician by performing inferior covers, or your favourite local pub is bought out, converted to a 'pizza bar' and stocked with under-dressed, over-melanin-ed 'socialites', you will recall their explanation in these pages. If someone famous like Nelson Mandela or Oprah Winfrey didn't say 'understanding is a bridge to unity' then they should have because bogans need new tattoo sayings. *Boganomics* is the bricks and stanchions of that bridge for all bogans and an important sociological exploration for non-bogans. Read this book to broaden your knowledge, pass the time with many pretty graphs, pictures, charts and diagrams, as well as the occasional activity to help you on your way, and immerse yourself in the science of things bogans like. It might help you sell stuff, or get on better with your in-laws. Hopefully it will provoke debate, dissension and the occasional laugh.

It may, in fact, kill fascists.

Intravenus De Milo, Enron Hubbard, Michael Jayfox, Flash Johnson, Hunter McKenzie-Smyth and E. Chas McSween.

Dublin   Trieste   Paris

1
HISTORY

The bogan is not a recent phenomenon. In its many forms and incarnations, the bogan has been around since the dawn of time. It has gone by many names — *homo boganus, mobile vulgus, el bogo* and *la bogue* to name a few — and many faces. But the annals of history are filled with peoples who bear the unmistakable mark of the bogan: an aversion to hard work; an inability to take responsibility for their own failings; a relentless desire to do everything on a leviathan scale; constant searching for shortcuts; overconsumption of resources; tendency to resort to anger and violence; and a penchant for garish fashion and crude sexploits.

The bogan hasn't always resembled the creature which menaces Australia today. The twenty-first century bogan is a sort of superbogan — the terrible culmination of thousands of years of evolution (or devolution, depending on your perspective). Just as humans evolved over millions of years through the process of natural selection, the bogan too has undergone a (slow) transformation since its emergence 30 000 years ago.

Rather than survival of the fittest, however, the bogan's story is one of survival of the loudest, laziest and most obnoxious. This might seem to fly in the face of evolutionary theory, but the bogan has always defied logic and science. In its various manifestations the bogan has been present across civilisations and epochs; a kind of cancer exhausting resources, destroying culture and undermining order. Throughout all of this it has contributed precious little to the sum of human knowledge, proving a constant impediment to progress and doing its best to destroy all that is beautiful, tasteful and aesthetically pleasing in this world.

This is the history of the bogan.

Ancient history

The bogan's story begins some time during the middle to upper Palaeolithic era, the period termed by historians and anthropologists as *ante-historique*. The earliest anatomically modern humans, *Homo sapiens*, emerged out of the earlier members of the genus *Homo* about 200 000 years ago in Africa. Around 70 000 years ago, these early humans are believed to have migrated out of Africa, subsequently spreading throughout Asia and, later, Europe. However, parts of these continents were already habited by an earlier member of the genus, *Homo neanderthalensis*. Between 70 000 and 30 000 BCE the two races coexisted, then the Neanderthals suddenly disappeared around 30 000 BCE.

Why did this happen and, more importantly, what in science's name does this have to do with the bogan?

Fortunately, the groundbreaking work of pioneering boganologist Pierre Yoplait provides an answer to both questions. Yoplait asserts that the Neanderthals interbred with the *Homo sapiens*, resulting in the Neanderthals' extinction and permanently altering the human genome. Yoplait posits the tantalising theory that this genetic transformation heralded the origins of a new subspecies, *Homo boganus*. Unlike the more dominant *Homo sapiens*, *Homo boganus* were generally shorter in stature, orange in hue and had smaller brains, making them more prone to anger and violence. Males of the species are believed to have had disproportionately large biceps and a highly carnivorous diet, while the females were smaller and more frail than their *Homo sapiens* equivalent, and more inclined towards hoarding shiny things.

From here the trail of the bogan goes cold for a while, as human beings reached what anthropologists call 'full behavioural modernity'. By this stage the human brain had fully developed, exhibiting abstract thinking and problem-solving abilities, while human beings began displaying so-called cultural universals including the use of language, the creation of sophisticated tools, the practice of music and figurative art, and the customs of burying the dead and religious worship. Early humans were hunter–gatherers, living in small nomadic groups and relying on most members of their primitive societies to forage for edible plants and animal carcasses, and to hunt for fish and other animals. It is believed the early bogans lived peacefully among these communities, unable to band together with other bogans due to their itinerant lifestyles and unable to be lazy or overly disruptive due to the overwhelming need to hunt for their own dinner and provide for their mates if they wanted sex that night. Still, archaeologists have found evidence of emerging behavioural differences between early bogan and early man, such as unusual distributions of crude, gaudy jewellery and head injuries found across burial sites in select parts of Upper Palaeolithic settlements.

Between about 9500 and 3500 BCE the human race entered a major period of change known as the Agrarian Revolution. During this period humans gradually transformed from transitory hunter–gatherers into members of sedentary societies with domesticated agriculture. This transformation was to have a profound impact on human development, allowing for the formation of urban settlements, the advent of specialised labour diversification and the development of technology, art and culture.

The Agrarian Revolution also played a key role in the development of the bogan. Whereas in the past the constant need to hunt for one's dinner, protect oneself and one's mate left precious little time for being lazy or obnoxious, now, for the first time in human history, a stable food supply and labour diversification meant that some members of the community could live off the hard work and innovation of others. The very early bogan was happy to oblige, quickly finding others like it in these developing communities with whom it could complain about, and blame its failings on, the more productive members of their community.

Gradually, the division of labour also meant that the more talented people in a community were able to specialise in what they were good at and, in some cases, receive recognition for their talents. This would force those less talented members of the community to seek other means to stand out, resulting in the early bogans becoming more concerned with their appearance, more self-centred and generally more intolerable.

From around 3500 BCE early urban settlements gradually developed into flourishing civilisations with complex political structures, social hierarchies and thriving cultures. In regions such as Mesopotamia, the Nile Valley, the Indus Valley, pre-Columbian America and early dynastic China, stability and human endeavour spawned major developments in art, science, technology, mathematics and medicine. But these cradles of civilisation also aided the ongoing evolution of the early bogan, who increasingly made its presence felt. Boganology and bogapology are still relatively young and emerging disciplines, with entire epochs of human history yet to be researched or studied at all. But even a cursory glimpse at early human civilisation reveals telltale signs of the developing bogan menace, including widespread contempt for the environment, the prevalence of conflict and an obsession with building big things.

One of the few early civilisations to be studied by boganologists is that of Ancient Egypt. During the period of the Middle Kingdom (2125–1550 BCE), working on the pyramids was akin to going to work in the mines, with pharaohs spending ridiculous amounts of money to help guarantee their entry into the afterlife. Early Egyptian bogans returned to Thebes from building the pyramids to blow their copper pieces on sick new rims for their chariots or a night on Egyptian-made Mesopotamian-branded beer and African slave girls. A low–cost chariot service sprang up to ferry early bogans to the pyramids, where they posed for papyrus scrolls that featured the bogan patting the Sphinx and holding up the Great Pyramid.

By the time of the Roman Empire, centuries of peace and stability had allowed the early bogan to grow lazier and more obnoxious than ever before. Historian Polybius refers to them as 'mobile vulgus' or, for those whose Latin is a little rusty, 'the fickle crowd'. We owe most of what we know about the Roman bogan (henceforth, 'brogan') to another pioneering boganologist, Maxamillion T. Reme. Reme likens the late Roman Empire to 'ze golden age of boganity' and has written extensively about the brogan and its role in the decay and fall of Rome.

Brogans lived mostly outside of Rome in sprawling McVillas, only coming into the city to visit the Forum to buy slaves (the brogan wanted as many slaves as possible), garish tunics and sandals; to complain about immigrants from provinces driving up the prices of grain and property; and for entertainment. With the legions usually away fighting barbarians or trying to recover lost standards, the emperor and senators were wary of the brogan and tried to keep it happy and distracted by offering a variety of entertainment. While it shunned the classics of Homer, Virgil, Ovid and Livy, the

brogan enjoyed watching crude comedies at the theatre, such as those starring Charlius Sheenius; engaging in ill-informed gambling on horse and chariot races at the Circus Maximus; and watching gladiators, slaves and wild animals slaughter each other at the Colosseum.

The gladiators were incredibly popular with brogans. They appeared in Latin trash magazines and made appearances at social engagements with their glamorous partners. According to Roman historian Tacitus, the most famous gladiator of all was Brendonius Fevolius, the only gladiator to wreak more damage outside the Colosseum than inside it.

In 476 CE, the Roman Empire (at least, the important part) fell to invading barbarian tribes. While historians have put forward countless theories as to the reasons for this (all wrong), Max T. Reme sums it up in the introduction to his groundbreaking work *Not Your Bro, Man*: 'It voz ze brogans, ztupid.' Over the 200 years or so leading up to Rome's fall, brogans gradually grew in numbers and influence until they outnumbered all other Roman citizens. Besides slowly destroying the Roman language and culture, and drawing the Roman numeral X everywhere, brogans required more and more of the empire's resources be thrown at them to keep them happy. This, combined with the brogan's elaborate methods of tax avoidance — rendering the empire's coffers empty — left Rome's borders unprotected, allowing lots of angry German dudes to barge in and slaughter everyone.

The Middle Ages

The fall of Rome was an epochal event, heralding the end of classical antiquity and plunging Europe into the Dark Ages, a period of economic disarray, cultural degradation and generally bad stuff that lasted for hundreds of years. The fall of Rome also proved a cataclysmic event for the evolving bogan. Without the protection and assistance of the Roman state, early bogans were once again forced to fend for themselves. Proving to be bigger fans of watching blood sports than taking part in them, they fled their McVillas in terror and scattered across the barbarian-ruled kingdoms of Europe. During the next 500 years, boganic tendencies were forced to take a back seat to conflict and chaos. Then, just as monarchs like Charlemagne and Alfred appeared to restore order and give the bogan some breathing space, Vikings began raiding and trying to cut the bogans' heads off.

As the Dark Ages gave way to the Middle Ages, the bogan found relief in God ... well, sort of. Across time, the bogan has never been particularly pious, but it occasionally embraces religion when it suits it. With the Catholic Church and the papacy increasing their power and providing some degree of unity and order in an otherwise troubled time, the bogan once more sought refuge in Rome.

In 1096 Pope Pius II called on western Christendom to embark on a crusade to save Jerusalem from Islam. Greedily eyeing off the promised forgiveness of its many sins and the opportunity to pillage the Holy Land and make its fortune, the bogan signed up faster than an Arts student enrolling in Postmodern Literature 101.

Leaving the crusades with a fatter wallet and a new-found hostility towards Muslims that would last until the present day, the bogan returned to a period of relative peace and prosperity. Northern Europe was becoming increasingly urbanised, the populations of most major cities attaining levels they would not reach again until the nineteenth century, while stability made possible a number of human achievements including the Magna Carta, the works of Dante, the Cathedral of Notre Dame, scholasticism and the invention of gunpowder. After years of hibernation, the bogan was finally reawakening. But then, in the early fourteenth century, it all went decidedly pear-shaped once more. First the Great Famine then the Black Plague decimated Europe, wiping out half of the population and sparking another long period of social unrest and perennial warfare, epitomised by the Hundred Years War (1338–1453). The bogan would have to crawl back into its hole and wait a little longer for its day of glory.

During the early modern period, three major events transformed the world the bogan lived in, with varying ramifications for it. Emerging in the mid-fourteenth century, the Renaissance was a cultural movement that transformed how Europeans thought and this marked the shift from the Middle Ages to the modern era. It began in Florence, Italy, and featured the intellectual and artistic contributions of such famous names as Leonardo da Vinci, Michelangelo, Machiavelli and Raphael. Partly thanks to the invention of the printing press in 1440 — which would eventually allow the modern bogan to buy box sets of *Twilight*, that trilogy by the dead Swedish guy and other books that have been adapted from successful motion pictures — the movement gradually spread throughout Europe during the fifteenth and sixteenth centuries, spurring major developments in philosophy, art, politics, medicine and science, and indirectly influencing authors like Cervantes, Shakespeare and Milton.

The bogan played absolutely no role, nor did it show anything more than the most fleeting interest, in any of this. Of only

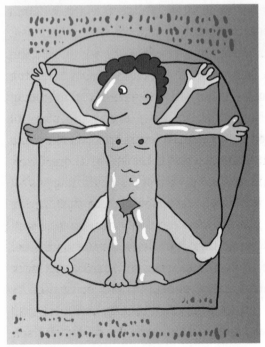

Thanks to Dan Brown, the bogan recognises this picture as being historically significant.

marginally more interest to the bogan was the other major intellectual development of the age, the Reformation. While it loathed theology, the bogan did not like its local priest after he told it off for stealing from the collection plate; therefore, the bogan was initially in favour of the Reformation. But when it realised that as a Protestant it couldn't do even more things it wanted to do, the bogan threw its support behind the Counter-Reformation, only to lose its zeal again as Europe descended into years of religious wars, culminating in the Thirty Years War (1618–1648).

The final major development of the early modern era was of the most interest to the bogan. After the fall of Constantinople to the Ottomans in 1453, Europeans were forced to find new trade routes to Asia, launching what would later be called the Age of Discovery. Being a generally myopic and inward-looking creature, the bogan cared not for development in navigational instruments, maps and sailing techniques, the discovery of the Americas or the voyages of Vasco da Gama. But this soon changed as the fabulous wealth brought back from the New World transformed Europe, ushering in a new Age of Commerce. The establishment of trading posts and, later, colonies across the New World saw an explosion in international trade and, gradually, the development of banking, insurance, paper currency, stock exchanges, listed companies and economic theory to support it. More immediately, this resulted in far greater supply and easier access to a whole range of new products the bogan hadn't realised it needed, including exotic spices to increase sexual performance (the erectile dysfunction nasal spray of its day), expensive pottery and silks, oriental wall hangings and new foodstuffs like coffee, cocoa, potatoes and corn. Much to the bogan's chagrin, the Portuguese also brought back the chilli, which would prove to be the bogan's nemesis at eateries and restaurants for the next 400 years. While it went unnoticed at the time (as it still is today by the bogan), this period also saw Willem Janszoon discover a new island south of New Guinea in 1606. In 1644, another Dutchman, Abel Tasman, charted the east coast of this island, later naming it *Nova Hollandia*.

Modernity

The next major movement to shape human history — but rather bypass the bogan — was the Enlightenment. Emerging in the coffee houses, salons and debating clubs of Paris, London and Amsterdam, the Enlightenment was a philosophical, political, cultural and scientific movement centred on reason and rationality. It questioned traditional structures and morals, urging ideas of freedom, democracy, secularisation and, ultimately, revolution. The bogan has long resented intellectualism and had no time for Voltaire, Rousseau, Kant, Montesquieu or Locke. But when the Enlightenment culminated in revolution in America and then France, *la bogue* quaffed a few bottles of Burgundy red and stormed the Bastille, not for *liberté, egalité* or *fraternité* but to loot and pillage. However, it quickly lost its revolutionary zeal when Jacobins and Girondins started trying to decapitate it as the revolution descended into the Terror. By the time Napoleon threw the continent into war once again, Euro-bogues tossed away their berets and fled across the Channel to England.

By the turn of the nineteenth century, most of the world's bogan population suddenly found itself in Britain. As history would have it, this proved a rather fortuitous time to be in Britain, which became the United Kingdom in 1801 after the short-lived union with Ireland. With the rest of Europe decimated by the Napoleonic wars and wealth streaming in from its colonial possessions around the world, Britannia was on the cusp of its Victorian golden age, when it became the most powerful nation on the planet.

Around this time Britain was also the stage for one of the most important historical developments in the history of mankind and one which would play a vital role in the evolution of the bogan: the Industrial Revolution. Between the late eighteenth and mid nineteenth centuries, a series of inventions and discoveries transformed Britain from manual and animal-based production into an industrialised economy. Major developments in textile manufacturing, coal mining, steam power, iron founding, transportation and machine tools fundamentally transformed the way humans worked and lived. Spreading through Europe and North America and later resulting in the inventions of steel, electricity, the internal combustion engine and the production line, the Industrial Revolution led to an unprecedented improvement in living standards for all people, beginning two centuries of gradually increasing average incomes and population growth across the developed world.

These changes would have profound implications for the bogan. Slowly increasing wealth would allow the bogan to spend money on things it didn't need, while the development of machines and tools would increase leisure time and allow it to be lazier and more inactive than ever before. Advances in manufacturing would facilitate the production of processed foods and gaudy homogenous fashions, while the invention of the engine would result in high-speed, fossil-fuel-guzzling recreational vehicles. Finally, the harsh conditions endured by many during the Industrial Revolution would drive improvements in labour practices, leading to the formation of trade unions and the expansion of government welfare, all of which the bogan would learn to exploit for its own selfish needs.

The history of the bogan in Australia

This is all very interesting, oh learned author, but then why didn't the bogan end up drinking warm beer and tea, eating roast beef and crumpets and whingeing about the weather in the UK? Well, dear reader, there was still one more major upheaval for the bogan to overcome: the great bogan diaspora. In what is still one of the great unexplained mass migrations in human history, large numbers of bogans waved goodbye to the cold climes of Britain

and Ireland and set sail for the antipodes, to the recently settled colony of New South Wales, and later, all the others.

Our understanding of this monumental event is still limited. What we do know we owe to the work of bogan migration expert and part-time alpaca breeder Sir Francis Sidebottom II. Sidebottom, who also invented the teabag, breaks down the bogan diaspora into three groups or phases. The first were convicts, mostly petty criminals from the cities of England, Scotland and Ireland. Of the approximately 161 000 convicts who travelled to Australia between 1788 and 1868, Sidebottom completely arbitrarily estimates that over 40 per cent were bogans, going some way to explaining the modern bogan's love of stealing bar mats, street signs and other items for their home bar. The second group, according to Sidebottom, was a large number of intoxicated bogans who, on their way to a buck's night in Austria, boarded the wrong boat. The final group travelled to Australia during the mid nineteenth century, either to make their fortune during the Victorian gold rush or to flee the potato famine in Ireland. The former accounts for the disproportionately high number of bogans in this author's home state, Victoria, while the latter explains the modern bogan's annual habit of pretending not to hate Guinness, wearing green and trying to glass c***s. Together, these distinct but similarly obnoxious groups of bogans formed the direct ancestors of the modern Australian bogan.

Contrary to most modern bogans' beliefs, Australia was not discovered by Captain James Cook in 1788. As we've already seen, Dutch explorer Willem Janzsoon was the first European to set foot on the continent in 1606, but he and subsequent Europeans were unimpressed by the lack of (discovered) resources or other Europeans to trade with, and Australia was left alone for a time.

In 1770 Cook discovered the east coast of Australia while searching for the mythical southern continent, *Terra Australis*, which — he'd overheard at his local one night — was filled with hot mermaids horny for British guys in uniform. Seventeen years

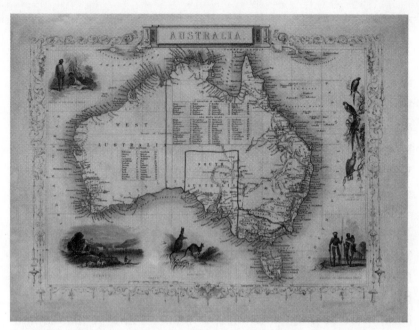

A suitably old-looking map of Oz that shows Aboriginal people on it.

later the British government decided to beat other European powers to it and establish a colony in Australia.

In 1788 Captain Arthur Phillip landed the First Fleet at Botany Bay, but when this proved unsuitable he instead landed at Sydney Cove, where he established a penal colony (when bogans learn this at school they usually snigger at the word 'penal'). Contrary to another bogan misconception, Australia was not inhabited by 'a few abos' at this time; rather, it contained up to 500 000 Indigenous people whose ancestors had been on the continent for somewhere between 40 000–60 000 years. (Bogans refer to this time as the 'dreamtime' or BC — Before Cook.) During the next century, European diseases and conflict would reduce this Indigenous population to less than 50 000.

Early convict-populated Australia was a harsh, unforgiving place for the bogan. Convicts were treated brutally by their British overseers and only 20 per cent of them were women, resulting in many frustrating nights at the Ball & Chain and a high number of glassings. Boganologists suggest that this goes some way to explaining the modern bogan's attitudes towards women.

The severe conditions in the early settlements led many bogans to resort to crime and corruption, culminating in the Rum Rebellion of 1808, where the notorious New South Wales Corps deposed then Governor William Bligh (of HMS *Bounty* fame) when he tried to crack down on their illegal rum-smuggling activities. This would set an early precedent for bogan uprisings: where other famous uprisings were fought for independence, workers' rights or suffrage, bogans fought for rum.

In future years, bogans spread across the land, inhabiting the 'outback' which it now eschews, but covets the idea of. Governor Macquarie sent explorers into Australia's vast interior, establishing the first inland city at Bathurst, which would later become a bogan place of worship. It was near Bathurst in 1851 that Edward Hargraves found a speck of gold in a waterhole, sparking the next chapter in the story of the bogan.

The discovery of gold transformed the fortunes of early Australia. Discoveries in New South Wales were soon dwarfed by

'Twiggy': the bogan's favourite Forrest since Gump.

those at Ballarat and Bendigo, and Victoria was quickly gripped by gold fever. Coming shortly after a global depression and the early success of the Californian gold rush, the Victorian gold rush lured immigrants from all over the world; 370 000 arrived in 1852 alone. Being huge fans of get-rich-quick schemes, bogans from all over Australia and beyond were lured by the promise of instant wealth.

While a few made their fortunes, working on the goldfields was less glamorous for most. Camps were overcrowded, conditions were cold and damp, and disease and crime were rife. Finding gold was difficult, requiring hard work and a lot of luck. Bogans expecting to find giant gold nuggets walking home from the pub soon became irritated and angry. They quickly found convenient scapegoats and a channel for their anger in the 40 000 Chinese miners who had also travelled to the goldfields. Unlike the bogan, the Chinese didn't spend all day at the pub quaffing cheap rum and they were well known for their work ethic. Scared of competition from those prepared to work harder than them, the bogan first threatened and bullied the Chinese, and, when this didn't work, they loudly lobbied the government to expel the foreigners. Bogan miners also became angry at the licensing fees they were forced to pay the government which left little money for boozing, gambling and working out.

Tensions soon boiled over, culminating in an organised rebellion by bogans in Ballarat who built a piss-weak stockade, unfurled a flag with only the Southern Cross on it and were promptly crushed by proper soldiers, resulting in 28 deaths. The Eureka Stockade, as it is popularly called, has since been mythologised by unionists, nationalists and bogans who all characterise it as a struggle for democracy and human rights; as the very 'birth of Australia'. In reality, the rebellion was a bunch of angry bogans who were jealous of Chinese workers, didn't want to pay tax and wanted free land. The Southern Cross continues to be a symbol of 'Aussie pride' and immense racial intolerance for bogans today; it is likely to be the last thing you see on a bogan's tattooed bicep before it glasses you.

The Eureka flag: first raised at the Eureka Stockade and now often seen on the arm or shoulder of the bogan to signify its willingness to kill you.

The gold rush spurred an economic boom that lasted for 40 years, improving greatly the bogan's standard of living and allowing it to buy things it hadn't known it needed. The boom peaked during the 1880s, culminating in a speculative land boom late in the decade. Bogans who had made mad cash during the gold rush eagerly embraced this boom and the great bogan dream of owning as many houses as possible was born.

With Melbourne suddenly one of the richest cities in the world and property prices expected to rise forever, nothing could possibly go wrong. Yet, in 1891 the land boom ended abruptly, sending sixteen banks and 133 companies into bankruptcy, leading to the Australian banking crisis of 1893 and depression of the 1890s. This was completely different to today and should not be viewed as a parallel of any sort. Definitely not.

Depression hit the bogan hard and many found themselves out of work, leading the nascent trade union movement to complain that the Chinese were taking their jobs. This would result in the *Immigration Restriction Act* of 1901; one of the first pieces of legislation passed by the new parliament after Federation, it restricted immigration to people of European origin.

The Commonwealth of Australia was born on 1 January 1901 when the six states were federated under a single constitution. Widespread nationalist sentiment led the bogan to greet this event enthusiastically, but its interest in the political structure of the country soon dwindled when it realised that Federation made little material difference to its wellbeing. It should be noted that despite never having seen or read anything about the Australian constitution, the bogan will frequently claim that things it doesn't like are 'unconstitutional'. When pushed on why this is the case the bogan will invariably look down and mumble something vague about the 'first amendment' and 'paying taxes'.

The first decade of the new century was relatively uneventful but beneficial for the bogan, as the growing manufacturing and agricultural sectors provided jobs and boosted incomes. This changed dramatically in June 1914, when the assassination of Archduke Franz Ferdinand of Austria sent Europe spiralling into the Great War. Two months later Britain declared war on Germany and Australia was enjoined. The war was greeted with enthusiasm by bogan and non-bogan alike, and such was the demand to enlist that many enlistees were turned back. Despite far more significant and telling contributions on the Western Front and in the Middle East, the Australian involvement at Gallipoli in 1915 is remembered as the most historic of the war. As part of a campaign to capture Constantinople, the capital of the Ottoman Empire, the British organised a joint campaign with French plus Australian and New Zealand (ANZAC) troops to take the Gallipoli Peninsula in western Turkey. Intended as a swift operation, the campaign failed due to poor planning, bad luck and the unexpectedly fierce Ottoman resistance; after an initial slaughter it turned into a bloody eight-month struggle that took almost 9000 Australian lives and ended in retreat and failure. Today the modern bogan celebrates this historic military campaign by travelling to Turkey, getting trashed and trying to root other bogans before passing out on the graves of fallen soldiers.

By the time the terrible war ended with the Paris Peace Conference in 1918 and the Treaty of Versailles in 1919, some 400 000 of the nation's five million people had served, with 60 000 killed and 156 000 wounded.

After the horror of war, the 1920s were a peaceful and relatively prosperous period for the bogan. With the economy continuing to develop and governments spending big on civil projects like roads, railways and the Sydney Harbour Bridge, the bogan's life was slowly changing for the better. An increasingly consumerist culture saw the introduction of products which made the bogan's life easier, including the radio, gramophone, toaster and the model T Ford (the Holden Commodore wasn't invented for another 30 years). However, this all came to a grinding halt in 1929 when the Wall Street crash sent the US and the world tumbling into the Great Depression. Due to its dependence on agricultural exports like wool and wheat, Australia was hit particularly hard by the Depression.

This was a devastating time for the bogan. Skyrocketing unemployment — almost 30 per cent in 1929 — led most to live in abject poverty and sent many to wander rural areas in search of work. Bogan demographer Barry Pepper believes that this total lack of idle time sent bogan numbers falling to their lowest point since settlement. Those who did survive sought refuge in sport, cheering on the heroics of Don Bradman and Phar Lap. The latter's death in 1932 led bogans to claim that the horse was poisoned by the Mafia, one of the first recorded instances of bogan conspiracy theories.

Then, in 1939, just as the country was recovering from the Depression and bogan numbers were picking up, events in Europe were to again take precedence as the continent entered war once more. Over one million Australians served in the Second World War, fighting the Germans across Europe, the Middle East and Africa, as well as the Japanese throughout the Pacific. The horrific conflict, which claimed another 39 000 lives, would mark the low point for the bogan.

The postwar period was a bountiful one for the bogan. Under Australia's longest-serving prime minister, Sir Robert Menzies, surging migration and a baby boom, major expansion in the manufacturing sector, strong spending on public works like the Snowy Mountains Hydroelectric Scheme and a sharp rise in housing construction underpinned a twenty-year period of prosperity and full employment. The bogan suddenly had more disposable income than ever before and, following the introduction of commercial television in the late 1950s, much higher exposure to advertisers imploring it to buy their products. The bogan happily acquiesced, spending large on new Holden cars, a growing array of domestic appliances it didn't know it needed and copious amounts of hair product.

The period also witnessed a boom in house construction, with home ownership rising from 40 per cent in 1945 to over 70 per cent by 1960. Unable to afford to live in the inner city and unwilling to compromise on its dream to live in a seven-bedroom McMansion with a triple garage, the bogan moved into new suburbs emerging on the fringes of cities and promptly complained about the lack of services and the commute time. This process would continue to repeat itself for the next 50 years, with the bogan and suburbia moving further out, while Holden developed progressively bigger and louder cars to make the commute more tolerable.

Under Menzies, Australia also developed closer political ties with the USA, resulting in Australian involvement in wars in Korea and Vietnam as well as the growing influence of US culture. As US television, movies and music came to dominate the cultural landscape, the bogan's interest in US film stars, musicians and other celebrities grew, spawning another bustling bogan ambition that would reach its zenith in the modern era: the insatiable desire to be a celebrity.

Also of interest to the bogan at the time was the 1967 invention of the stubby holder and the disappearance of the PM Harold Holt — who, in the bogan's ill-informed opinion, had clearly been abducted by a Chinese submarine. In 1972 Australia elected its first Labor prime minister in 23 years, Gough Whitlam. Whitlam was initially popular with the bogan when he introduced fee-free university and universal health care, the latter causing the number of sickies and back-related workplace injuries to soar. But by the time Whitlam was dismissed by the governor-general in 1975, the bogan had lost interest and was too busy watching *Homicide* and *Hey Hey It's Saturday* on its new colour television.

The bogan today

Here we are, then. The fourth quarter. The final straight. The last stage in the bogan's evolution from innocuous ape to terrible modern superbogan.

During the 1980s Australia entered another period of prosperity, driven by key economic reforms instituted under the governments of Bob Hawke and Paul Keating, including the deregulation of the banking system and the floating of the dollar. This was a decade of corporate excess, rampant consumerism, and cultural glitz and glamour. Computer games, VCRs and home computers became must-have accessories for the bogan, and the rise of junk food and takeaway restaurants changed bogan dietary habits. A stockmarket boom enticed many bogans to 'play the market' for the first time, leading many to claim to their friends that they were becoming the next Alan Bond, only to be proved prescient when the stockmarket crash of 1987 sent the fortunes of both plummeting.

In 1989 the Berlin Wall came down, signalling the fall of communism and the end of the Cold War. However, this was overshadowed by another symbolic barrier that tumbled down when Australian cricketer David Boon shattered fellow cricketer Doug Walters's record by drinking 52 cans of beer on the flight to London during the 1989 Ashes tour. The world was truly changing.

In 1991 the property bubble burst, sending Australia into 'the recession we had to have' and proving the end of corporate raiders like Alan Bond and Christopher Skase. But while things appeared bleak, this was far from the end of the great bogan dream. After a tough period in the early '90s, the economy soon bounced back. Elected in 1996, the Howard Government continued the reform agenda of its predecessors and — better yet for the bogan — showered its subjects with the baby bonus, superannuation contributions and the first-home-buyers' grant. Videos gave way to DVDs and home theatre systems; televisions got wider; McMansions

**David Boon: 52 cans.
Enough said.**

got bigger; the growth of the Internet allowed the bogan to keep in touch with celebrity news and surf for porn 24/7; and relaxed credit standards and Gerry Harvey allowed the bogan to take on more debt and buy more things it didn't need than ever before. But things were only warming up.

From around the turn of the century, surging Chinese demand for Australian resources spurred unprecedented investment into the mining sector and resulted in the greatest resources boom the country had ever seen. After the terrorist attacks of September 11, 2001, reminded them that they didn't like Muslims, bogans around the country were flown to Western Australia and paid mad cash to hold traffic signs. Incomes and McMansion values continued to increase and bogan numbers grew to record levels.

Realising that its time was at hand, the bogan began baying for more. It wanted to stand out more: it began buying Ed Hardy T-shirts, Louis Vuitton bags and anything containing the word 'couture'. It wanted to be unique: it named its child Kylee and tattooed the Bhutanese word for 'universe' on its arse. It wanted

to be exotic: it travelled to Bali and started drinking Corona with a slice of lime in it. It wanted to be bad: it started watching *Underbelly* and glassed a c*** who cut in front of it at a bar.

In short, it wanted to be maxtreme. And even the global financial crisis couldn't stop the bogan as Chinese demand for iron ore and coal helped the economy avoid recession and power on. This only furthered the bogan's belief that it was more awesome and more deserving of awesomeness than other people and nations.

Thus, after 30 000 years of evolution, the bogan's journey was complete. As it powered down the thrust on its jet ski after singlehandedly exterminating three marine species, it took a rare moment to reflect on how awesome it was.

It had won.

Knowing how the bogan has evolved, it is now necessary to look at the habitat of the new maxtreme bogan and its offspring. Hence the title of the next chapter: Geography.

2
GEOGRAPHY

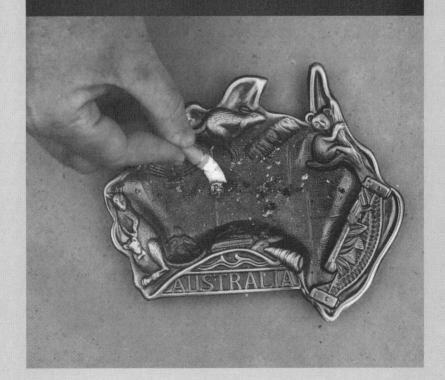

Back in the early days of Australia, boganism was a strictly local affair. Without the technology to consume petrol as a form of recreation, bogans stayed close to home, doing stuff like cutting down trees and glassing each other after drinking crudely fashioned beer and rum. This was soon to change, though, for in 1856 a gentleman named James Holden started a saddlery business in Adelaide. While bogan ancestors enjoyed the velocity of horse riding, it was physically tiring and minimal amounts of fossil fuels were consumed in the process. Responding to market demand, James Holden invented the automobile. Heretically, his company assembled car bodies for Ford Australia early in the twentieth century, until bogans stormed the factory and threatened to burn the place to the ground.

Due to these events, the great bogan institution of Ford versus Holden was created; more importantly, automobiles made the bogan a mobile force across the countryside. A bogan could wake up in its house in Geelong, eat breakfast and be glassing someone on crudely fashioned beer and rum at a pub in southern New South Wales by lunchtime. This changed the bogan's worldview. Sydney bogans no longer holidayed in Gosford — they could load the whole family into the Holden and turn up in Queensland.

Clutching to its heart this new-found ability to traverse large distances, the bogan soon set about customising its vehicle to make it an extension of its soul. This was achieved via such means as painting a stripe on the car, hanging unusual artefacts from the rear-view mirror or affixing stickers conveying impractical political or general statements to the rear bumper. That way, whenever a bogan chariot rolled into town, the locals could examine its particular boganic customisations in much the manner of two newly acquainted dogs jamming their snouts into each other's arseholes at the park. But another innovation had also occurred which would change the bogan's horizons forever.

In 1920 a door-to-door shoe salesman and Lithuanian immigrant named Andrius Qantas invented the aeroplane in rural Queensland, using three sheets of iron and a lawnmower engine borrowed from his older brother, Victa Qantas. He went on to create one of the world's iconic airlines — and one which was responsible for ferrying the bogan to Bali and Thailand for the very first time. No longer needing to spend four months on a smelly ship in order to pour beers in London, the bogan was able to stride purposefully onto the world stage, glassing all comers on whatever crudely fashioned beer and rum was favoured by the locals.

In the decades to the end of the twentieth century, the prohibitive cost of airline travel restricted many bogans to only occasional flights, but global tranquillity was ruined by Sir Richard Brandsome with the launch of Virgin Blue in 2000. This was soon followed by Qantas subsidiary Jetstar, then Tiger (though by the time this book hits the shelves it might have disappeared).

With a low-cost network now spanning Australia, Asia and, more recently, England and the USA, bogans no longer need particularly compelling reasons to venture far from home. While James Holden, Andrius Qantas and Victa Qantas have all been dead for hundreds of years, they remain unforgivably culpable for mobilising the bogan. Due to the increasing complexity of the bogan's domestic and international distribution patterns, further investigation is warranted.

Domestic distribution

Due to the enabling factor of both land and air transport, the bogan has colonised a broad geographic range of the Australian landmass. In Australia's tropics the warm weather enables the bogan to be shirtless, while in the southern reaches of the continent, the bogan is also shirtless, and attempting to convince others that it is impervious to the cold. Figure 2.1, below, details the parts of Australia where bogans have settled and where bogan sightings have been reported.

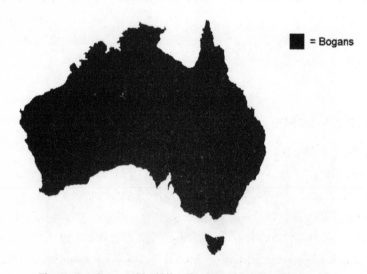

Figure 2.1 Geographical distribution of bogans in Australia

In addition to the land areas included in Figure 2.1, the invention of the jet ski by the Melbourne band Jet about fifteen years ago has enabled the bogan to confidently explore Australia's marine areas, either alone or in pairs. The rise of the jet ski imperilled dolphins and other aquatic life even more than the speedboat, which was invented by Brisbane reggae trio REO Speedwagon in 1971.

Fond of the habitat of Australia's largest cities, the twenty-first century bogan is not confined to a particular suburb or side of town. While infamously fond of anywhere it is able to build a massive McMansion, the bogan can be found in the inner suburbs near trendy bars, in the suburbs miles from anywhere interesting or out of town trying to build a maxtreme dirt jump for its car. The broad geographic and financial range of the modern bogan means that whoever you are, and wherever you live, you may well be enduring one or more bogans next door.

The bogan has a different philosophy to the non-bogan when it comes to choosing a place to live. While the non-bogan will weigh up the local amenities and linkages of an area it wishes to reside in, the bogan will purchase whatever allows it to fit the largest McMansion it can afford, and will then expect the government to magic-wand all imaginable services to the boganic doorstep. This inherent lack of pragmatism and logic when selecting a residential address is a key reason why bogans can end up pretty much anywhere.

State by state

New South Wales

New South Wales is home to almost a third of Australia's population and also a bridge that Paul Hogan used to have a job painting. Thanks to the state being the site of Australia's first British colony, it is overwhelmingly likely that the first ever Australian bogan arose in New South Wales. The time since then has seen the state develop immensely, which was validated by the fact that Russell Crowe (one of Australia's foremost adopted bogans) chose to settle in New South Wales when he left New Zealand as an adult.

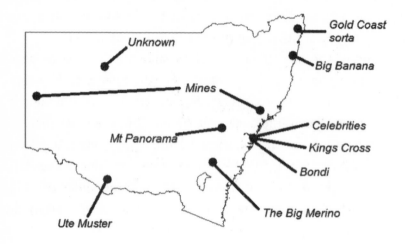

Figure 2.2 New South Wales

WHAT'S IN IT FOR THE BOGAN?
The diversity of options available in New South Wales means that the bogan's short attention span need not be an obstacle to keeping occupied. Bogan-approved activities include vomiting in Kings Cross, trawling for Swedish backpackers at Bondi Beach, perspective-based photo opportunities at the Big Banana in Coffs Harbour, drinking at bars at Thredbo, and getting sunburnt on a part of the Gold Coast (albeit the boring bit).

Victoria
While Victoria is further from Bali and Phuket than any other mainland state, it is still a region that is prized by the bogan. In addition to the illustrious tales of Ned Kelly and Chopper Read, pretty much all of the stuff that happened during the first season of *Underbelly* happened in Victoria, so the bogan knows that

Australia's south-east corner is capable of delivering maxtreme bogan-friendly crime. Home to Australia's largest brewing company, Victorian liquor has also been responsible for millions of unplanned bogan pregnancies.

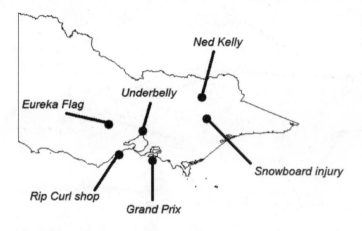

Figure 2.3 Victoria

WHAT'S IN IT FOR THE BOGAN?
Featuring two different grands prix, a massive casino that shoots balls of flame and a 100 000-seat shrine to Shane Warne and Brendan Fevola, the bogan is often willing to forgo its constitutional right to get sunburnt during winter in order to spend time in Victoria. If sunburn is still required, the bogan can head to Bells Beach during its summer holidays and fall off its surfboard.

Queensland

Australia's sunshine state has lured bogans for generations with the dual promises of Bundaberg Rum and cola on tap, and melanomas. Oh, and the Gold Coast. While the dominant local beer is only mid-strength in order to reduce glassings, the weather is warm enough for the bogan to drink at a phenomenal pace, easily offsetting the weaker beer. Severe flooding during the wet season is often counterbalanced by severe footy-trip flooding during the dry season, leaving precious few months a year in which Queensland's non-bogans are safe from disaster of some sort.

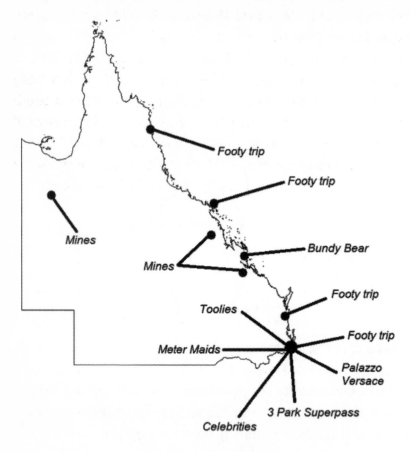

Figure 2.4 Queensland

WHAT'S IN IT FOR THE BOGAN?

Heaps. The home of schoolies, IndyCars, and meter maids, the Gold Coast offers almost everything that the bogan could possibly want. These expeditions to bogan paradise are often funded by going to work in the mines, which the bogan can also do in Queensland. A visiting bogan can acquire a Three-park Superpass, stay where the celebs stay at Palazzo Versace, check out the place where a stingray got the better of Steve Irwin, or visit the Bundy factory to see where the magic happens.

South Australia

As Australia's only state that wasn't founded as a convict settlement, it can be argued that boganism came later to South Australia than other areas. Despite this, the bogan has still managed to have a major impact. The South Australian bogan has endured significant setbacks in recent years, with the F1 Grand Prix being poached by Victoria, and hometown hero Lleyton Hewitt's tennis career stagnating. But — proudly for the bogan — Lleyton's lack of success on the court has coincided with a stunning level of success at becoming a bigger bogan. South Australia was also Julia Gillard's childhood home, and is presumably responsible for her accent.

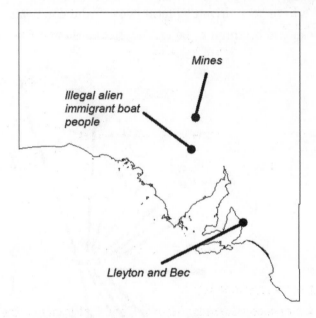

Figure 2.5 South Australia

WHAT'S IN IT FOR THE BOGAN?

There's not too much here for the visiting bogan, aside from the chance to drink Coopers at its source. While the state currently serves as the second-favourite butt of interstate jokes, the future expansion of BHP Billiton's massive Olympic Dam mining project promises to change the bogan's perception of South Australia. As a result, now is a good time to open a jet ski dealership and corner the market.

Western Australia

The Promised Land. Covering a third of Australia's landmass, Western Australia is universally considered by male bogans to be the solution to all of their self-inflicted problems. Going to work in the mines can make even the least meritorious of bogans wealthy, allowing them to fly into Perth, lose at poker, smoke cigars and then glass someone in Northbridge at 2 a.m. At various points in its history Western Australia has had a secessionist movement, believed to have been driven by local bogans who don't want their eastern-seaboard brethren to be cashed up like them.

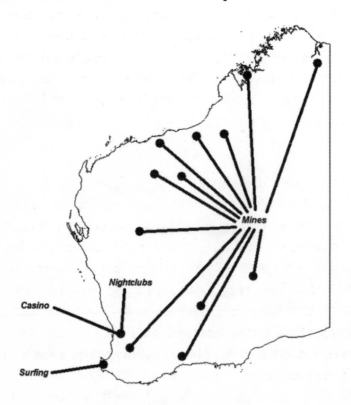

Figure 2.6 Western Australia

Pretty much everything it's ever wanted. More coastline than you can poke a jet ski at, more underpoliced highway than you can poke a bright green HSV at, and more six-figure semi-skilled jobs than you can poke a poker table at. Probably the main downside to the mining regions is the dearth of young bogan women, causing squabbles and many glassings. This is generally offset by flying to Perth and spending the night at the strippers' club.

Northern Territory

Thanks to the bogan's intuitive feel for the Australian outback, it doesn't have to actually travel to the Northern Territory in order to confidently comment on the people or places therein. This is fortunate for the bogan, who — in the event that it visits the NT — finds the lack of giant shopping centres and entertainment complexes to be quite disappointing. Other downsides of the Northern Territory in the bogan's mind include the eventual discovery that Uluru is located many hours from Darwin and, for nonindigenous bogans, the regular presence of Indigenous Australians who have neither won Olympic gold medals for Australia nor presented on *The Great Outdoors*.

WHAT'S IN IT FOR THE BOGAN?

While the shopping centres aren't big enough, the crocodiles are. Numerous visiting bogans touring the Top End have endured severe injuries courtesy of crocodiles too stupid to understand that the bogan was 'just having a laugh'. Injuries aside, the crocodiles are quite big. Also big is Uluru, which the bogan can climb on or pose for perspective-based photographs in front of. In January 2007 the open speed limit on the Territory's rural highways was abolished, which consequently abolished one of the key reasons why a bogan would want to visit.

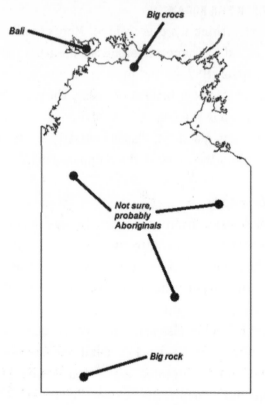

Figure 2.7 Northern Territory

Tasmania

The geographic isolation of Tasmania is believed to have allowed a different, more inbred strain of bogan to evolve — that is, if you ask a mainland bogan. Rather than a place to visit, mainland bogans primarily regard Tasmania as a concept whose mention can turn a terrible joke into a brilliant one. While the bogan is incorrect on this count, it is closer to the mark in its assumption that Tasmania contains little of interest to a visiting bogan. Eric Bana imitator Mark Read moved to Tasmania in the late 1990s, but left after a few years due to boredom. The bogan knows that legendary beer pit David Boon is down there somewhere — but he, like the thylacine, is rarely sighted.

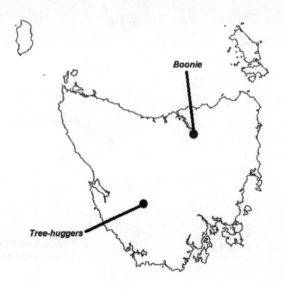

Figure 2.8 Tasmania

WHAT'S IN IT FOR THE BOGAN?

The bogan is aware that Tasmania produces good beer, but most of these products are sent to the mainland, thereby neutralising the incentive for the bogan to fly south to consume. The bogan's love of maxtremely big things does not extend to towering stands of eucalypt; in fact, the relative prominence of conservationists in Tasmania displeases the bogan. To conclude: while there are indeed bogans living in Tasmania, there is little reason for non-Tasmanian bogans to be sighted there.

Australian Capital Territory

The Australian Capital Territory covers an area of 2358 square kilometres and was carved out of New South Wales in 1911 to house a city that would go on to impose limits upon the bogan. Canberra is the demonic vacuum that removes the bogan's hard-earned taxpayer dollars, for which the bogan vows it sees so little in return. In a bid to sweeten the deal and prevent bogans from laying waste to the city, the finest bogan bribes that the bogan has seen have originated from within the ACT, generally around election time. For the other 2.7 years out of three, the bogan knows that the entire Australian Capital Territory needs to be sacked.

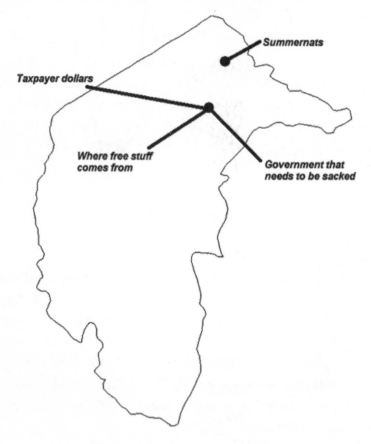

Figure 2.9 Australian Capital Territory

WHAT'S IN IT FOR THE BOGAN?

A bogan visiting Canberra cannot expect to receive additional bogan bribes as a result of its journey, making a visit a reasonably pointless undertaking. On the plus side, the city is home to the time-/bogan-honoured institution called Summernats, where bogans can spend days on end watching other bogans do burnouts and then do some of their own. Parliament House is also host to the largest potential flag cape in the world.

International distribution

While the bogan has made great strides in spreading itself across the Australian landmass, its international progress has been considerably less impressive. During the twentieth century this was largely due to the bogan not being sufficiently cashed up. The subsequent cashification — which also coincided with the emergence of international discount airlines — has cruelled the portions of international community with more bogans than ever before. However, while a number of overseas destinations have been ruined by bogan hordes, vast tracts remain unacknowledged by bogankind. What's this all about?

Figure 2.10 The bogan world, shown to scale

The bogan on tour

You will generally not find the bogan hiking the Mongolian steppes, nor will you spot a bogan assisting in the construction of shelters at a refugee camp in eastern Chad. For when the bogan passes through the gates of justice that it recognises from *Border Security* it is on a quest to become more of a bogan, not less.

Sporting historical knowledge, including Australia's triumph over the Nazis at Gallipoli, the neo-colonialist bogan is keen to re-enact fifteenth to nineteenth century scenes in which rich Europeans with guns sailed into far-flung lands and flexed their financial and technological muscle over primitive tribesmen. In the bogan's twenty-first century remix the role of the tall ship is performed by Jetstar, the roles of the primitive tribesmen played by any foreigner with less cash-flow than the bogan and the role of the guns by an iPhone capable of instantly informing Facebook of how hard the bogan was able to haggle with an impoverished shopkeeper.

It is, however, an oversimplification to suggest that the bogan selects its travel destinations solely by its capacity to exploit an income disparity that it was born onto the right side of, for the bogan has numerous other needs. Foremost among these needs is the requirement to be constantly near other bogans. This requirement is a major reason why the bogan's travel adventures are routinely unadventurous. Australian bogans comprise barely one-thousandth of the world population, making it a statistical necessity that they must holiday in no more than twelve overseas places in order to retain a critical boganic mass at each location. In the event that one of these places manages to become overwhelming and confusing for a travelling bogan, the bogan's anxiety can be swiftly soothed by yelling 'Aussie Aussie Aussie', safe in the knowledge that someone within earshot will validate its boganity in three barked, nasal syllables.

A bogan-tested way of reducing the risk of cultural shock in overseas places is to ensure that any and all overseas places visited have at least one Australian-themed bar. These bars allow the bogan to pay $9 for a VB and to watch repeats of Australia succeeding in sports. While far more interested in Hilltop Hoods and Powderfinger when it is at home, Australian-themed bars provide the bogan with a stupefyingly short playlist of songs such as 'Khe Sanh' and 'Down Under', both of which will make the bogan shed a tear as it thinks about the nation that it flew out of as little as 72 hours prior. It is believed that the Walkabout Pub in the Shepherds Bush area of London contains a higher concentration of homesick bogans than the *Big Brother* house at Dreamworld, seasons one through eight.

Another thing that the travelling bogan requires at all times is the native language invented in Australia: English. While the bogan steadfastly expects that anyone in Australia — residents and visitors alike — should be fluent in English (and preferably restrict their conversation to bogan-compatible topics), the bogan's refusal to learn anyone else's language means that its foreign sojourns are limited in scope. Parts of the world that speak Australian are acceptable, meaning that the bogan can happily visit the UK, Ireland, New Zealand and North America. While an Australian-speaking country, South Africa is generally placed in the too-hard basket due to the distressing South African famine in Ethiopia.

There are, however, also other parts of the world which are linguistically suitable for the bogan. These places — such as Thailand, Bali, Vietnam, and Laos — have little form on the English-speaking front, but their bogan-approved beach or party scenes, combined with the poverty of the locals, have proven an irresistible inducement for local businesspeople. These people will generally learn some rudimentary English in a bid to improve their standard of living, creating an exciting opportunity for bogans to snidely mimic their attempts at communicating in English. At the conclusion of the conversation the bogan will mispronounce one of the two Thai words it learned at the Australian-themed bar, then congratulate itself on its worldliness.

Even for a creature as fond of its cultural comfort zone as the bogan, occasionally a yearning will develop for something more: an interaction with cultures that offer the bogan neither English conversation nor 40-cent beers on the beach. This is the bogan equivalent of a journey outside of the Solar System and requires a special protective suit. One even more protective than an

Australian flag cape. Oddly, this protective suit was first provided by a Kiwi half a century ago. When John Anderson conducted his first guided Contiki Tour of Europe in 1961, an entire continent that was previously blacked out due to its un-Australianness suddenly fell into the reach of the bogan.

Now the bogan could pose in a perspective-based photo in front of the Eiffel Tower — but not until it had had a quick vomit in a nearby garden bed due to the amount of cask wine it had consumed in the bus overnight. The next major innovation came in the mid '90s, once the fall of the Berlin Wall allowed Contiki to ferry the bogan to a perspective-based photo on the far side of said structure; also to the cheaper beer in Prague. The bogan witnessed this new development and groped the other bogans on the bus approvingly. Indeed, the Contiki Tour is a valuable cultural exchange for the bogan, allowing Australia's bogans to interact with boganesque representatives of other cultures in a chaperoned, booze-slicked environment. Subsequent expansions of the Contiki empire to Egypt and Asia have generated thousands of shithouse photos featuring bogans kissing the Sphinx or humping a terracotta soldier.

When the bogan is travelling, as in many of its other endeavours, there is an immense need to use Facebook. This often results in bogans complaining on Facebook about how the funny foreign keyboards make it hard for the bogan to complain on Facebook. The speed of Internet connections in south-east Asia is also routinely unacceptable to the bogan, who, along with its adjacent friends, is attempting to simultaneously upload thirteen boast-related Facebook statuses, seven complaint-related Facebook statuses, and 1739 photos of sunburnt drunk bogans posing in front of stuff.

Specific sightings

As we have established, the bogan's hard-wired needs eliminate large tracts of the planet from its travel itineraries. But of the places that theoretically offer bogan-suitable habitat, the distribution and density of bogans still varies wildly. Upon closer analysis, the secrets of the migratory bogan can be uncovered, revealing six key Bogan Overseas General Attendance Necessities (or BOGANs) that lure the bogan like bogans to a velvet rope. It is simply inconceivable that you will find a bogan at an overseas location that doesn't feature at least two of the following BOGAN factors.

THE MAXTREME

A bogan will not go to all of the effort of travelling overseas unless the destination provides the bogan the chance to max out to the max. The bogan's desire for the maxtreme does not tend to extend to mountain climbing, trekking or any form of maxtreme endurance — the bogan wants to max out *right now*. Activities such as bungy jumping appeal more: the bogan stands on a ledge and gets pushed by someone who says 'fush and chups'. Other maxtreme activities coveted by the bogan include the physical maxtreme of shooting an AK-47 assault rifle near the killing fields of Cambodia, the physical maxtreme of consuming 26 shots of Bundaberg Rum at an Australian-themed bar in London and the fiscal maxtreme of betting everything on black in Vegas.

HAIR BRAIDING

While unconvinced by the fashion merit of braided hair when in Australia, the bogan delights in seeking out holiday locations where it can swan around with its hair in cornrows. Observed in both male and female bogans, the cornrows are merely a symptom of the bogan revelling in its capacity to pay a small brown person to squat by its side for four hours while its hair becomes more like a rapper's, and therefore totally gangsta/celeb. Most of south-east Asia offers the bogan the opportunity to become temporarily infatuated with this hairdo.

Both male and female bogans will braid their hair on holiday — though they'd never dream of doing it at home.

ANNUAL PARTIES

If a place is host to an annual party, the other 360 days of the year disappear into a boganic blindspot, never to be seen again. Conditioned by a domestic calendar featuring the Big Day Out, the Spring Racing Carnival and St Patrick's Day, the bogan knows how to fleetingly fire up for something it doesn't otherwise like. Oktoberfest is the only reason a bogan would ever visit Munich, and the bogan's deep need to attend one-off parties is sometimes even strong enough to have it overcome its deep suspicion of South America, so that it can get hammered at the Rio de Janeiro Carnival. Via a process understood only by bogans, Gallipoli has now also become an annual bogan party location and the only reason a bogan would ever declare an interest in visiting Turkey.

CHEAP LIQUOR

The bogan is routinely willing to pay $9 in Australia for a bottle of locally brewed foreign-label beer, but once overseas the bogan will become acutely price sensitive about the very same matter. Due to the neo-colonialist bogan's need to haggle and scrimp when overseas, a bar selling local beer for $1 will be bogan free if there is a nearby bar selling it for 90 cents. The ultimate bogan drinking vessel is better known for its capacity to carry sand for golfers, but the intrepid bogan considers writing itself off on two buckets of vodka and Red Bull to be the ultimate Thai spiritual experience.

SHINY THINGS

Due to its multi-year project to cripple its attention span via a diet of Jägerbombs, graphic pornography, *Two And A Half Men* and general maxtremity, the bogan needs regular stimuli of flashing lights and shiny things in order to be happy on holiday. This means that bogans are rarely found holidaying in non-urban areas. Beach raves can sometimes be an exception, where the bogan requires fireworks, flares and a black shirtless man doing fire twirling. Las Vegas and New York are world leaders in the provision of flashing lights, while Phuket and Ibiza do their darndest to adorn their sands with a cloak of epileptic strobes.

META-FACTOR: OTHER BOGANS

This BOGAN factor transcends all of the others and scores triple points on the bogan importance scale. Even if a bogan managed to find a magical wonderland where all five of the aforementioned BOGAN factors coexisted in perfect harmony, there is a real risk that the bogan would not want to be there unless there were other bogans onsite also. There are many reasons for this, ranging from 'oi oi oi' chants as back-up in the event of glassings, right through to the capacity to form a boganic voting bloc when lobbying a DJ to play Kings of Leon. The unwillingness to be away from other bogans at any time is a key appeal of Contiki Tours. Roaming in a pack also reduces the probability of a bystander taking a bogan to task for being a bogan.

The ultimate boganic destination

Armed with this knowledge of what the bogan requires from its travels both at home and abroad, it is possible to create a travel and hospitality venue that can extract more bucks from the bogan than the bogan possesses, both now and in the future. As has been touched on in the explanations of the BOGAN magnetism factors, the bogan's behaviour — while constantly boganic — does change when it travels overseas. Therefore it is first important to establish whether, as a bogan-mustering entrepreneur, you are asking the bogan to travel domestically or internationally in order to offer its dollars to you.

Domestic

The bogan knows that it can't get its hair cheaply braided into cornrows in Australia, but that's okay because it doesn't want them anyway. Instead, the bogan is interested in looking as celeb as possible. This is generally done by locating itself near expensive things such as premium retailers, French Champagne and other bogans wearing clothing from premium retailers and drinking French Champagne. Ideally this destination will be familiar to the bogan because TV crews film it. Charging a high entry price is desirable because it helps the bogan to convince itself that it is doing something elite. The element of maxtremity is also desired, often via consuming luxury to the maxtreme.

While numerous people may be aware of the need to offer the bogan this type of domestic destination, relatively few have a sufficiently large bunker of cash to execute the plan. James Packer — one who has never lacked the bunker — owns arguably Australia's two finest domestic bogan hot spots. Crown Casino in Melbourne is Australia's largest casino by size and the venue for the Logie awards, and it features a riverside promenade that shoots giant balls of flame into the night sky. When this is paired with the prospect of Shane Warne being somewhere in the building losing a poker game while wearing a Lycra tattoo sleeve, bogans will travel from far and wide to attend this giant, gaudy, shimmering mecca packed to the gills with shit nightclubs, high-end retailers and resultant swarms of bogans.

Brian McFadden may have won this hand, but he lost Delta's.

While Burswood Casino isn't quite as large and offensive as Crown, it makes up for it in other ways. The complex features a large entertainment arena which during 2011 alone has played host to bogan-approved activities such as monster trucks, WWE wrestling and Usher. It is also newly home to the Rockpool Bar and Grill, which offers the Western Australian bogan the chance to pay $110 for a steak and then complain that it's too raw. Burswood's Perth location makes it the ideal choice for cashed-up mining bogans who fly in for the weekend from the Pilbara, and easily enables the bogan to burn through upwards of $5000 in a 72-hour period. Star City Casino in Sydney is the next best bogan option, and while it admittedly lacks giant balls of flame and direct flights from the Pilbara, it does have the word 'star' in its name, and celebrities have probably been there.

While a trip to a Packer-owned casino ticks all the boxes for a bogan night out, this sometimes leaves the bogan at a loss during the daytime. Each springtime this problem is solved by the Spring Racing Carnival, which leaves the bogan at a loss via a different method: uninformed gambling. A day at the races allows the bogan to be near designer clothes and French Champagne; there is expensive food, expensive horses and expensive ways to gamble.

Television crews are routinely onsite, sharing in the bogan's eternal quest to spot celebrities. Flemington Racecourse is the foremost bogan raceday venue, with tens of thousands of bogans sighted in peach-coloured polyester suits, or with giant feathers pinned to the side of their heads.

How to attract a bogan to a venue, party or state

Do:

- Ensure that reality television contestants are seen at the venue.
- Furnish the venue with as many unnecessary red carpets and velvet ropes as possible.
- Provide a VIP area where the mini spring roll platters have an extra type of dipping sauce.
- Attempt to incorporate some form of pyrotechnics, regardless of relevance.

Don't:

- Market the destination as affordable — the bogan wants to pay as much as possible.
- Locate it somewhere outside of mobile phone range — the bogan needs to upload pics to Facebook so everyone knows it's there.
- Stock Champagne brands the bogan hasn't heard of — they are of no value to the bogan, regardless of quality.
- Close early — you will make most of your money from the bogan once its fifth Jägerbomb sends it maxtreme.

International

As already mentioned, the bogan overseas feels liberated from its normal need to be seen as classy and celeb. When a bogan leaves our shores it devolves into the ultra-bogan. Gone are the fancy clothes, fancy booze and desire to hire limousines. In its place is a bogan swigging cheap liquor from a bottle while it rides shirtless and helmetless on the back of a motor scooter, yelling unintelligibly at anyone unfortunate enough to walk up a street shared by the motorised bogan. The bogan abroad feels anonymous, bulletproof and able to ascend to new boganic heights. As a result, an expensive Australian-based bogan shrine such as Crown Casino would be unlikely to have the same capacity to hypnotise bogankind if it was located overseas.

Aside from London — where the bogan's preferred neighbourhood of Shepherds Bush has been remodelled to be as un-overseas as possible — south-east Asia surely holds the title as the ultimate bogan overseas destination. Due to poverty the area remains as cheap as hell for the bogan, ensuring that even bogans who work in hospitality back home can leverage their spending power to act appallingly to local staff.

While Australia's climate affords the bogan ample opportunities to get sunburnt, the ferocity with which the bogan applies itself to this task increases considerably when in south-east Asia. If provided with a destination featuring immense volumes of sun, the bogan will stay longer, drink harder and spend larger. Aside from the increased costs for bouncers and security staff, venues generally want the bogan to spend until it vomits, and then for at least a couple of hours after that. This process can be enhanced by watering down the bogan's Jägerbombs and buckets, thereby acquiring more bogan bucks per stomach pump.

The relaxed road laws in south-east Asia allow the bogan to hire 100 cc scooters and draw on their minimal scooter-riding experience to tear around blind corners at speed. The heterosexual bogan male would never be caught dead on a scooter in Australia (where they're only for fags), but the amount of hobbling, bandaged bogans wincing their way to Australian-themed bars in south-east Asia is testament to the number of bogans almost literally caught dead on these scooters overseas.

Bali was the original bogan destination, with a track record stretching back decades. The rest of Indonesia is too confusing and Islamic for the bogan, so the next destination to develop was Thailand. The presence of Thai ladyboys is a bottomless source of bogan laughter, as is the bogan's first run-in with magic-mushroom milkshakes. In recent years the bogan has caught wind that Laos, Cambodia and Vietnam are even poorer than Thailand and offer the bogan cheaper beer and massages. Tourism workers in these countries have striven to lift their English language skills to the sweet spot where the bogan can understand them yet still laugh at them. Political problems in Burma have kept that country off Jetstar's (read: the bogan's) radar, though this may change in the future. Singapore's locals are too rich to exploit and the country has too many rules for the bogan's maxtreme taste.

How to attract a bogan to your country

Do:

- Stock Australian liquor at high mark-ups.
- Ensure that you stock white singlets bearing the name of the cheap local beer that made the bogan vomit four times in a week.
- Lobby Jetstar to get it to fly to a nearby airport.
- Redouble your earlier efforts to get Jetstar to fly to a nearby airport.

Don't:

- Have too many foreign words on the drinks list or menu — a few is fine, but keep them easy.
- Let the ladyboys get too realistic, for it will result in immense bogan shame.
- Tell the bogan what to do, just bandage it at the end of each night.
- Forget to lobby Jetstar to fly to a nearby airport.

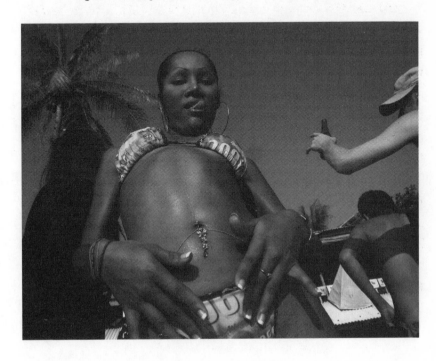

The well-travelled bogan will Facebook loudly about their latest trip to drink, shop and sunbake but once they are home they are ready to sit back on their faux leather L-shaped lounge and watch their 'no deposit, no interest, no repayments for eighteen months' massive home theatre TV screen. Here they can safely be bombarded with ads for things they have to have during the multiple ad breaks of *Two And A Half Men* and the latest *Underbelly* instalment. As many tourist operators have discovered, marketing to the bogan is a highly lucrative business. This niche segment of boganic understanding is covered in Chapter 4.

3
ECONOMICS

Fundamental to the bogan's economic existence is the need to buy things. Descartes' 'I think, therefore I am' was quickly replaced with 'I consume, therefore I want'. This was to be the shrill catchcry of the nouveau bogan, a voice that was heard loud and clear by many a rogue marketing graduate. At the heart of the study of bogan economics — or boganomics — is the way in which the bogan chooses to buy, heedless of the limits imposed by trivialities such as income or available credit. As the following principles of boganomics will show, the magnetic forces of needs, wants and credit combine to form the flypaper to which the bogan is inexorably drawn. Consequently, the science of economics has warranted a change in definition, scope and application in order to reflect the new Armani-clad participant and its impact on commerce as a whole.

At this point it is pertinent to ask whether or not this sort of arcane theorising is beneficial to anyone. Does it matter that the bogan is here, and spending? The answer is a resounding yes. Analysing the impact of a new market entrant in an economic system is best compared with studying the effects of the introduction of the cane toad into northern Queensland. Evolutionary biologists have long been documenting the effects of an introduced species into an existing ecosystem in order to assess their potential for disrupting biodiversity. Where the cane toad (*Bufo marinus*) promptly establishes a beachhead before proceeding to eradicate whole species of quoll and goanna, the bogan (*Boofhead marinara/Homo boganus*) establishes a line of credit then proceeds to eradicate vast swathes of consumer goods from shop displays. The results, while shocking, reflect a deep social malaise, one in which ideals such as rationality and intellectualism have been trumped in favour of myopic self-interest and gluttonous materialism.

Definition

Economics is the study of the allocation of scarce resources in the most efficient manner possible. Boganomics is the study of the perceived absence of scarcity of resources. It is a multidisciplinary science that tackles the irresponsible allocation of land, labour and capital resources due to the actions of certain economic agents collectively known as bogans. Using various methods of investigation and critical analysis, it explains the workings of the economy; interaction between its agents (bogans), and the helpless attraction to Harvey Norman's financial instruments.

Classical economic theory burdened itself with concepts of wealth distribution and equality, ideals that are rendered useless when considering the bogan of the twenty-first century. Like David Ricardo in the late nineteenth century, the bogan also sees an inherent conflict between landowners, people who want to own land and people who own guns. Boganomics ignores the absurd idea that resources are finite — because the bogan's needs are not. Therefore, as the bogan's consumption increases, thus do the world's resources grow exponentially. This curious marriage of variables is a seminal constant in the realm of boganomic thought, and thus is important to understanding subsequent chapters of this text.

As illustrated in Figure 3.1, the bogan's needs tend to comprehensively outperform global variables of population growth, available resources and the perception that these resources are renewable and limitless. Complex mathematical modelling techniques have shown, however, that at least 70 per cent of the planet cannot in fact be reproduced, regrown, regenerated or remixed on a scale that can sustain the bogan's consumption needs. This has created a boganomic quandary that can only be understood by delving into the inner sanctum of this new and exciting discipline in order to understand its mysterious dimensions.

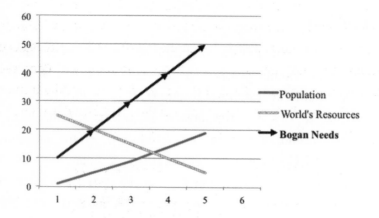

Figure 3.1 Relationship between the bogan's needs and forecast world conditions

Demand and supply

The theory of demand and supply is a (dis)organising principle to explain prices and quantities of goods or services sold in order to determine an equilibrium point. As a rule of thumb when supply exceeds demand for a given product, price will fall. When demand exceeds supply, the bogan gets extremely angry. When prices also increase it grows even more irate and this almost always results in an external variable being glassed.

EXAMPLE

The bogan likes to drive. Everywhere. This requires petrol, which costs money. Sometimes other people also *need* to drive — say, to see their terminally ill mother or when milk needs to be transported from cows into flavoured milk. Eventually lots of people require dairy-based beverages and lots of sick people require seeing. This results in the demand for petrol exceeding its supply, thus raising the price. This occurs because there are only so many Gulf countries that can be invaded at any given time and it takes longer than an episode of *Border Security* to economically refine crude oil.

In the meantime the angry bogan has already purchased its new V16 Turbo Max Subaru, determined to get to places faster so it won't use as much petrol. On its next refill the bogan realises that nothing has changed: prices have gone up again. Confused and livid, it switches on *Today Tonight* for answers. Luckily it finds a scapegoat — the government is to blame. It drives down out to the local pub to ease the tension. A c*** is glassed.

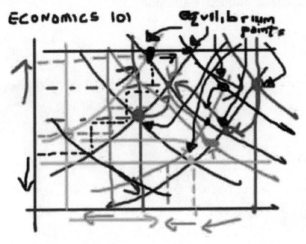

Figure 3.2 A simple graph plotting the demand and supply schedule

Elasticity

Elasticity is a central concept to supply-and-demand theory. It swiftly determines the extent to which demand will respond to the change in the price of a good or service. An elastic good is one for which a price rise will result in far fewer people wishing to purchase it — say, a diamond ring. An inelastic good is something people buy at almost any price, such as petrol or milk. Bogan elasticity, however, is not linked closely to price but, rather, to proximity to celebrities, and demand from others. In effect, the bogan will buy whatever it wants at any price so long as it wants it. If it considers the price to be too high, it will then complain about it on Facebook.

While normal people will question the economics of paying $250 for a T-shirt with an aborted dragon on it, the bogan will remain confident that it scored a great deal because somebody once spotted a celebrity wearing it. This is a telling sign of the power of marketing and gimmicks on the haplessly malleable neurons trapped inside the bogan mind. It is hardly surprising, then, that people who have understood this boganomic abnormality have exploited it to make ridiculous amounts of money. Examples include fashion labels, musicians, sports personalities, beverage producers, chefs, publicists and God.

Figure 3.3 The bogan will understand elasticity only if the concept is explained with this picture

The principle of elasticity in conventional economics assumes a rational and logical consumer. Seeing as the bogan is neither rational nor logical, this concept has had to be turned on its head (see Figure 3.3). This has resulted in an upheaval of the traditional rules of the market, which held that people were assumed to only disregard price for essentials such as cancer medication or disposable nappies. Bogans, however, like a congress of baboons that have recently stumbled upon a large, flowering acacia tree, have blindly stripped the tree of bargains (i.e. raised prices for everyone else) due to their primordial need for unrepentant consumption.

As observed in Figure 3.4, the demand for brand X is impervious to changes in price when endorsed by any celebrity. Driven by cleverly engineered promotional messages combined with strategically placed shots of celebrity cleavage, marketers have reaped enormous rewards from this relationship. This differs markedly from the dynamics expressed in Figure 3.5, where the bogan is terribly sensitive to the sartorial goings-on of Fred Down the Pub. The more Freds it sees sporting brand X, the less inclined it is to follow suit. This is because Fred is not Fred Durst or Fred Perry and the bogan does not want to be seen as, well, a bogan. In an uncharacteristically complicated web of thinking, the bogan feels inviolable in the collective validation of celebrity but distrusts the opinion of the 'common man' it so loathes. The need to be different, while still being part of the safe and popular celebrity-endorsed majority, is one of the defining hallmarks of this virulent creature.

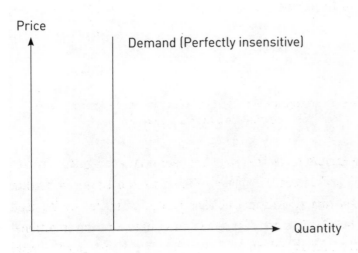

Figure 3.4 Elasticity of brand X when worn by celebrity Y

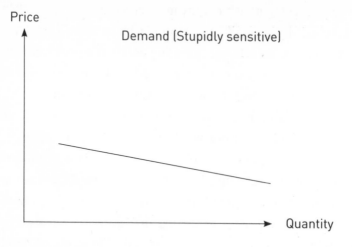

Figure 3.5 Elasticity of brand X when worn by Fred Down the Pub

In this instance, the elasticity of the product Fred is wearing is quite high — the bogan desires to wear something better than what Fred has. This most often results in the bogan purchasing a T-shirt of similar branding to Fred's but in a brighter colour. This indicates the presence of the *Durst–Gaga colour/elasticity spectrum*, (Figure 3.6) which indicates decreasing elasticity commensurate with vividness of pigment.

Lady Gaga regularly blows the Durst–Gaga spectrum.

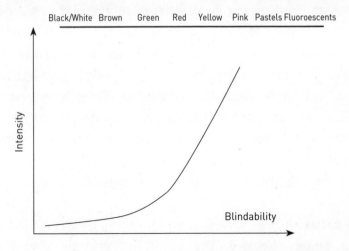

Black/White Brown   Green   Red   Yellow   Pink   Pastels Fluoroescents

Figure 3.6 Durst–Gaga colour/elasticity spectrum

There is one other factor that can greatly alter any given good or service's elasticity: competition. When the bogan wants something that is in front of it, there are few barriers — short of all seven credit cards being maxed out — that will stop it having that thing. The possibility that the same thing will be available at a different price a short distance away, however, changes the dynamic significantly. The greater that distance, though, the more inelastic the demand for that product becomes — drastically so. As a rule of thumb, the bogan will not travel more than 300 metres by foot or 30 minutes by car (the bogan measures distance travelled in cars by a unique timing system) before the product's elasticity precludes making the trip, and the bogan purchases what is in front of it.

Case Study 3.1: The credit malaise

The bogan was responsible for the global financial crisis. Of course, it takes a creature infinitely more strategic than the mere bogan to manufacture a virus that could infect the world's economic system; therefore, it sought help from people it typically derided for being smart. These people came in the form of bankers, marketers and publicists who were nursing an affliction of another global epidemic: greed. The marriage of credit and greed created some interesting outcomes, least of which was credit cards and the fallacious idea of interest-free loans which, in the bogan's mind, translated as 'free stuff' and 'more free stuff'. In order to sufficiently understand the bogan's economic habits it is necessary to view the impact of marketing in tandem with its resultant consumption patterns. The following examples illustrate these twin concepts seamlessly working together like the turbines of an offshore German wind farm.

Credit cards

As abundantly discussed, the bogan is decidedly devoid of foresight. This enables it to make decisions in the present while completely disregarding the future consequences of making those decisions. Therefore, the idea of credit fits in gloriously with this line of thinking. The very idea that one can procure funds to upgrade from a 36" plasma TV to a 58" plasma TV in a mere six months *without actually paying for it* filled the bogan with uncontainable glee. Banks and credit institutions were only too happy to cater to this goldmine and wilfully doled out credit cards, personal loans and other conveniences that were eagerly lapped up like a dog does its own sick.

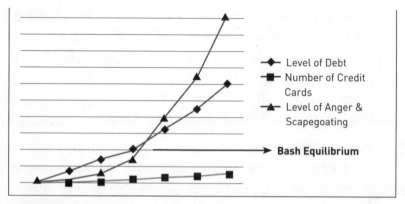

Figure 3.7 Relationship between debt levels and number of credit cards acquired by the bogan

After purchasing everything it thought it required but did not need, there eventually came a time when the bogan was politely asked to actually pay for some of it. Confused and angry, it demanded that it receive another credit card and quickly forgot about those pesky and corrupt banks. This happened a few times, but the idea of debt was never fully registered as a concept of 'that which is owed'. Figure 3.7 plots the relationship between debt levels and the number of credit cards acquired by the bogan over a three-year period.

As shown, the level of anger and scapegoating exceeds the level of debt around the acquisition of the fourth credit card. This point shall henceforth be known as the 'Bash Equilibrium', largely because of the inherent rage contained within the bogan and its propensity to bash anyone soliciting their rightful dues (so named for Nobel Prize winning economist and mathematician John Forbes Bash, who was immortalised in film by Russell Crowe in *Romper Stomper*). Furthermore, being the myopic creature that it is, the bogan necessarily requires a scapegoat on which to blame its hardships. Consequently it will come full circle and finally and squarely blame the very banks that made the purchase of its third jet ski, *Speed Tiger*, possible.

THE ECONOMICS OF SHINY PLASTIC

In a gloriously perverse example of a boganic feedback loop, banks have informed the bogan that it can finance its immediate need for attention via a platinum credit card. Originally the domain of high-net-worth individuals, the race towards the mass market commenced when banks and credit-card issuers realised just how much extra the bogan is willing to pay in order to go platinum. For example, HSBC's platinum Visa card is open to people with just $50 000 of annual income, despite being marketed as 'exclusive, elusive, and not for everyone'. Even this modest level of exclusivity bothered some bogans, who demanded awesome celeb platinum status regardless of their personal circumstances.

Enter bogan Bali facilitator and discount-doling magnate Jetstar, with its Jetstar Platinum Mastercard. The card features an income requirement of $30 000 per year, an exclusive threshold far above the $29 714 per year set by Fair Work Australia in June 2010 as the minimum legal full-time salary. Just like the systematic pillaging of all meaning from the term 'couture' undertaken by fashion marketers over the past fifteen years, the bogan has commissioned and achieved platinum status by stealth. It only has to pay $149 to Jetstar each year, compared to $49 for the non-platinum card. And pay 7 per cent more interest on its purchases of P!nk albums. A truly magnificent piece of marketing. Or a truly heartbreaking display of stupidity. You decide.

Case Study 3.2: Discounting the future and other tales of immediacy

Key to the bogan's survival is its ability to discount the future and revel in the power of now. It is likely that it once purchased Eckhart Tolle's self-help bestseller *The Power of Now* and decided to misguidedly embrace the title after a brief glance at the blurb on the back cover. Not being one to rely on a carefully constructed philosophical or ideological framework, the one thing the bogan knew was that it wanted things badly and it wanted those things *now*. This was duly noted by people who sold things, who were looking for a way to sell more things. After not much deliberation, they realised that stressing the power of immediacy in procuring things would comfortably negate any logic or reason that is normally associated with the purchasing process. Medical science has related this sort of impulsivity to be a major component of various neuropsychiatric conditions such as ADHD and bipolar disorder. The bogan, however, suffers from none of these. Its brand of sickness stems from an addiction manufactured only to perpetuate its love for maxtreme acquisitions.

Consequently, various vendors have told the bogan that it would not have to pay a cent upon the purchase of its new home theatre system/gargantuan built-in wardrobe/jet ski for eighteen months. Unable to contain its excitement at this act of benevolence, it failed to read the fine print that also mentioned the 35 per cent monthly interest that started accruing immediately when the bogan missed the first payment or the 65 per cent interest payable once the eighteen months were up.

Then came the apocalypse. First it received a letter from Harvey Norman stating that it owed them $1800 more than the original cost of its now outdated home theatre system. Ignoring this, it was sent a second letter demanding some manner of payment, as it had failed to make any in the preceding eighteen months. Livid at these pesky turns of events, it sought justice the only way it knew how: by contacting *Today Tonight* and *A Current Affair* to register a lengthy and vociferous complaint about the deception inherent in Big Business. When that failed to deter some brawny gentlemen from knocking at its door, it promptly applied for a new credit card and temporarily forgot about its financial woes.

This is largely due to the fact that when presented with a credit agreement from GE Finance, all the bogan sees is this:

$$\nabla P(x, y, z) = \left(\frac{\partial P(x, y, z)}{\partial x}, \frac{\partial P(x, y, z)}{\partial y}, \frac{\partial P(x, y, z)}{\partial z} \right)$$

$$\nabla^2 P(x, y, z) = \frac{\partial^2 P(x, y, z)}{\partial x^2} + \frac{\partial^2 P(x, y, z)}{\partial y^2} + \frac{\partial^2 P(x, y, z)}{\partial z^2}$$

$$\frac{\partial P(x)}{\partial x} = \lim_{\Delta x \to 0} \left[\frac{P(x + \Delta x) - P(x)}{\Delta x} \right]$$

$$\frac{\partial P(x)}{\partial x} \approx \mathbf{D}_x P(x) = \frac{P(x + \Delta x) - P(x)}{\Delta x}$$

$$\frac{\partial^2 P(x)}{\partial x^2} \approx \mathbf{D}_x \mathbf{D}_x P(x) = \frac{\mathbf{D}_x P(x + \Delta x) - \mathbf{D}_x P(x)}{\Delta x}$$

$$\frac{\partial^2 P(x)}{\partial x^2} \approx \mathbf{D}_x^2 P(x) = \frac{P(x + \Delta x) - 2P(x) + P(x - \Delta x)}{\Delta x^2}$$

It then refocuses, and finally sees this prior to signing the contract:

AWESOME!!!! 👍

Boganic Future Value (BFV), however, does not take into account anything but the present and can, therefore, simply be equated to *awesome* (mathematically denoted as infinity, ∞). Rudimentary pricing theory suggests that the more one has of a product (marginal utility), the less valuable it continues to become (total utility). For example, if a four-person household has four televisions, then it is *reasonable* to assume that *Two And A Half Men* does not become quadruply funnier by purchasing an additional four TVs. In the bogan's mind, however, this is not true. There is a direct relationship between the quantity (i.e. more) and value (i.e. happiness/outrage) of any product that it desires.

By definition, marginal implies small. But there is no such concept in the bogan's economic vocabulary and all references to *small* are thought to have been replaced with *more* or *big* over the course of this rapid evolution. In fact, the Law of Infinite Wants has made life rather uncomfortable for the bogan, as it now constantly hovers in a state of hopeful desperation in order to get more stuff in order to be happy. This has created a proverbial fix, as the Hills Hoist of desire and happiness swirls around in a circle of futility, like a cat chasing its own tail.

In Table 3.1 there is a direct relationship between the number of televisions and level of total and marginal fear instilled in the bogan. As the capacity to screen more episodes of its favourite show, *Border Security*, increases with the number of TVs, the bogan is more fearful that Australia is being invaded by rice-smuggling foreigners. We see that the level of total fear is greater by a factor of 50 when it has six TVs in its McMansion, indicating that at this point it will emit a noise equivalent to the Krakatau volcanic eruption of 1883. Of course, should this be extended to ten TVs, the levels of fear also increase exponentially.

Table 3.1 Relationship between Total and Marginal Value as expressed by Fear

Number of Televisions	Capacity of McMansion to screen *Border Security* (per week)	Total Fear instilled (Decibels per television)	Marginal Fear instilled (Decibels per television)
2	2	20	0
3	4	40	20
4	8	70	30
5	10	150	80
6	12	300	150

Great economists and why the bogan loves/hates them

John Maynard Keynes (1883–1946)

British economist John Maynard Keynes was one of the most important figures in the history of the discipline of economics. His ideas had a profound impact on the theory and practice of contemporary economics, especially in relation to fiscal and monetary policy. It has been said that 'his radical idea that governments should spend money they don't have may have saved capitalism', as he advocated the outrageous contention that spending more money in times of less money will ultimately lead to more money.

WHY THE BOGAN IS A KEYNESIAN

The bogan doesn't care for intellectual debate or thought. However, the recent global financial crisis (GFC) — which it helped create — revealed that the bogan is, in fact, a subscriber to the Keynesian school of thought. Keynes's idea of a government-sponsored fiscal stimulus during times of economic difficulty was grounded in the premise that increased spending by consumers and investment in public infrastructure will, in the long term, benefit the economy as they create tax revenue and jobs.

The bogan loved the idea that it was going to get *free* money for causing the very thing that necessitated the money. It also saw global investment banks and local commercial banks also receiving money as a result of their misbehaviour. Thus encouraged, the bogan now interpreted Keynesianism as 'reward for misbehaviour'. And loved it. The Australian federal government's stimulus package in 2009 was thus engineered to ensure that its biggest client remained loyal, so cheerfully gave it $900 and insisted it spend it all at once. The bogan, stupefied at the turn of events, was now a certified Keynesian.

WHY THE BOGAN IS NOT A KEYNESIAN

While the bogan wallet briefly bulged with the government's generosity and it flirted with the idea that this stimulus stuff was indeed the best course of action, it was quickly disappointed. It was furious when it realised it was not going to receive all of the $42 billion devoted to the stimulus package, and that some of it was going to abstract indiscretions such as public infrastructure on the rationale that it would be prudent for long-term job creation and tax revenue. Immediate gratification was denied. The $900 was spent on hair gel and a new pair of paint-splattered jeans in the hope that the bogan would get more free money, *because that's what the government said*.

Like the flash of a neutron ray, the bogan hated this Keynes poof and busied itself looking for someone to blame.

Adam Smith (1723–1790)

 A moral philosopher, often called 'the Father of Economics and Capitalism', Adam Smith is one of the bogan's favourite economists. Unbeknown to the bogan, Smith's magnum opus, *An Inquiry into the Nature and Causes of the Wealth of Nations*, is a guiding light in its philosophical journey towards its present state of being. Of course, like all things cognitive, the bogan doesn't really know for sure. Smith is, however, most famous for his much-quoted concept of the 'Invisible Hand', in which he contended that in seeking to fulfil his own self-interest an individual unintentionally promotes the interest of others and, thus, of society at large. The bogan's favourite invisible hand is the Stranger that it will perform on itself on lonely evenings. (See *Things Bogans Like*, published by Hachette in 2010 or you can Google it if you don't know what this is.)

WHY THE BOGAN IS A NEOCLASSICAL ECONOMIST

The bogan cares not for anyone but itself, ruthlessly acting to satisfy its own interests. It is, indeed, guided by a very *visible* hand of greed and selfishness, with no intention whatsoever of advancing the greater good of society. This, is turn, has meant that retailers, producers and marketers of every boganic stripe have greatly benefited — albeit accidentally — from the bogan's need for consumption. When capitalism works in favour of the bogan — extending credit lines, approving loans, discounting airline tickets and granting bonuses for mining jobs — it is, in essence, a neoclassical economist basking in the rewards of the laissez-faire market. Self-interest has prevailed, society has benefited and the bogan proudly announced to its barbecuing friends that it 'loves this capitalism business, eh'.

WHY THE BOGAN IS NOT A NEOCLASSICAL ECONOMIST

Should the normal tides of free-market economics not favour the bogan, it will scream and label its participants — such as banks and multinational corporations — greedy corporate fat cats. When it discovers that a fad-based product that it paid $250 to acquire because it was 'limited edition' dropped to a sixth of its price in four weeks, it will insist it got ripped off by greedy capitalists. Being characteristically short-sighted, it is hardly a surprise that when long-term financial commitments (such as shares) that are also subject to the vagaries of free markets go awry, it will cry foul and blame its mate, from whom it sought informal advice. Or the greedy executives who, it will allege, are making too much money, despite the bogan having purchased its third ute from the dividend proceeds of the same company. In these cases the bogan is a free-wheeling socialist, one who fights for the common man's rights to equality.

Andrew Bolt (1959–Present)

Newspaper columnist, radio commentator, climate-change scientist, economist, theoretical physicist, anthropologist and movie star, Andrew Bolt is the catheter of reason through which the bogan forms its opinions. Being the associate editor of the country's largest-selling newspaper, Melbourne's *Herald Sun*, Bolt commands a readership of 1 500 000 a week in addition to writing a popular online blog, making regular television appearances on channels that the bogan loves and saving the world from refugees. While his views are generally considered to be conservative, information scholars have recently found that they are, in fact, inconsistent. In a spectacular display of author–audience convergence, Bolt's opinions are just as fickle as the cancerous tides of populism and convenience that he so effortlessly rides.

WHY THE BOGAN LIKES BOLT

There are about eight million reasons why the bogan likes Andrew Bolt. First, his last name is Bolt, which conjures up images of vascular Jamaican sprinters, lightning or some such maxtreme phenomenon. The other 7 999 999 reasons have, in varying fashion, to do with Bolt's ability to selectively prey on facts and summarise them into easily digestible, highly quotable rants expressing outrage at pretty much everything that the bogan is also outraged by. Wearing a finely woven veil of reason, he asks the difficult questions: 'If parts of Afghanistan are safe enough to build a new housing project to house rejected asylum seekers, why do we take any Afghan refugees at all?' Because the bogan wants to also feel worldly and erudite, it will greedily scan the comments section for answers. Stumbling upon Shazza from Brisbane's reply of 'Bloody oath, let's take care of our own people before we go around caring for others', the bogan is convinced that Australia's refugee policy is far too relaxed.

In Bolt, the bogan has finally found someone it can relate to. Someone that is smarter than itself, yet one who does not challenge its own preconceptions and ideas about the universe. One who presents majestically worded, Year 12–grade arguments about everything that is important in the bogan's world. Its own intellectual ambassador has arrived, riding a horned steed of reason that spits fire at anyone who dares to ask for clarification. The bogan likes Andrew Bolt.

WHY THE BOGAN DISLIKES BOLT

Not applicable to bogans.

Milton Friedman (1912–2006)

Nobel laureate, Presidential adviser and American, Milton Friedman was the leader of the infamous Chicago School of Economics and possibly the most influential economist of the twentieth century. His work largely dealt with extolling the virtues of free-market economics and fervently argued against any government intervention. A strong opponent of Keynes, Friedman argued that increasing the money supply was the only sensible policy and that the government should stop pretending to know what it was doing. Among his other accomplishments was his role in abolishing mandatory conscription, and living till 94.

WHY THE BOGAN LIKES FRIEDMAN

As noted above, Friedman constantly argued against government intervention in economic policy and insisted that an economy be governed by the forces of the free market. This idea appealed enormously to the bogan, because it hates the government and is a neoclassicalist libertarian at heart (for a detailed explanation of boganic libertarianism, please refer to the Politics chapter). Until, of course, it has to pay bank fees or notices that the price of petrol has risen by two cents — then it demands that the government 'do something about it because it pays its taxes'. Another reason that the bogan likes Friedman is because he proposed renegade ideas such as a negative income tax, volunteer military and education vouchers, all of which serve to exonerate the bogan from taking responsibility for itself. More importantly, the bogan likes Friedman because he starred in its favourite movie, *The Shawshank Redemption*.

WHY THE BOGAN HATES FRIEDMAN

The bogan will profess to hate the government and love Friedman's free-market economics as long as the capitalistic tides gently bathe its feet. However, should it be swept away by its own torridly desirous currents of consumption, it will demand that the government help. Usual allegations of 'nanny state' quickly abate when the cost of living increases primarily due to the bogan's own rabid love for acquiring things. At this stage it will promptly expect the government to intervene and lower the price of petrol, reduce food costs, give it free money and cut taxes. It also wants more doctors, nurses, teachers, schools, hospitals, roads, freeways and bridges; a higher dollar, a lower dollar; really, really fast Internet, and no more immigrants.

David Koch (1956–Present)

David Koch is the country's foremost authority on finance, economics, banking, property, tax, saving money and loving life. Having co-hosted a morning breakfast TV show for a decade and completed a bachelor's degree in accounting, Koch's grasp of the global financial market is categorically unrivalled. While occasionally criticised for his 'homespun' approach to dispensing financial advice on national television, Koch's experience as a cadet business journalist at *Business Review Weekly* (*BRW*) afforded him the necessary expertise to tackle vexing questions such as, 'If the exchange rate is AUS$1.00 = US$0.95, why is it that when I want to purchase US $1, I can only get $0.92? I do not understand', with characteristic incisiveness: 'Because it's a rip-off by the currency traders. I will be talking about this on *Sunrise* tomorrow and doing a blog about it. My sister-in-law got hit with the same thing.' Besides being a financial heavyweight, Koch is a published author, humorist and above-average Aussie bloke.

WHY THE BOGAN LOVES KOCHIE

It is not hard to see why Koch is among the top 50 most-respected people in Australia. He is white and balding, wears glasses and hosts a television show. In addition to fighting for the rights of the 'common man' — the same commonality that the bogan strives tirelessly to better — Koch provides a safe air of mediocrity around all of his endeavours. Constant reminders of his devotion to family and kids further assure the bogan that this man is indeed the one qualified to tell it how to invest its life savings. Having walked the Kokoda Track and climbed Mt Kilimanjaro, Koch has convinced the bogan that it should purchase a copy of *Kochie's Guide to Keeping It Real* in order to obtain advice about its financial future. Key to Koch's advice is that the bogan invest in property and blue-chip shares, and siphon more funds into superannuation because 'they all go up'. With heretofore unprecedented ability to detonate all of the bogan's trigger points, Koch is, without question, the bogan's favourite economist.

WHY THE BOGAN HATES KOCHIE
Not applicable to bogans.

Activities

1. Define boganomics and explain why it is important to the future of the human race.
2. What determines the quantity of a good that a bogan demands? Please draw a demand-and-supply schedule using the example of Ed Hardy T-shirts, and hair gel.
3. What is meant by the term 'elasticity'? Describe the effect of Lara Bingle sporting a certain brand of lingerie on the female bogan's credit rating.
4. Please identify the level of outrage as a result of the following events:
   a. Jet ski producers outsource their manufacturing operations to a country the bogan hates (e.g. Saudi Arabia).
   b. There is a sharp spike in the price of petrol upon aggressive nationwide discounting of Hummers.
   c. The price of paint-splattered jeans declines dramatically due to a study that exposes the spurious nature of the garment.

4
MARKETING

Like its modern cousin, the bogan of decades past believed in nationalism. But its relatively smaller world meant that it also very strongly represented its own state and town. Convincing a Melbourne 1970s bogan to drink a Brisbane beer was an exercise in marketing futility, because the bogan vehemently believed that the brewery in its own town was the greatest brewery in the world. Also, aside from whatever sportswear company sponsored its hometown football team, the twentieth-century bogan had little need for clothing that wasn't made by Bonds, Holeproof — and perhaps Levi Strauss. Its car was locally manufactured and 'eating out' meant fish and chips, or a counter meal at the local pub.

Overall, the bogan's broad philosophy towards consumption was 'oi oi oi', modulated by the proximity of the good or service's origin to the bogan's place of residence. However, the second half of the twentieth century saw the rise of very cheap manufactured goods from Asia, and also coincided with the emergence of truly global brands such as McDonald's, Nike, Sony and News Corp. These companies, along with countless others, very much wanted the bogan's bucks. This proved difficult at first, as the bogan wasn't accustomed to the flotilla of exotic brands and couldn't see why rice wrapped in seaweed could possibly be considered edible when compared to a meat pie and sauce.

Enter marketing.

Marketing is the process of inducing the bogan to purchase goods and services that it not only doesn't need but doesn't yet even know that it wants. To people without a background in marketing such things to the bogan, the process can seem daunting. Later in this chapter, bogan marketing will be broken down into a series of steps that will make it possible for you, too, to connect your goods and/or services with the bogan's greasy mitts.

The land since time

Before we go into *why* things have changed in bogan marketing circles, let's quickly cover the progress made by marketers in the recent past. The bogan has been turned from being a sceptical, set-in-its-ways luddite into an extremely malleable piece of consumption-hungry clay that marketers contort into ever more ridiculous shapes each year. This has been achieved by seizing control of the bogan's self-esteem.

Prior to modern times the bogan derived its sense of wellbeing from sporting teams, its mates and cooking food. Nowadays that elusive sense of wellbeing comes from purchasing sporting-team merchandise, impressing its mates by looking celeb and watching people cooking food on TV while eating takeaway.

This is a remarkable achievement by the marketing profession, presumably inspired by the great thinkers who shuffle down the hallowed hallways of the world's finest tertiary institutions. Here is a quick review of the iconic body of academic work relating to marketing.

Marketing – an intellectual pursuit

Academics and professionals have devised a mystifying number of conceptual models and multistep processes with the aim of demystifying marketing. Conventional marketing wisdom suggests that the marketer should conduct focus groups, examine reams of data, create gargantuan spreadsheets and compile dossiers on the strategies of competitors. One of the most famous marketing concepts is the hallowed 'Four Ps'. These Ps — Price, Product, Promotion and Placement — claim to be the ultimate pathway to marketing success. Sensing the power of numerous dot points starting with the same letter, other academics have tried to tack on extra Ps to gain notoriety for themselves. These have included clumsily shoehorned concepts like People, Process and Packaging. Academics with minimal bogan knowledge will plead with you to give Ps a chance.

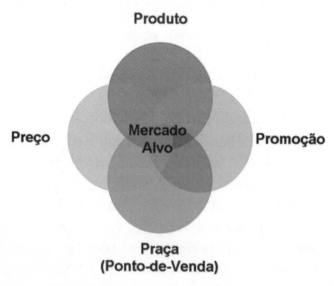

Produto

Preço

Mercado Alvo

Promoção

Praça (Ponto-de-Venda)

Figure 4.1 The Four Ps. The fifth P is Portuguese

However, a Ps offering to the bogan does not, and will not ever, work. While academic textbooks contain many important-looking diagrams and checklists, the reason they are rarely found anywhere other than in academic textbooks is because they offer very little insight into the staunchly anti-intellectual world of the bogan. The bogan aspires to be maxtreme in all areas of its life, and it needs something with a bit more 'X factor' than the application of sensible measures like deciding how much to sell a product for and where to sell it.

Market research and the bogan

There are millions of them, many of them are cashed up, and pretty much all of them like buying stuff when such acquisition cannot be justified by rational means. But why do bogans do this, and what are their preferred *irrational* means? Enslaving the bogan is a key objective of marketing professionals in the twenty-first century; bogans are a juicy market segment that will spend up to and often well beyond its capacity. A marketer's degree of success in this endeavour can be the difference between the product becoming a surprise hit (see Power Balance) or fundamental failure (see *Waterworld*).

Figure 4.2 A sheep, segmented

An important part of being a modern bogan involves not forming independent opinions on a majority of matters. Some people view the behaviour of the bogan as being sheeplike, but the simile goes much further. The bogan is a cumbersome, suggestible, dull animal found in vast numbers in Australia and, like the sheep, it grows a fleece out of its body that needs to be regularly shorn in order for the bogan to remain happy. This fleecy crop is bogan bucks. In order to efficiently extract bogan bucks, marketers and advertising professionals (regrettably) need to spend time inside the bogan's mind, identifying the bogan's trigger points in the hope of outmanoeuvring their commercial rivals so they can own the bogan.

The traditional method of understanding the bogan has been immersion: the marketer simply had to conduct endless carefully segmented focus groups with bogans, attempting to filter mountains of nonsense into usable opinions, motivators and trigger points. Another alternative was to go undercover, don the accepted bogan attire of the day and spend hours in shopping centres and nightclubs while whispering notes into a hand-held audio recorder. These repetitious and inefficient processes were ultimately unacceptable, mainly due to the sheer quantity of bogan interaction required.

A better way

As a response to these problems we have developed a model to assist the marketer to understand the bogan. Not an academic model — a model born from the 'real world' that the bogan will staunchly vow it not only inhabits, but reserves the right to be the sole spokesperson for. Our X Factor model, Figure 4.3, contains five bogan trigger points which stimulate the reward centre in the front of the bogan brain, targeting the relentless pursuit of crass instant gratification that is the soft underbelly (as opposed to the totally hardcore *Underbelly* from TV).

The obvious common theme of the model is the letter X. This is, by some margin, the bogan's favourite letter. Numerous marketers have identified this and incorporated it into product names, without realising that the bogan's underlying behaviour is also driven by the eXcitement derived from these five X Factors. The following pages contain an analysis of these five boganic trigger points.

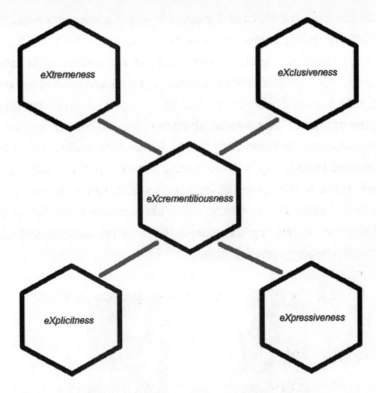

Figure 4.3 The X Factor model. Hexagons = gravitas

eXtremeness

Years of taking things to the max have created fundamental chemical changes in the bogan, and these changes are particularly pronounced in the male. Its brain does not respond well to the prospect of subtlety; the bogan craves the eXtreme in order to send it soaring to dizzying heights of pleasure. As such, any product pitched at the bogan needs to announce the bogan's consumption in the most radical (yet conformist) manner possible. If a lawn mower requires a 6-horsepower engine to cut grass, sell the bogan a 35-horsepower model that runs on higher-octane premium petrol. For twice the price. Then tell the bogan that the sliver of lawn in front of its McMansion will be cowering in fear every weekend, hoping that the 'Grass Thrasher 4000 Demon XT' isn't wheeled out of the garage. To the eXtreme.

If you are seeking to sell a car to a bogan male, do not call it 'the leisure cruiser'. Cruising suggests to the bogan that it would be able to proceed at a leisurely pace, at harmony with its surrounds. Instead, call it 'the ROCK-KRUSHER'. The excited bogan will instantly picture itself dominating its environment in a stunning display of power. The promise of a product allowing the bogan to become the alpha male in its locale is remarkably compelling to the bogan mind. In case the bogan is still unable to visualise the scene, there is the option of creating an advertisement depicting the bogan male scaling Uluru in its eXtreme ROCK-KRUSHER, in the process pulverising the monolith into a red sandpit suitable for female beach volleyball players.

REAL WORLD™ BOGAN EXAMPLE: PEPSI

The male bogan will not purchase Diet Pepsi with its angelic white background, rounded girly font and implication that the bogan is trying to become less manly. Pepsi figured this out in the mid-1990s and released Pepsi MAX, which allows the male bogan to take its low-calorie cola consumption to the eXtreme. In 2011 Pepsi MAX sponsored a V8 Supercar, covering the car in eXtreme graffiti. This proves beyond all doubt that even the girliest of products can be made eXtreme for the bogan, and that the bogan will then purchase it.

eXpressiveness

The bogan is desperate for everyone to know the full extent of its prosperity and personality. It sees no logic in purchasing something expensive unless one (and preferably more) of an onlooker's senses is bludgeoned by the eXhibition of that something. Therefore, any product pitched at the bogan *must* be a loud statement of some sort.

While often happy for the eXpressiveness to be a statement relating to the bogan's mastery of one of the other four X factors, at other times the bogan feels no need to understand the nature of its statement at all. Any bogan wearing a brightly coloured T-shirt with 'Rio de Janeiro Championships Princess 86' emblazoned across it is unlikely to have been to Rio de Janeiro or to understand any of the slogan.

Marketers can appeal to the bogan's quest to overgarnish itself, devising nonsensical slogans, designs and methods with which, via consumption, the bogan may express the process of expression. A female bogan will not pay $1000 for a Tiffany & Co. bracelet unless it is eXtravagantly branded, preferably in letters larger than the bracelet itself. The bogan will generally only be happy once it is a blinding peacock monument to all of the things it has purchased.

REAL WORLD™ BOGAN EXAMPLE: PERSONALISED NUMBERPLATES
Unsatisfied with the amount of eXpression that is made possible by spending thousands of dollars modifying a car and then covering it in stickers of the various brands it wants to boast about, the bogan also requires a six-letter statement to the world to be displayed on its numberplate. State-based road and traffic authorities have recognised this bogan need and now charge the bogan hundreds of additional dollars per year so that its vehicle can be called '2SXY69'.

eXclusiveness

Because celebrities have eXclusive things, the bogan wants them too. While millions of bogans acquiring an eXclusive product will serve to systematically strip the product of any of its eXclusivity, this does not deter the bogan. The reason many of these things are difficult to acquire is their high price. No matter: the bogan has a great willingness to bridge the gap between its needs and wants via credit cards, thus obtaining products that it deems to be eXclusive.

One definition of eXclusivity relates to products or services that are hand or custom made, or only available to certain people who have achieved things. The bogan has little time for this definition, as its interpretation of eXclusivity is generally 'fashionable, factory made, heavily marketed and very eXpensive'. To the bogan, eXclusiveness is interchangeable with eXpensiveness.

Real estate salespeople, often being bogans themselves, understand the bogan's desire to think that it possesses things that are hard to get. If a new apartment development is constrained in size by factors such as land size or height restrictions, the salesperson will go to great pains to portray each apartment as 'eXclusive'. This is true to the extent that external factors excluded the developer from making more money by adding four extra floors to the building. Undeterred, many real estate developments are declared to be exclusive even if they're sprawling campuses of poor-quality cement sheeting and pine floorboards.

Similar to the word 'couture', the bogan has minimal grasp of the word 'boutique'. The blame for this can largely be laid at the Italian leather shoes of marketers, who have been valiantly trying to convince the bogan that small things called 'boutique' are as good as big things that are maxtreme. The bogan generally remains unconvinced.

REAL WORLD™ BOGAN EXAMPLE: TOOHEYS EXTRA DRY PLATINUM

In May 2006 Tooheys Extra Dry Platinum, a beer with increased alcohol content of 6.5 per cent, was launched, with the first shipment selling out in days. The 'platinum' branding completely changed the bogan's attitude to a beer brand that was otherwise quite mundane, producing sales results which warrant further investigation of the power of platinum. The beer is also sold in eight-packs, as opposed to the traditional six-packs of most bottled beers. Besides appealing to the bogan who generally believes more is better, this makes it difficult for the bogan to calculate whether it is getting a good deal or not, leading it to conclude that because the product is platinum, it is a very good deal indeed.

eXplicitness

This X posits that a product that allows the bogan to become more crass is a product that the bogan wants. Any idea that takes more than five words, five seconds or five brain cells to convey is likely not to resonate in bogan circles. In order to connect a product with the bogan audience it needs to be reduced to a pixellated caricature of something good. Something that locks onto the animal urges of the bogan. And while the bogan has numerous animal urges, one stands above all others.

Brothels have known for millennia that sex sells. This hypnotic effect is particularly pronounced in the bogan, who will be far more likely to purchase anything that brings with it the vague promise of more sex with hot people. Accordingly, in order to sell something as remarkably nonsexual as cold and flu tablets, the bogan requires a marketing angle that directly connects clear sinuses with getting max laid.

It is, though, not enough to just bombard the bogan with unlikely scenarios that link consumption with sex: the bogan wants to *be* the sex. In its ongoing quest to remove dignity from its life, a bogan female's willingness to pay for a swimsuit is inversely correlated with the amount of fabric in the swimsuit. A similar phenomenon is regularly noted amongst male bogans, where a male who has decided to get huge in the gym will then wear a T-shirt whose sleeves are too small for it. In its bid to convince onlookers that it is extremely sexual, the bogan will thus seek to provide an overwhelming volume of evidence.

REAL WORLD™ BOGAN EXAMPLE: LYNX

For years deodorant manufacturers have used the suggestion that their fragrance might enhance a man's chances with members of the opposite sex. Global consumer products giant Unilever had long used this strategy, to moderate success, with its Lynx range of male deodorants. But, unhappy with their share of the bogan market, the marketing gurus at Unilever launched a new campaign in 2007 entitled 'the Lynx effect'. Dispensing with any notions of subtlety or realism, the new ads featured increasingly absurd depictions of nerdy-looking guys picking up really hot chicks due solely to the seemingly magical properties of their Lynx body spray. This culminated in an advertisement featuring hundreds of bikini-clad beauties navigating difficult geographical terrain in an attempt to sexually devour a particularly nerdy-looking Lynx wearer.

eXcrementitiousness

The attainment of this fifth and final X factor is often a product of an unpleasant combination of numerous other X factors. In order to embrace a product, the bogan does not apply normal tests of utility, quality, affordability or modesty, rendering the bogan very prone to embrace things that are shit. Indeed, this grand tradition of shithouse product consumption stretches back into the depths of bogan history. A landmark event in eXcrementitiousness occurred in 1954, when, to commemorate the Queen's visit, Crown Lager was first released to the Australian public. This product was expensive, erstwhile, exclusive and bore a large gold label. Predictably, this shit product became a bogan staple for decades hence and a valuable blueprint for product marketers seeking to endear eXcrementitious products to the bogan (see Chapter 10, Food and Drink, for more detail).

In a crowded product marketplace it is sometimes difficult for the bogan to sort the wheat from the chaff. Products endorsed by credible scientists or relevant experts are reasonably likely to be good, but of little interest to the bogan unless the product also satisfies numerous X Factor criteria. More reliable in terms of successfully locating terrible products are the paid opinions of celebrities, good-looking people and pseudo-experts.

REAL WORLD™ BOGAN EXAMPLE: POWER BALANCE

In the period before they were punished by the ACCC for running a major scam against bogans, the distributors of Power Balance wristbands promised the bogan up to '500 per cent more power, flexibility, and strength' courtesy of wearing a $60 rubber wristband with mystery holograms on it. Approved by leading scientists such as Brendan Fevola and Benji Marshall, this product surely has to rank amongst the shittest things that the bogan has ever purchased.

Selected other tools to court the bogan

Premiumisation

Because of the bogan's steadfast belief that it 'deserves' things that are far in excess of what it actually needs, marketers are presented with a valuable opportunity to not only induce the bogan to consume phenomenal amounts of goods and services but convince the bogan that the things it is being asked to consume are a lot better than they actually are. If the bogan is told by a marketing campaign that a product is of premium quality, it will generally accept that assurance without further analysis.

If a marketer was tasked with getting the bogan to purchase clothing, an easy way to simultaneously increase the bogan's willingness to pay, along with the quantity demanded, is to include the term 'couture' somewhere in the branding. The bogan is aware that the word revolves around the concept of awesomeness, and the bogan does certainly wish to be awesome. While any genuine couture clothing is likely not to be famous enough in bogan circles to gain the bogan peer recognition that motivates expensive fashion purchases, any old factory pap from Guangzhou branded as couture can command a mad bogan cash premium.

Similarly, Australian-based brewers' purchases of the right to brand their products as Stella Artois, Beck's and Heineken has been a fantastically effective way of extracting a new bogan cash premium for something that the bogan has always had. While these beers routinely taste different to the same products brewed in their respective homelands, bogans do not care. Recently liberated by marketers from the obligation to drink the local beer from their home town, the bogan is now willing to pay more money to get smaller bottles of beer with world-famous premium logos on them ... but probably brewed in their home town.

Premiumisation, in the bogan's mind, is generally only achievable via the butchering of a brand or concept with which it is already familiar. But in another wonderful beer stunt, the launch of Pure Blonde by Carlton United Brewers in 2004 saw the product branded as a 'premium lager' from day one, despite the fact that it was sold at similar prices to the brewer's other base-rate beers and didn't contain any extra ingredient or even employ any markedly different production process to justify this premium label. It is at this point that the word 'premium' loses any lingering meaning — which is not to say that the bogan will not continue to fall for it.

Wary (needlessly) that the bogan would one day wake up to the emptiness of the term 'premium', savvy marketers have also prepared a contingency plan: another word that means 'premium', but is arguably more celeb: Platinum (see Real World™ bogan example on page 92).

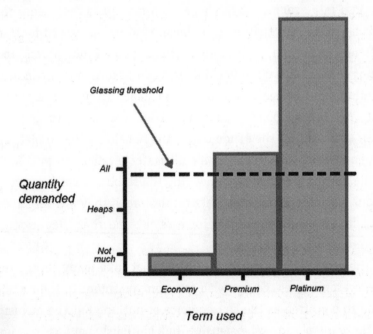

Figure 4.4 Premiumisation and consumption, boganic

Unless there is an unlimited quantity available of a product that is branded as 'premium' or 'platinum', problems will result. The ferocious demand for 'premium' and 'platinum' causes the bogan to become aggressive and competitive, and very likely to glass bogans and non-bogans alike. As illustrated in Figure 4.4, the glassing threshold is situated at a demand level just below 'the bogan wants all of this'.

The bogan, one of the most abundant elements on the Australian continent, has been instructed to swathe its existence in one of the rarest elements in the earth's crust (at just 0.0005mg/ kg). While the bogan is aware of its natural aptitude for going to work in the mines, it has only a vague awareness that platinum is a metal that comes from mines and riverbeds. This is because 90 per cent of the world's platinum is sourced from Russia and South Africa, and these countries are unwilling to pay bogans enough money to purchase jet skis. However, this is not to say that the bogan is not a platinum enthusiast.

In a rare example of the bogan subscribing to the theory that it is better to give than receive, bogankind has bestowed fourteen different platinum sales accreditations upon P!nk, seven upon Kings of Leon, five upon David Guetta and dozens more upon other fleeting chart sensations who have managed to press the bogan's buttons. Female bogans have also tried very hard to convince their spouses that they should give the female a $10 000 platinum diamond ring from the bogan's ultimate jeweller, Tiffany & Co. While bogans are generally unwilling to establish what it might be about platinum metal that makes it desirable, they are very aware that it is a synonym for 'awesome celeb', and that they urgently require it in their lives.

However, marketers have ensured that, like many things that are awesome celeb, things with the word 'platinum' in their names tend to be (often as the consequence of nothing but the inclusion of the word 'platinum') expensive. In a gloriously perverse example of a boganic feedback loop, banks have informed the bogan that it can finance its immediate need for platinum stuff via a platinum credit card. Originally the domain of high-net-worth individuals, the race towards the mass market commenced when banks and credit card issuers realised just how much extra the bogan is willing to pay in order to go platinum. Wisely, most marketers have managed to resist the temptation to brand all products 'platinum' at this time, instead seeing it as a 'break glass in case of boganic consumption emergency' back-up.

Buying the boast

In light of the previous discursion on premiumisation, it's worth explaining the principle that the bogan does not purchase so-called premium products because they're better than non-premium products. Nor does it purchase premium products primarily to enjoy the perceived luxury of consuming them. No, the bogan purchases premium products with the express aim of alerting as many people as possible to the fact that it is consuming a premium product. The bogan is buying the boast, not the product.

As the bogan is generally unable to differentiate between personal enjoyment and the enjoyment of boasting to friends and strangers alike, it would be highly difficult for even a skilled marketer to convince the bogan to pay premium prices for something if it couldn't then boast. Therefore, the more that the marketer can help the bogan to boast, the more the bogan is willing to pay.

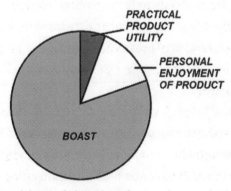

Figure 4.5 Breakdown of the value of a premium product, bogan-style

In the instance of high-end Champagne, it is common for the bogan to gain no additional quenching or taste enjoyment from a $90 bottle over a $40 bottle. Both bottles are 750 ml in volume, so the marketer must supply the bogan with a bogan-boast value of $50 or more in order to induce the bogan to make the purchase. The Veuve Clicquot brand, trying to lure the bogan away from its default of Moët & Chandon, occasionally helps out the bogan with fluorescent orange sleeves, made out of stubby holder material, for its bottles. But well into the twenty-first century, the bogan marketer can do so much more to facilitate the bogan-boast.

A recent and highly effective method for marketers is to create fake Facebook or Twitter profiles to engineer 'organic' fan groups or tweets for their expensive products. Naming them something like 'If you do not select Bollinger Champagne, you're not worth partying with' is likely to appeal to the bogan. At this point the appeal can be ratcheted up a few notches by inserting a spelling/grammatical error and/or an example of text speak. This will connect the group to the bogan's Real World. Example™: 'OMG if u havent got bottles of Bolly at ur party I'm totes not coming!!' This will allow the bogan to confidently join the group and in the process spam up its friends' news feeds with boasts about their affiliation with your product, creating immense value for the bogan and the marketer alike.

The scientific term for this process is 'free viral advertising to infect exponential quantities of bogans via bogan-boast'. Other proven methods include providing branded stickers with the product, bundling the product with low-quality luggage and making the branding as eXpressive as physically possible.

Limited edition

While the bogan loves jumping aboard meaningless consumption bandwagons more than almost anyone, sometimes it will be slow to comprehend the nature of a product being pitched to it. Alternatively the product may be placed at the back of a purchasing queue, behind other things that are also being pitched at the bogan's inflamed credit-card statement. A few bogan-savvy marketers have figured out an amazing loophole that has the capacity to induce the bogan to buy their products immediately, without question and at inflated prices: they tell the bogan that the product is limited edition.

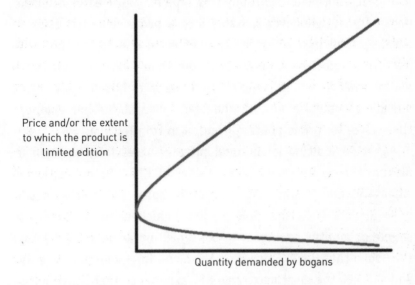

Figure 4.6 The limited edition demand curve

'Limited edition' is the boganic equivalent of a squirrel hoarding walnuts ahead of a blizzard. The bogan is stung into maxtreme action by the mere mention of not having the future option of buying something that it does not need. The 'limited edition' can be limited to a particular quantity of the product or a limited time that the product is available for, or it can mean that the product is so limited in its appeal that only a bogan could possibly justify its purchase.

Robert B Cialdini, Professor of Psychology and Marketing at Arizona State University (Cialdini, R.B. (2001). The science of persuasion. *Scientific American*, 284, 76–81) has undertaken extensive research into the concept of 'perceived scarcity', the theory that the bogan's behaviour will fluctuate wildly depending on how much it thinks it is able to consume. Cialdini observed that 'items and opportunities [are] seen as more valuable as they become less available', and evidence of this process can be found in many aspects of the bogan's life.

It is not currently known which multinational conglomerate is manufacturing black men, but this type of man creates a female bogan frenzy whenever it walks into a bogan-favoured glassing barn. Spurred into action by the perceived scarcity of the black man's rumoured giant genitals (bigger than Richard Wilkins's no matter what Karl Stefanovic says), a swarm of bogan females will quickly accumulate around the black man, bickering amongst themselves for prime pouting position in front of him.

Another multinational conglomerate successfully engaged in making the bogan panic is the owner of KFC. For no particular supply-related reason, KFC's stores in some parts of Australia only intermittently sell its Hot & Spicy chicken. For a period of a couple of months each year or so, hyped-up advertising informs the bogan that Hot & Spicy is on the menu for a limited time only, and that it's the most maxtreme KFC experience that bogan bucks can buy. Instantly the bogan will drop everything and sprint (drive) down to suckle on the Colonel's oily and temporarily spicy teat. If Hot & Spicy chicken was available at all times, the lack of its scarcity would likely result in bogans becoming bored with it, and they would move on to daring each other to pour Tabasco sauce under their eyelids. Perhaps fortunately for the bogan, KFC's marketing department knows just which boganic buttons to push.

While KFC succeeds in extracting $10 from the bogan with its limited-edition pitch, the stakes can be far higher. Each summer, on a pitch of a different sort, Mark Taylor and Richie Benaud will goad the bogan to purchase a 'limited edition signed panoramic photo' of Shane Warne taking a wicket somewhere in the world. In a panic due to only 500 of the photos being available, the bogan will announce its credit card number on the phone, becoming $700 poorer in exchange for the 'rare' opportunity to acquire an autograph that can often be obtained for free at the next Crown Casino celeb poker tournament.

The power of limited-edition anythings to induce bogan expenditure reaches its logical conclusion with 'limited editions' of everyday products. Something as banal as a diabetes-inducing breakfast cereal will announce a limited-edition packet featuring a different colour scheme relating to a current event. After its enthusiastic purchase the bogan will then trudge through 805 grams of Nutri-Grain and throw the box in the bin. A few hours later the hungry bogan will prowl its local supermarket or fast-food outlet for the next item that a marketer has declared to be a fleeting, shimmering comet streaking across the empty expanse that is the bogan's imagination.

The innovation adoption curve

The bogan wants to fit in by consuming things that other bogans are already consuming, and it is not accustomed to utilising independent thought to determine its consumption patterns. Its inexperience makes deviation from that pattern very risky — that's why it needs other people to go first. In music, it's the people who seek out unknown bands in back-street pubs. In fashion, it's the people who support a struggling designer selling their first-ever collection in a plain inner-urban boutique. It is not structurally possible for these people to be bogans.

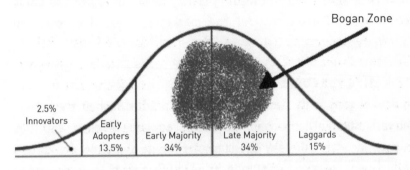

Figure 4.7 Technology adoption life cycle (after Rogers)

A young American sociologist named Everett M Rogers charted this phenomenon in 1962 (Rogers, Everett M. (1962). *Diffusion of Innovations*. Glencoe: Free Press). His segmentation of a market into Innovators, Early Adopters, Early Majority, Late Majority and Laggards has become crucial to an understanding of how to get the bogan to buy things.

Products used by Innovators and Early Adopters are expensive, and the bogan likes expensive things. But they're generally not expensive due to prime-time television ads and huge marketing budgets, more to small production runs, low competition and higher risk on behalf of producers and retailers. The bogan is uninterested in these factors, and thus its zone is considerably further into the adoption curve.

Modern bogans can be found around the middle of the innovation adoption curve, with a moderate skew to the late-majority side. Once a product nears its peak the newly interested bogan will jump on board the bandwagon and ride it all the way to oblivion. Indeed, it can arguably be said that the big winner in Triple J's Hottest 100 on 26 January each year is commercial radio, which instantly acquires dozens of tracks that are now ready for the late majority.

This curve theory is all well and good, but sometimes the Innovator and Early Adopter phases take too long to arrive for marketers to wait for them, and the big bucket of bogan bucks isn't accessible until the feeding frenzy near the top of the curve commences. Fortunately for the marketer, there does exist an alternative.

DEFEATING THE CURVE

Since bogans only tend to consume products that they have already seen other bogans consume, an odd 'chicken and egg' situation arises whereby the marketer has to somehow convince a first bogan to take the plunge. Offering free stuff to the bogan is one way to get the ball rolling, but it hampers any future effort by the marketer to premiumise the product in the bogan's mind. The marketer instead needs to target the hybrid bogan–early adopter. This very rare subspecies of bogan retains some capacity to think for itself and is hence not a full bogan.

In order to connect with the hybrid a restrained, dignified version of the X Factor marketing model needs to be employed. No balls of flame, no screaming — just less maxtremity overall. The pitch needs to imply these things without specifically pointing them out. Using a relatively obscure manufacturer of motorcycles as an example, a branding and marketing angle using subdued colours, fewer stupid stickers and an emphasis on high performance allows the hybrid bogan to purchase a model called 'Calibre' in a moderately discerning manner. As soon as it gets home with its new bike its inner bogan will take over, and the bike will be tearing up the street on one wheel at 90 km per hour. Bogan bystanders will see the nature of the maxtreme bogan feats attainable on the new motorcycle, and it is at this time that the marketer will release the 'Demon Banshee XXX' edition of the bike onto the market. The Demon Banshee XXX is the same as the Calibre, but with lightning bolts, shiny stuff, an abrasive advertisement and heaps more uses of the letter X. This product will succeed, thanks to the bogan-aware marketer.

If a product is so stupid that only a complete bogan could possibly ever purchase it, this can present a significant hurdle when viewed through the prism of the product adoption curve. How does the marketer propel a product through the Innovator and Early Adopter phases, when none of these people would want a bar of it? The answer is — as it so often is — celebrities. By paying celebrities big dollars to wear, purchase, or do something ridiculous, the marketer will soon recoup its initial outlay when thousands of bogans rush to the stores, beating each other up for the chance to be first onto the hot new bandwagon.

Maxximising the bogan opportunity

Marketers should never, ever view the bogan as a problem. The bogan is an amazing opportunity. Other market segments that marketers deal with are likely to be more discerning, more logical and more restrained. When faced with the chance to pitch to the bogan, the opportunity needs to be maximised to the power of max.

BOGAN MARKETING: NOVICE LEVEL

The basic view of marketing involves making your product stand out amongst competitors', and appealing to the target audience in a way that makes the audience more likely to plump for your product instead of something that isn't your product. Take, for example, a hungry bogan. One who wishes to plump for its own plumpness.

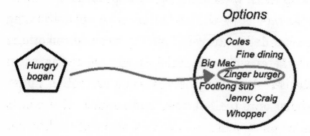

Figure 4.8 Bogan marketing, novice level

As portrayed in Figure 4.8, a marketing strategist for KFC aspires to instruct the bogan that it should not go to the supermarket, nor should it sample fine dining, go to a competitor or go and do something about its waistline. Instead of any of these things, the bogan needs to want a delicious Zinger burger. The easiest way to do this is to apply as many of the X factors as possible from our proprietary X Factor bogan-wrangling model.

BOGAN MARKETING: INTERMEDIATE LEVEL

The novice marketer to the bogan may think that he or she has done a wonderful job by convincing the bogan that it should eat a Zinger burger at KFC. In truth, the marketer's performance has been woeful, considering the opportunity presented. The bogan has little capacity to differentiate its wants from its needs, and its own opinions from those opinions which it is instructed to possess. A higher level of bogan marketer appreciates these facts and will use them to achieve a higher level of success.

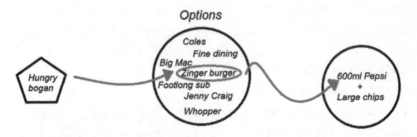

Figure 4.9 Bogan marketing, intermediate level

The intermediate-level bogan marketing diagram demonstrates the ability to make the bogan choose KFC for its burger, and then inform the bogan that it also needs something else in order for the Zinger burger to be truly satisfying. This can be done by packaging the products together and calling this package 'deluxe' or 'value'. The bogan will never evaluate whether the package of products is indeed deluxe or good value, so there is no need to discount or add quality. When packaging the products together the bogan marketer should consult the X Factor model to ensure that the package comes in a brightly branded carry box. Another highly effective method is informing the bogan that the deluxe value meal, while comprising three regular menu items, is available for a limited time only.

BOGAN MARKETING: ADVANCED LEVEL

The bogan marketer who has achieved the intermediate level of upselling, packaging, or expanding the bogan's perceptions of its needs has reason to feel proud of his or her work. A marketer at this level is likely to be promoted to middle management and go on to forge a solid career assisting the bogan in believing that marketing and advertising are instruments that help the bogan, not control it. If, however, the marketer wishes to progress to the top of the tree, they need to abandon any quaint idea that they work *with* the bogan, instead embracing a gloriously depraved hegemony over the bogan's hopes and dreams.

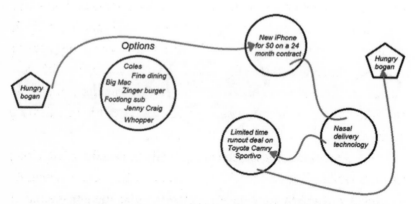

Figure 4.10 Bogan marketing, advanced level

The diagram for the advanced level of bogan marketing shows that the bogan's hunger should not be acknowledged by the marketer. Hunger for food can generally be satiated for $15 or less, and the bogan has more bucks than that. These bucks are the rightful property of the marketer and need to be removed from the bogan promptly. The advanced-level bogan marketer interprets the bogan's hunger not as a hunger for food but a hunger for consumption. For example, a bogan marketer with multiple clients should include in its KFC advertisement a plug for an iPhone app, an app which would allow the bogan to summon a Zinger burger to its couch with little more than a wave of its finger. Now that the bogan is thinking about the benefits of advanced telephony, it is ripe to be sold a poor-value, multi-year phone contract with an overloaded telco. This phone advertisement needs to follow the KFC advertisement swiftly, before the bogan forgets what it has been told it wants.

Stage one complete, the elite bogan marketer will conjure up a nonsensical branding alliance between the phone retailer and the provider of dubious and extremely expensive medical suppliers who promise that they will assist the bogan to have maxtreme sex. The branding alliance does not need to make any sense at all — the bogan is still hungry and confused, and its credit card is warm from previous swiping. An equally meaningless connection can then be made to a car manufacturer via a method such as an 'everyone wins something' raffle or lottery, where the bogan's supplied contact details are then used to pepper it with any number of unrelated marketing schemes. The bogan's hunger has continued to grow, and the idea of a fast car to get it to a feeding venue is likely to be of appeal.

At this point the bogan's bucks are likely to be exhausted, along with its various lines of credit. A $15 hunger has been completely ignored by the advanced-level marketer, who merely viewed it as the soft underbelly of a cash chamber worth approximately $45 000. The chamber thus emptied, this zen marketer can choose to retire to the Bahamas. If, however, the marketer has become so hooked on exploiting the bogan that he or she can derive joy from nothing else, he or she can then sell a 26 per cent interest 'Deluxe platinum' credit card to the bogan, because the bogan is still hungry and Zinger burgers ain't free.

Activities

1. Explain three ways in which the bogan's marketing needs differ from those of the non-bogan.
2. Referring to the X Factor model, identify a bogan-treasured product or service that embodies all five of the X factors and is therefore revered by the bogan.
3. Devise a new product or service in accordance with the X Factor model, preferably in a product category in which existing products achieve only some of the X factors.
4. Develop this product or service, pitch it to the bogan using advanced-level bogan marketing strategy, and attempt to become incomprehensibly wealthy in the six- to twelve-month period before the bogan's short attention span shifts elsewhere. Then, once the bogan bucks begin to evaporate, sell franchises of the product or service to bogans. We will then sue you for 30 per cent of all takings.

With hunger satiated, a bogan likes nothing more than to settle back on its L-shaped faux leather lounge suite it bought from Harvey Norman on eighteen months' interest free at the same time as it bought the home theatre system, and watch the news and then *Today Tonight* or *A Current Affair* (depending on whether they think Tracey is a good sort or not). The bogan prides itself on knowing all about what is happening because of these programs and listening to either Andrew Bolt, Alan Jones or the news guy on Triple M. The bogan's political bents and proclivities are revealed in the next chapter.

5
POLITICS

Bogans occasionally drive through Canberra, the nation's capital, on their way to various other locations. Most often they will buy some fireworks and pornography, stop off at Parliament House, walk away thoroughly disappointed and resolve that they do not like the place. However, none of this is to suggest that Canberra does not like bogans. On the contrary, bogans are the cornerstone of any successful political campaign.

The bogan — with its congenitally limited attention span, disinterest in all things beyond page three of its local News Limited newspaper and near-superhuman self-interest — is the definition of the modern swing voter. While most other members of the national electorate carefully review their political affiliation every three years, weighing up the policies of the competing parties and reaching a considered conclusion, the bogan waits until the day before any given election, turns on the news and asks, 'What's in it for me?'

In 2010 we saw an election campaign in which two political parties, hamstrung by an obsession with budget surpluses and a brief flirtation with words like 'austerity', found themselves short the requisite coin which has been historically hurled at bogan votes in swing seats. The result was that bogans nationwide, forced to consider things like the national interest and effective policy implementation, delivered a minority government, so incapable were they of collectively picking a side.

However, before we delve into the murky morass that is the bogan political mind, let's regress somewhat and look at how we, and the bogan, got here.

The bogan's politics

Over the centuries, political thought has been refined to numerous diverse theories, intended to help us differentiate between clashing ideologies and to refine our own approach to politics. All of these theories coalesce in a swirling maelstrom of ignorance and fury to form one political theory that, as yet, has not received the thesis treatment by a Nobel laureate: neo-boganism.

The reason that this particularly virulent strain of political thought has received so little attention is most likely the bogan's sub-Orwellian capacity to hold so many apparently inconsistent — nay, contradictory — ideas simultaneously. Neo-boganism manages to cobble together elements of such seemingly disparate schools of political thought as classical conservatism, neoliberalism, socialism, nationalism, majoritarianism and a brand of faux-libertarianism adapted from their American cousins, resulting in a mishmash of irony-defeating beliefs that always result in someone being deported.

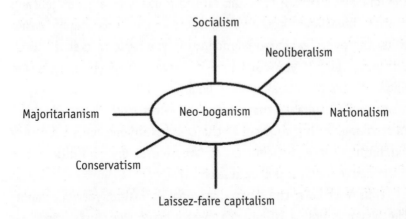

Figure 5.1 Neo-boganism

The bogan, however, sees nothing unusual in this Molotov cocktail of incoherent beliefs. Indeed, to the bogan it is not only sensible but unavoidably, cosmically true that it should pay no tax, receive sumptuous amounts of public money for doing things of little to no social value, receive subsidies for private education and insist on other people's behaviour being regulated, all the while decrying the tyrannies of the 'nanny state'. Any attempt to decipher this political coagulant should begin by breaking it down into its component parts, to better understand how it functions as a whole.

Nationalism

The bogan knows it probably can't ban non-bogans from voting, but it can bloody well try to stop them coming to Australia in the first place.

Nationalism suggests that political outcomes be dictated by the identification of political actors with an entity defined in national terms. More specifically, nationalism is rooted in the idea that a specific ethnic group (bogans) has the right to statehood, or that citizenship should be limited to that same group. Nationalist political thought also places a premium on the primacy of a geographically specific homeland, a thought process made considerably easier when there are no shared boundaries in the nation. In short: 'Fuck off, we're full'; 'If you don't love it, leave, and if you stay, speak English!' This process allows the bogan to self-identify with any of a series of personality traits it opts to select from the spectrum of Australiana, with the bogan at the centre. Anyone not sufficiently exhibiting these behaviours is, therefore, by definition not Australian enough and should leave.

Thus was born the Australian flag as fashion accoutrement. The bogan is not satisfied with merely *being* the most awesomely maxtreme Australian ever — it requires all others to understand this fact, and there is no better way to do this than for the savvy boganista to drape itself in a colourful announcement of its 'patriotism'. When Samuel Johnson said in 1774 that 'patriotism is the last refuge of a scoundrel', he should have added that 'patriotism is the first and only refuge of a bogan'. The bogan knows that wearing its national flag as an item of beach wear is in no way disrespectful but, rather, proof positive of its commitment to the cause. What that cause is, exactly, is a subject for a different book.

What the bogan does not, in all likelihood, realise is that the first prominent Australian to wield the flag in this manner was Cathy Freeman, after she won gold at the 1994 Commonwealth Games and the 2000 Sydney Olympics. After an Australian won an event for Australia in Australia's largest city and celebrated by wearing an Australian flag, the bogan was naturally furious: Freeman toted an *Aboriginal* flag on her shoulders for her victory lap, as well as the defaced Blue Ensign. This perceived subordination of the sacred by the profane was enough to drive the bogan horde into a frenzy, a righteous fury only extinguished by the lingering memory that it could now lay claim to another gold-medal winner — without poaching an Eastern European track and field athlete.

Nationalism can also build a collective consciousness around a semi-fictional imagining of a national identity, most commonly founded on historical events, particularly military battles. But where historians might point towards Australian troops' vital role in key battles across numerous conflicts, for the bogan military accomplishments begin and end with the Gallipoli campaign in 1915.

The godfather of bogan-baiting political sloganeering, John Howard, realised very early in his term the power of attaching the bogan's perception of itself to the military and notions of heroism. Decades of education have begun to remind the bogan that Australia's storming of the beaches in and around Anzac Cove on Turkey's Gallipoli Peninsula actually resulted in a grinding, drawn-out slaughter of the misdeployed Australian troops. While it was initially disheartening for the bogan to learn that Australian soldiers hadn't heroically trounced the towelheads, after watching the movie *Gallipoli* it realised that Gallipoli was all the fault of the pompous British, which allowed it to reinforce yet another long-entrenched prejudice against people who are not Australian.

As a result the bogan will always encourage further defence spending, until it impacts on the bogan's rate of taxation or the level of welfare it feels it is entitled to. A larger military can achieve many things that bogans deeply appreciate, such as stopping boats and cultivating the notion that the bogan is considering joining the army. The bogan will, however, reserve the right to complain about wasted spending. A key example from recent history was Australia's Collins class submarines, which the Trashmedia (see Chapter 6) happily touted as a monumental waste of bogan bucks. That money could have been better spent cladding more bogans' children in khaki to stop more boats.

In the present day of much more sanitised war efforts, the bogan has needed to associate itself with as many proxy wars as possible (particularly on Anzac Day), in between mouthfuls of Doritos and proclamations of its deep-seated desire to do its patriotic duty and become a reservist. Accordingly, the bogan will follow victorious Australian sportsmen (not women) who do not drape themselves in foreign flags. In the bogan's worldview, war and sport are entirely synonymous, and within this paradigm the greatest success story of all has been Lleyton Hewitt.

Hewitt's rise to the apex of the tennis world simply involved too many uses of the word 'battler' for the bogan to resist. From his victory as a fifteen-year-old at the Adelaide International to his maiden grand slam triumph, Hewitt roused the competitive patriotism of the bogan by screaming a lot, calling linesmen 'spastics' (before being cowed into repentance by the nefarious forces of political correctness), and appropriating a Scandinavian hand gesture as a fist pump. (The bogan had not seen this reverse gooseneck when employed by Jonas Björkman so, much like the pavlova, embraced it as an Australian invention.)

While Hewitt was winning, the bogan associated him with the rousing success of its default view of Australia; while he was desperately climbing the rankings, routinely losing to superior opponents, he was our little digger. Periods of mediocrity — characterised by his various stretches spent in the world-ranking wasteland of 100–30 — coincide with periods during which Hewitt is strangely absent from the bogan's self-perception. It is at these times that Hewitt must resort to the Trashmedia to get the attention he feels he now deserves — an effective analogue of our leading politicians.

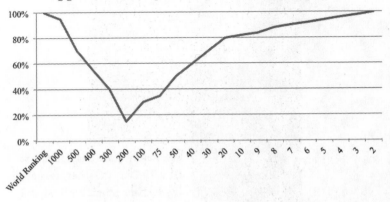

Figure 5.2 Approval rating of Lleyton Hewitt

Neoliberalism

One thing should be noted at the outset: the bogan is in no way neoliberal. Indeed, in all likelihood very few bogans would self-identify as such. Yet neo-boganism features such a hearty helping of neoclassical economic thought (as distinct from action) that it simply must be dealt with here.

Neoliberalism is the application of neoclassical, or free-market, economics to issues beyond simple budget deficits and broadening the tax base. That is not to say that the bogan does not subscribe to the notion of Australia being a pure meritocracy. The bogan, comfortable in the knowledge that it can do anything it puts its mind to — wisdom inherited from the various self-help books gathering dust in its formal lounge — believes in the inalienable likelihood that it will be the beneficiary of the free market. Because it is not an alien.

Neoliberalism, however, moves beyond the notion that private enterprise, left to its own devices, will ensure bogan prosperity in perpetuity, and applies this non-interventionist approach to all matters economic, political and cultural. In essence, neoliberalism

The nanny state has nothing to do with Fran Drescher, except in the bogan's mind. But Fran did host Brynne Edelsten's wedding to Geoffrey, which has nothing to do with anything, really.

dictates that the government should stay the hell out of the affairs of private citizens. The bogan has distilled this branch of political philosophy, developed over more than 100 years, into a two-word complaint: 'nanny state'. A complaint delivered at a similar, ear-threshing volume to Fran Drescher at the height of her fame.

To the bogan, the nanny state encapsulates everything bad about a society that prevents it from doing things that it wants to do. Should the bogan receive a speeding fine, it is the result of the nanny state's revenue raising. The bogan, in its own vacuous mind, has no obligation to anyone else and is unlikely to feel any negative repercussions resulting from its inclination to be places sooner than it otherwise could be. The bogan's need to arrive faster has led to countless thousands of deaths on Australian roads, but the nanny state's insistence on mandating speed limits and seatbelts leaves the bogan aghast at the intrusiveness of government. In order to prop up its argument that it is being needlessly oppressed, the bogan — who has never travelled further from home than Phuket — will refer to the autobahns of Germany (which, incidentally, frequently fall victim to multi-hundred-car pile-ups) and America's absent seatbelt laws and state that they do just fine.

According to the data that can be found if you look, the bogan is correct: Germany does indeed have a lower road toll than Australia per 1000 people. But this oversimplifies the matter. The essential point here is that the neoliberal theory that people can be trusted to make responsible decisions bears out, provided that most of those people aren't bogans. Moreover, the safety of German cars is likely to mean that any driver in an accident is less likely to suffer injury in the form of death than a bogan in a Maloo.

The bogan, of course, also claims to subscribe to the economic theories of Friedman, Menger and Stigler. Although not in those words. When the bogan is employed it decries the expense of paying unemployment benefits to 'bludgers', as it feels its tax dollars are being wasted on reprobates. Likewise, the bogan is an avowed enemy of 'foreign aid', as countries that are insufficiently maxtreme as to provide for themselves have done little to earn a precious slice of the bogan's taxpayer dollars.

However, the minute the absence of government intervention or financial support ceases to benefit the bogan, its tone radically alters and the bogan becomes a slavering, rabid socialist. This is not a sentence that the bogan likes to hear, as it simultaneously holds the Cold War–era belief that communism is an evil force, and that communism and socialism are entirely synonymous. Yet a closet socialist the bogan truly is.

Neoliberalism vs socialism — the bogan's Faustian pact

Money is wasted when not spent on the bogan: if the bogan's prevailing politico-economic outlook could be swiftly encapsulated in one sentence (it cannot), this would be it. With the notion entrenched in modern society that governments have money and can spend it in manners both judicious and craven, the bogan's political beliefs skew towards the idea that government money should indeed be spent. Just not on others. The bogan has sold its soul to the socialists.

Australian politics has long had a collectivist bent: the Labor party of yore was an avowedly socialist party, professing a desire to limit the expansion of business owners (whom the bogan of today refers to as 'fat cats') into controlling the factors of production. While not going so far as to blatantly support an Australian Marxist uprising, Labor ensured the entrenchment of the idea that the government's responsibility is, to some degree, to support the nation's disenfranchised.

If Australia has a collectivist tradition, the bogan has jumped on the gravy train — it just loves collecting. Even as, over the past few decades, Australia's average income has soared and the bogan has become comfortably ensconced in the middle class, it still requires constant — and substantial — subsidisation by other people's tax dollars. The bogan requires official aid to buy a home, to pay for health insurance, to have a family, to buy its investment properties, to educate its children, to conceive its children and to pay for its dodgy accountant mate, who will dedicate himself to compiling an elaborate web of fibs in order to minimise the bogan's contribution to the government that it receives so much from (see Table 5.1 for a breakdown of the communal funds the ordinary bogan family can receive in a year).

Table 5.1 Funds available to the bogan

First Homeowners' Grant (Federal)	$7000
First Homeowners' Grant (State)	$7000
Health Insurance Rebate	$600
Negative Gearing	$30 000
Family Tax Benefit (A)	$6900
Baby Bonus	$5000
Private Education Subsidy	$6300
Total	$62 800

The bogan even sees the need to socialise charity. Due to the bogan not possessing a moral compass that extends beyond its own self-interest, the Australian government realises that it has to give away FREE MONEY in order for the bogan to act generously. Thus, charities the nation over will routinely advertise that any donation to their cause is tax deductible, leading the bogan to greedily hoard the receipt from its $5 donation to Channel Nine's flood appeal program. In the same breath, however, that the bogan will loudly promote its philanthropy, it will decry the fact that its taxpayer dollars are being spent on those unable to 'drag themselves up by their bootstraps'. This is the only known occurrence of a bogan using the word 'bootstraps'.

The bogan also unwittingly associates with a traditional strain of communist/socialist thought: class warfare. The bogan believes that the 'wealthy' should not receive any assistance, in keeping with broad socialist thought, but no bogan has ever — *ever* — self-identified as being wealthy. Shane Warne himself, when asked about his station in life, would no doubt shrug and mumble something about 'making ends meet'. Even when the median bogan household income is approaching $70 000 a year (an income that disqualifies the bogan from exactly none of the above-mentioned government subsidies), it views itself as the 'Aussie Battler'. This is one point of differentiation between Australian bogans and their American equivalents. In America, those who detest governmental interference do so on the grounds that they truly imagine they will one day be in an income bracket that high taxes would inhibit. Bogans, however, want all the support they can get on their way up the ladder before pulling it up after them at the point that they feel comfortable. That point has yet to be discovered.

Despite all of this, the bogan, when asked, will dissociate itself from socialism, communism or any synonym thereof. As the bogan is reluctant to deal in abstract notions and theories, it is bereft of any cohesive, consistent, overarching political belief system. The resulting ideology, neo-boganism, is therefore distilled to the present selective socialism we see today.

Majoritarianism

Majoritarianism is a theory asserting that the will of the majority deserves some measure of primacy in determining the political direction of the state. Alexis de Tocqueville, after his nineteenth century travels around the nascent United States, returned to his native France filled with the fear of what he labelled the tyranny of the majority. Burgeoning democracies frightened and infuriated the monied nobility of Europe, mortified as they were by the likelihood that the unwashed, uneducated masses would vote only in their own self-interest, subsequently leading to the collapse of civilisation. Tocqueville didn't know it in 1835 but he was identifying the onset of bogan politics more than a century before anybody tattooed their allegiance to their shoulder blade in constellation format.

Likewise, the bogan does not know it but it represents majoritarianism in action. While the bogan is inherently self-interested, it is also deeply insecure. It always wants more stuff, although it will only ask for it if the majority agrees. As the majority of voting Australians tends to at least periodically exhibit bogan tendencies, the bogan feels comfortable demanding things that it wants. Loudly.

If a man complains really loudly in the middle of a forest with a megaphone, and no one is around to hear it, does it make a sound?

This ties in with a deep-seated by-product of the bogan's majoritarianism: anti-intellectualism. Bogans do not think deeply about things, preferring instead to rapidly develop opinions based on little more than pre-existing prejudices and facts that can be researched in the summary section of a Wikipedia page. This sits poorly with intellectuals' means of proffering statements, which is to amass evidence, carefully consider multiple competing arguments, then formulate an opinion. The bogan is having none of that. Intellectuals are, almost by definition, not part of the majority. The bogan is. The bogan is right, the intellectual is wrong. QED.

One possible benefit of neo-boganism's majoritarian streak is that the bogan can, sometimes, change its mind. While the bogan will happily and fiercely hold its beliefs in the face of stiff opposition, incontrovertible proof and even bribes, there is one thing that the bogan's Araldited belief system cannot withstand: majority opinion. In particular, majority opinion with a celebrity mouthpiece.

Oftentimes, the bogan will, rather than actually change its mind, simply cease proclaiming its opinions quite so vociferously, but sometimes it has been reported that bogans will alter their not-very-deeply held opinions in the face of overwhelming public disagreement.

Democracy

The bogan believes that it believes in democracy — but it in no way believes in the rights of other people to believe in things that it does not. While democracy is a form of majoritarianism, in any instance where there are more than two alternatives (the Greens being a third party, for example), or opinions, the majority can suddenly swing wildly away from the bogan's position. Confronted by the fact that the society in which it exists is capable of holding more than a binary discussion on any topic rattles most bogans, and leads them to make statements like 'sometimes I reckon this dictator thing doesn't sound too bad'. Coming from a bogan — whose intrinsic desire to never be told what to do by anyone is at the bottom rung of its hierarchy of needs — this would seem to make little sense, but in the bogan's mind the dictator would think and act in exactly the manner that the bogan would wish.

Incidentally, much as the bogan cares not for the Senate, it is also ill-informed regarding state governments. To the bogan, state government does not matter because the bogan doesn't know what it does, except build lots of freeways and allow developers to build new houses in places far away from public transport, amenities, services and jobs. Once it has moved into the newly built cheap housing in a paddock 20 kilometres from the nearest train station — but 20 metres from the nearest Krispy Kreme — the bogan then blames the federal government for its employment situation, and the fact that it commutes through heavy traffic for two hours a day. Then demands more police.

In the end, though, the bogan lives in Australia's federal constitutional monarchy under a parliamentary democracy. The socialist recoils at the banks that are unregulated and charge too much for it to borrow the money it needs for its negatively geared investment house. The neoliberal sighs at the government that tried to tax a mining industry that clearly rescued Australia from collapse. The nationalist roars in fury at the approach of boats that clearly should be stopped. The libertarian groans at the compulsion to vote, but vote it must. Having mapped the bogan's political philosophy, we next take a look at how the bogan votes, and it is not pretty.

BOGAN VOTES
Why does the bogan vote the way it does?
Before any attempt to apply this neo-bogan philosophy to bogan voting behaviour, a more pressing question should be asked: why does the bogan vote at all? While the bogan is fundamentally driven by self-interest, it is at least tangentially aware that it is likely to be the recipient of some rather juicy bribes by the major parties no matter what, so there is little motivation to drag itself, hungover, out of bed on a Saturday morning and exercise its right and duty as a citizen of a democracy.

Perhaps anticipating this outcome, Australia's founding fathers, writing the constitution of the federation they were birthing, presciently mandated voting. Bogans ever since have mourned this fateful decision. It bears pointing out, however, that even with compulsory voting, at the 2010 federal election 7 per cent of the population failed to attend, and another 5 per cent failed to vote properly. This suggests that the threat of a fine only serves as part of the reason bogans attend the booth twice every three to four years. That reason can be broken down thus:

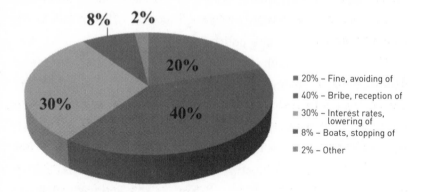

Figure 5.3 Bogan voting motivations

As can be seen, avoiding a fine comprises only a minor slice of the bogan's voting motivation. As most bogans, faced with a letter from the Australian Electoral Commission announcing that it has been fined $50 for failing to attend a polling booth, will simply discard the letter and ignore its contents, the threat actually has less impact than the $50 may suggest.

The bogan, once it decides who it will vote for, always dresses for the occasion.

It is the largest slice of this pie that is most important in our discussion of bogan voting. The bogan wants, as we have seen, the largest slice of the national pie, and the capacity of politicians to cater to this need with succulent bribes is at the heart of the bogan's politics.

Bogan bribes

The capacity for politicians to offer investment in targeted projects for targeted constituencies is nothing new, but if any political trend mirrors the rise of the modern bogan it is the alacrity and enthusiasm with which today's politicians toss out ever-more-bountiful bribes at ever-better-targeted bogan marginal seats.

Indeed the bogan, with its constantly shifting ideological sands — and no overarching, cohesive political theory to underpin its decisions — is by definition a swinging voter. It will sway this way and that, assessing the personal benefit to itself and the withholding of benefit to others in each party's bribes. Thus, marginal seats tend to exhibit a very high bogan quotient. Any seat that is safely in one party's grasp is, almost by definition, ideologically consistent and therefore lacking in neo-bogan thought. The bogan, however, will happily vacillate, ensuring each bogan seat sits on a margin of 0 to 5 per cent, capable of swinging any which way. This, of course, is not to say that all marginal seats are bogan — but all bogan seats are marginal.

It is this paper-thin margin that the bogan can wield as a form of electoral blackmail, ensuring that every three years (and, increasingly, every year in May at Budget time) there is a substantial carrot or two on offer to entice the bogan to put a '1' in the correct box. Please note: the bogan will never, ever, vote below the line on the Senate ballot.

The history of bogan bribes

The first bogan bribe occurred when a snake said to a chick called Eve that she could be more like God and never die, simply by eating some fruit that she had been expressly told not to eat. Eve's impatience and desire to take things to maximum lifespan and deification did not come without its consequences.

The first bogan bribe on Australian soil occurred when Edmund Barton promised Tasmania a bridge to the mainland in order to secure the Tasbogan's approval in entering into Federation. Each of the colonies also received equal representation in the newly created Senate, as proto-bogans of the time were concerned that their ability to extract future bribes from a national government would be hampered if their representative voice wasn't as loud and piercing as their neighbours'.

From the point that Australia became a sovereign nation, happily ensconced under the Southern Cross, the bogan began seeking bribes with which it could correct its wildly oscillating moral compass. After the initial period of dipping their proverbial toes in bogan-baiting waters, Australia's politicians stepped back from the precipice, as bogans between 1901 and 1945 were kept relatively happy by having multiple wars to cheer on and by the White Australia Policy. Then came Ming.

Sir Robert Menzies founded his Liberal party in the 1950s by appealing to a new constituency: the 'forgotten people'. The bogan of that era had long felt — as the modern bogan feels — that it received insufficient taxpayer funding to be maxtreme, and hence that it had been forgotten by successive governments. The new nomenclature was a genius move on the part of Menzies, as it didn't actually involve the granting of any particular bribes. The bogan was being bribed merely by being acknowledged. And so was born a record-setting period of Liberal party rule. The Libs then promptly forgot about the bogan for a few decades.

This could not last indefinitely, however, as even the most thick-witted bogan will eventually realise that the bribes it believes it is receiving are not, in fact, being received by it. After over 80 years of being told it was receiving excellent bribes in exchange for its vote, the bogan woke one day, stared at its solitary television and cried.

The bogan-baiting era peaked during the final years of the Howard Liberal–National government. In fact, for the first time a government realised that it had the ability to offer bribes without even pretending that it was being fiscally responsible.

Much like Eve's godliness and immortality, the Tasmanian bridge never eventuated; this speaks volumes about the early bogan's willingness to go along with the promise of political favours rather than actual bribes-in-hand. Once, the mere promise of a promise was enough to steer the bogan's hand towards the correct box come election day. Today, however, the bogan is more jaded, more aware and more avaricious than its Victorian-era counterparts.

The bogan's modern response has been to want its bribes paid up in advance. Much of the bogan's twenty-first century bribe mongering comes in the form of not allowing a government to repeal investments that were once good economics but which now exist as a means of funding bogan consumption. During the global mini-recession of 2000–2001, the Howard government wisely introduced the first-homeowners' grant, propping up the housing and construction sectors, which was enough to help prevent the recession's creep into Australian homes. However, as house prices (particularly in areas where cheaper houses were snapped up by property-hungry bogans) began to skyrocket, the prospect of removing the handout became politically unpalatable.

This is classical bogan bribe MO: take advantage of an offer, then threaten violent electoral retribution should it ever be removed. This escalated further during the 2008 global recession, when part of the new Rudd Labor government's stimulus package included temporarily doubling the federal contribution to this homeowners' handout. While this is by no means the sole manner in which bogans gain access to other people's taxpayer dollars, it is during election years. Should an existing offer be removed more than eighteen months prior to an election, bogan retribution is not incurred as the bogan is paying no attention.

By the time of writing, the flurry of bribes that took place in the preceding fifteen years has led to a rapid drop in the marginal value of bribes (see Economics, Chapter 3). For each dollar of bribes spent, fewer bogan votes are received, as opponents have come to the bribe party too and bogans will hold out for the juiciest offer. When Howard lowered the fuel excise for bogans looking to save a precious three cents a litre, there was no counteroffer to bring the bogans into a different camp. Today, the combination of competing bribes and surplus fetishisation have lessened the once-magical power of the bribe. It matters little, however, as there are several other things that can drive the bogan to vote one way or the other. And there is one factor in particular that sets bogans' pulses racing like few others.

Interest rates

In 2004 and 2007, bogans were surveyed by all major polling companies to determine their key voting issues in each election. The results remained exactly the same in each instance. Here are the results:

1. Interest rates
2. Interest rates
3. Interest rates
4. Aquatic policy
5. Maintaining the value of their house
6. Housing affordability
7. Cheap food
8. Cheap petrol
9. Cheap energy
10. 'The environment'

Bogans — while having a floating, ambiguous relationship with political thought — have an iron-clad grasp of economics. While the bogan behaves in a manner in keeping with wider economic thought, it also has a simpler approach. Much like it tracks the performance of its favoured athletes, the bogan is fixated on how well the economy is going, and there is only one true measure of economic performance and, therefore, political performance: interest rates.

The bogan knows that interest rates are the key measure of economic performance, as it can see it in the bills it pays on its highly leveraged home. Viewed through this prism, the economy becomes simple: high interest rates indicate a struggling economy in which it is increasingly difficult for the bogan to purchase things it likes on credit, while low interest rates indicate a fiscal utopia where the bogan may borrow unfettered, prancing gleefully among the fields of borrowed money.

The bogan — under the extraordinary levels of mortgage stress it inherited due to the policies of a government that has no control over interest rates — will then approach the bank, asking to fix its mortgage rate. It understands economics, but not fixed or variable mortgages. It resigns itself to watching the monthly announcement on the increase in interest rates and then whining noisily about how unaffordable housing is in Australia. The bogan's fear of losing its only appreciable asset is reflected in how it is treated by the nation's politicians.

Irrespective of all other alternatives that a government or opposition may have at hand, the level of interest rates in Australia will dictate how the bogan votes in the twenty-first century. If interest rates are high, the government will lose. This flies in the face of longstanding political wisdom, which dictates that a strong economy — which usually features higher interest rates — tends to result in incumbent governments remaining so. However, as the modern bogan's economic illiteracy becomes entrenched, it will assess the strength of the economy solely on how well it can meet its interest repayments on its Harvey Norman couch. Accordingly, governments no longer want to maintain a particularly strong economy. Thus, if interest rates remain below 7 per cent the opposition party must make the bogan afraid that they may go up again. Fear is the tool of the political party that can't wait for interest rates to go up.

The bogan will remove any parliamentary party from government once the RBA cash rate crosses that threshold. The fact that this tends to coincide with a natural peak in the rate set by the Reserve Bank, and that interest rates tend to slide thereafter, acts as a reaffirmation that the bogan's ousting of a government has had the intended effect of making shit cheaper.

FEAR! SOLUTION!

Beyond offering bribes, there is little a bogan demands of its politicians. Except ACTION. And LEADERSHIP. However, since there is little scope for either of those in the provision of tasty bogan schmackos, politicians find themselves at something of an impasse. Doing things can create a circumstance where things have a chance of being worse for bogans than before. However, this is unacceptable to the bogan, who insists that the politicians DO SOMETHING. Politicians are nothing if not wily, though, and there are six ways they can provide the aforementioned LEADERSHIP and ACTION:

1. Bribe the bogan.
2. Announce an investigation/commission into something troubling the bogan (for when bribes would be too expensive).
3. Point out that the other party will lead to higher interest rates.
4. Be filmed wearing an Akubra hat/hard hat, listening thoughtfully to bogans complaining about interest rates/the cost of living/boats.
5. Take part in a maxtreme athletic endeavour, preferably while displaying bare chest.
6. Point out that the bogan should be afraid of people poorer than it. Then resolve to wipe them out.

In a strange reversal of the semi-Darwinist, survival-of-the-fittest bogan's ordinary mentality, the bogan tends to view the poor and disenfranchised as a threat, whereas to the politician the poor and disenfranchised are the only members of the community who are in no position at all to offer any kind of threat whatsoever. Still, the politicians must choose a target in order to appease the bogan. And the easiest group to demonise is, of course, criminals.

Aided and abetted by the Trashmedia (see Chapter 6), politicians have managed to convince the bogan over the past few decades that despite consistently falling levels of violent crime, it is increasingly at risk of vicious murder at the hands of a psychotic, slavering, homicidal burglar–rapist.

Research conducted by the Australian Institute of Criminology[1] indicates that bogans all over the nation are increasingly terrified of crime. In fact, 38.8 per cent of bogans interviewed believed that crime had increased 'a lot' in recent years. According to the ABS, however, the only crimes to increase nationally since 2001 were blackmail and extortion, as more bogans spent their time accessing the Facebook profiles of loved ones and holding them to ransom.

Interestingly, the AIC's research also revealed that few bogans considered that crime had fallen over the equivalent period. The numbers indicate that the likelihood of actually falling victim to crime had dropped relatively sharply (car theft fell over 60 per cent), but no doubt the bogan knew someone who had been abducted a few weeks back.

This discrepancy between perception and reality means that politicians can appear on major Trashmedia outlets such as *A Current Affair* or *Today Tonight* and tell bogans how concerned they are about the rising crime levels. This choice of Trashmedia conduit means the politician will not be seriously questioned

---

1 *Trends & issues in crime and criminal justice no. 396*, Brent Davis and Kym Dossetor, July 2010.

before proposing to take action in an inexpensive and ineffectual fashion. Most often this involves banning something that was already effectively illegal, such as knives as weapons. Thus, without having done anything, the politician has convinced the bogan that it now sleeps safer thanks to the diligence of its elected officials.

One of the synergistic wonders of this process is that the bogan has selected two groups whom it knows are responsible for rising crime: drug users and the young. Politicians are thereby provided with two further groups with no political power nor right to vote to routinely vilify without risking electoral backlash. (By 'drug users', the politician is not referring to bogans who happily snort ice or put away fistfuls of arbitrarily labelled pills on a weekend. And cigarettes and alcohol don't count.)

This tactic can occasionally be a fatal error for politicians, however. While the bogan will happily speak loudly in public about the ills of drug use and their corrosive effect on society, it secretly hopes that the government will not show LEADERSHIP or take ACTION, as any targeting of police resources to limit the movement of drugs in Australia will likely hit the bogan's hip pocket quite hard, as restriction of supply necessarily drives up the price of the drugs. While the bogan will use this newfound hardship to make the case for LEADERSHIP and ACTION on spiralling food prices and the cost of living, it is concerned about its ability to fund its maxtreme weekends in the face of the full force of the fuzz.

A recent example of this kind of backlash was Senator Stephen Conroy's attempts to impose a filter on the Internet. Predicated on the need to remove smut from the web and 'protect children', Conroy thought he was on solid bogan policy ground. He was, however, new to the game and unaware of how the shifting sands of bogan ethics can harm the unwary political moraliser. When interviewed by polling companies the bogan would always indicate, in its socialist manner, that it favoured censorship on the Internet, the better to protect its children. At home, though, furiously pummelling away at itself as it watched 'Bambi' and 'Jessikah' apply various power tools to one another, the bogan grew greatly afraid. Sermonising notwithstanding, it could not bear to lose its porn. Thus was the ALP very nearly handed a first-term ousting at the hand of undersexed bogans nationwide.

Conroy's web filter is unlikely to block the recurrent nightmares afflicting anybody who's had the misfortune of seeing Warwick Capper's sex tape.

Porn loss is not the only thing that scares bogans, however. Sometimes, something appears on the political horizon so terrifying to bogans that it is all politicians can do to offer a sufficiently vindictive solution before bogans, in a frenzy of terror, begin self-immolating in the streets. And if there is one thing that sets bogans a-trembling, it is boats.

Stopping boats

If desperate foreigners arrived on Australia's shores via jet ski, the odds are that their arrival by water would not be a politico-bogan issue. But they do not and it is. This is a poorly understood and only sparingly explored facet of the bogan's psyche: it is terrified of boats. It is concerned that boats arrive on its shores illegally, that the boats' arrivals are harbingers of wave after wave of terrorism, and that boats will take its jobs and suck up its taxpayer dollars via welfare rorts.

That the boats claim to be victims of mistreatment elsewhere is of no interest to the bogan who, with its neo-bogan hat firmly on, insists that sparse government money should not be spent on these things; that it is government overreach. The bogan does, however, expect politicians to engage in a form of labour protectionism, artificially inflating wages, rather than have these boats move into its landlocked home and seek gainful employment.

Upon deeper inspection, however, it becomes apparent that it is not boats, strictly speaking, that bogans are afraid of; indeed, there is something of a polarisation regarding which boats bogans will allow on its shores and which it will not.

Boats bogans like = Jessica Watson's *Ella's Pink Lady*.

Boats bogans dislike = asylum seekers' boats.

Prior to 2000 the bogan cared little about the arrival of a fractional percentage of Australia's immigration intake at Christmas Island, as it had a job, was paying low interest rates and was far more upset about the GST.

The Howard government, having told the bogan that it would 'never, ever' introduce a consumption tax, introduced a consumption tax after being elected in 1998 by the barest of margins. Being a creature defined by its consumption, the bogan was outraged. The government was aware, however, that the bogan capacity for outrage — while nearly limitless — is also narrowly focused. The bogan can only channel its outrage at one or two things at once, so in 2001, when an opportunity appeared in the form of an unfortunate Norwegian sea captain following international ocean-going protocols aboard a ship called the *Tampa*, it was manna from heaven. The government told the refugees aboard the boat that they could not land, and sent the SAS to ensure that they did not. The bogan — whose attention was gained by the use of maxtreme military operatives on national news — suddenly became interested in why this boat was arriving. It grew afraid. When Howard subsequently told the bogan that 'we will decide who comes to this country, and the circumstances in which they come', all thoughts of the GST were banished, replaced by fierce patriotic pride in Australia's new-found ability to stop boats. Thus, when the election came around a few short months (and an intervening terrorist attack, making boats all the scarier) later, the Howard government — which had been staring into a GST-shaped abyss — was returned with an increased majority. This was also despite the fact that the ALP had campaigned on a platform of 'rolling back' the very GST that the bogan had bemoaned; by 2001, though, the bogan had forgotten that it had ever lived without a consumption tax.

Since that moment the bogan has had a fixation on stopping boats. It has little interest in stopping cars, trains or aeroplanes, which continue to move in and about Australia with unfettered ease. The freedom of boats to move about freely, however, must be limited, at all times and by any measure. As a result of the bogan's abnormally laser-like focus on this issue, it has become adept at ensuring that boats are stopped.

Presidential politics

As both major political parties become increasingly similar from a policy perspective, the bogan has been forced to develop new means of differentiating its two voting alternatives. The only option the bogan has conceived of has been to pay attention solely to the leaders that it has elected. Directly. Despite the failure of the bogan to even begin to institute this constitutional change in 1999, the bogan has come to believe that it has the right to elect the prime minister directly.

Upon Kevin Rudd's removal as leader of the parliamentary Labor party, and hence as prime minister, one of the key issues among the bogan electorate was dissatisfaction with the ALP for 'removing the man they elected prime minister'. A cursory reading of no less robust a source as Wikipedia could inform the bogan that it voted for nothing more than its local member, and that the party can do what it likes with its members. If the bogan doesn't like that it is free to vote for someone else or submit an invalid ballot. The bogan will not do that, however: it will vote for the leader of one of the two major parties, assuming that the name on the ballot is merely a proxy for the leader.

Moreover, the bogan's grasp of presidential politics is tenuous at best. Historical polling data shows one remarkable trend in the popularity of party leaders: the bogan's preferred leader of a party is the person who is the leader of the party. In the spirit of the bogan's love of parliamentary leaders, we will now take a look at prime ministers (and some opposition leaders) across the ages and how much the bogan liked them.

The bogan's leaders

When assessing the performance of anything, the bogan will insist on quantification. Anyone who has watched *20 to One* on the Nine Network knows that even arbitrary collections of distantly related things being grouped together must be ranked in a list of some kind. It is with this in mind that we close the Politics chapter with a list of the most bogan-friendly prime ministers this nation has ever seen.

10. JULIA GILLARD (2010–?)

The bogan got over its suspicion of women and redheads when Gillard showed it 'the real Julia'. Also helped by the fact that the bogan generally supports whomever is leader and interest rates were well below the 7 per cent threshold during the 2010 election.

Pros: She's a chick, allows bogans to make countless ranga jokes, supports the doggies.

Cons: She's a chick.

9. GOUGH WHITLAM (1972–1975)

Gough — as he is fondly known — is more famous for being booted out of office than for his attractiveness to bogans. He abolished the death penalty and appointed women to high posts. However, he increased government spending, forever endearing him to the bogan.

Pros: Won JJJ's Hottest 100. Lots of spending and tax cuts.

Cons: Forced bogans to learn about the 'Constitutional Crisis' at school, too tall.

8. HAROLD HOLT (1966–1967)

Holt went missing one day while going for a swim near Portsea, Victoria. Bogans believe he was abducted by Chinese submarines.

Pros: Likes the beach, lets bogans tell jokes.

Cons: Weak swimmer.

7. JOHN F. KENNEDY (1961–1963)

Strangely accented leader was famously shot while driving through Pearl Harbor, Darwin in November 1963. Bogans remember him for his grand speeches about bogan rights and for hammering on the Commies.

Pros: Good looking, protected rights, smashed Commies.

Cons: Un-Australian.

6. PAUL KEATING (1991–1996)

Labor leader who famously 'knifed' Bob Hawke to take the title; was known for his biting wit, which endeared him to bogans, and his love of French antique clocks, which did not.

Pros: Bit of a c***.

Cons: Bit of a c***.

5. SIR ROBERT 'BOB' MENZIES (1939–1941, 1949–1966)

Bogans like Bob Menzies because he is our longest-serving prime minister and managed to avoid serving during most of the war (fortuitously voted out in 1941), as the bogan also does.

Pros: The bogan can name him in order to sound smart.

Cons: When pressed, the bogan knows little to nothing else about him.

4. STEVE WAUGH (1999–2004)

Waugh led Australia through its period of international dominance for four years. The bogan loves a winner.

Pros: Great leader, epic ton at the SCG in 2004.

Cons: No tax cuts, spends too much time in India.

3. KEVIN RUDD (2007–2010)

K-Rudd, or Kevin '07, became popular with the bogan when he unseated John Howard, with whom the bogan had grown bored.

Pros: 900 reasons to vote Labor.

Cons: Mining tax, used too many words, nerdish, not enough ACTION.

2. BOB HAWKE (1983–1991)

Hawke was the bogan's champion for years, a man who proved to the bogan that it could achieve the greatness it knew it deserved while still sinking bulk piss.

Pros: Amazement at yard-glass and pint-drinking records, advocacy of sick days, introduced CGT and FBT.

Cons: Rhodes scholar, bogans blamed him for losing money in financial scams and high interest rates.

1. JOHN HOWARD (1996–2007)

Was there any doubt? The man wrote the book on bribing bogans in every conceivable way. He offered cash handouts even when there wasn't a global recession.

Pros: Bribed the f∗∗∗ out of every bogan in arm's reach, stopped loads of boats. Or told bogans he stopped lots of boats.

Cons: Can't bowl, can't field.

6
THE
TRASHMEDIA
KRAKEN

The Trashmedia Kraken is a much fabled but largely misunderstood beast. Although the bulk of its output appears to be unsophisticated and wilfully stupid, it is unwise to underestimate the arch intelligence of this malevolent creature. Nothing is more adept at harnessing the bogan for its own empowerment, and nothing knows the bogan better, than the Kraken. Indeed, to understand the Kraken's ways is to understand the bogan. But the task of understanding the Kraken is made difficult by the fact that its central nervous system lurks deep in some pitted crevasse on the ocean floor. Those seeking to understand the Kraken must instead inspect its multitudinous arms, which reach out into every bogan home.

It is from these tentacles that the bogan derives cultural nourishment, which gushes forth in a brightly coloured slurry

Figure 6.1 The Trashmedia Kraken: a metaphor, clearly

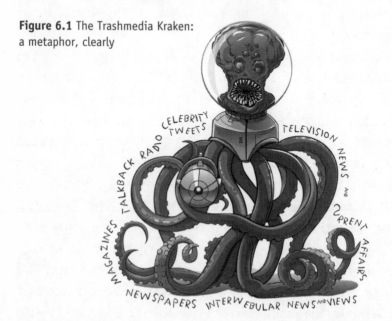

of hope, fear, excitement, shock and the vapid spectacle of celebrity reportage. It is tempting for non-bogans to discount these daily tentacle feedings as a harmless diversion that keeps the bogan on the couch, away from situations where it might do itself or others harm. But bogan scholars must understand the subtle pervasiveness of the nutrients contained within the Kraken's sugared gloop, which impart everything the bogan understands about the world outside its own tiny orbit. Because when the bogan ventures out into the world to work, play, share information, court and potentially breed, its every action will bear the suction-cupped mark of the Kraken's influence.

Diabolical and many-tentacled as it may be, the many Trashmedia appendages all connect to the head of the Kraken. While undoubtedly subtle and cunning, at a basic level all the conniving, devious designs in the Kraken's nervous system can be explained by one simple thing: its primary source of sustenance and sole motivation is cash, which comes largely in the form of advertising bucks. Without the steady stream of ad dollars that fuels the Kraken, its limbs would curl up like deflating party whistles and its dull eyes would roll back in its barnacled cranium for good.

Thankfully for the Kraken, however, advertisers are only too happy to keep feeding it cash. Because the Kraken gives them the ability to flog their wares to millions of people at once, it has made itself indispensible to advertisers. And thanks to the bogan's unrivalled status as a cash cow for those peddling overpriced and largely value-free consumer goods, advertisers seek max bogue exposure at all times. This, in turn, provides strong incentive for the Trashmedia to intensify its bogan-courting activities, which throws the entire system into a self-reinforcing spiral of boganity.

So the Trashmedia chases advertising bucks, advertisers chase bogan bucks and bogans chase boganic programming. This cycle ensures that Trashmedia outlets continue to scrap amongst themselves for the largest slice of bogan attention, each attempting to out-bogue the other. This classic race to the bottom happens to the detriment of informed comment, rational debate and the accountability of our elected officials. But although the entire industry is geared around the bogan and its tastes, the bogan does not control the Trashmedia networks. In fact, thanks to the bogan hivemind's unrivalled suppleness and malleability, its tastes, needs and wants are more or less open to negotiation. This task is one relished by both the advertisers and networks alike.

Plurality of opinion

Australia's federal government has legislation to ensure that a plurality of companies control the country's media landscape. However, power over the country's television and radio networks, newspapers and high-circulation magazines is, nevertheless, concentrated in a handful of players. Ownership of national and state capital daily newspapers is dominated by two companies — namely Fairfax and News Corporation. And the Australian television industry is little better, especially when the partially state-funded outlets are excluded — which is appropriate, given the fact that, in between soccer World Cups, most bogans have written off these channels as un-Australian and irredeemably biased. But more on this later. The remaining free-to-air stations collectively command over three-quarters of the country's television audience and approximately 99.65 per cent of the country's bogan television audience. This is why, many years ago, networks recognised that the best way to vie for market share is to vie for bogan share.

One crucial aspect of these Trashmedia channels is that, despite the fact that each network's programming shifts and adapts in an attempt to differentiate itself from others in the marketplace, and aside from some stylistic variations, the stations' news and current affairs offerings are identical. The bogan has learned to expect the familiar flavour of the Kraken's sugared gloop, no matter which Trashmedia appendage it is currently attached to. The bogan will respond with confusion and anger when startled by any substantive changes to this mixture. This is why networks tend to avoid nasty surprises of this sort, as bewildered and insulted bogans may migrate to other channels, decimating the network's bogan share and, thus, its value to advertisers.

This situation is hardly one conducive to forming a well-rounded, nuanced view of the issues discussed in news and current affairs programs. However, when discussing these topics the bogan likes to believe it knows what it is talking about. Perhaps this is because it thinks that by flicking between the Trashmedia networks, it is drawing its views on the world from multiple sources, thereby conducting exhaustive research. In fact, the bogan's engagement with the world's issues is largely conducted by sitting on a couch in a state of passive and uncritical thrall to a stream of news and opinion. It is only to be expected, then, that this news and opinion will pass into the bogan brain only to be repeated by the bogan in a garbled fashion whenever conversation alights on these topics.

Bias and the bogan

Despite its habit of regurgitating Trashmedia opinions in an uncritical fashion, the bogan is aware of the concept of bias in journalism. In fact, it considers itself something of an anti-bias crusader, vociferously decrying any example of journalistic prejudice it finds. But the key difference between the bogan's understanding of bias and the traditional one is that the bogan uses the word to define any position it finds disagreeable. Even the most rhetorical polemic may pass the bogan's bias detector, provided the bogan agrees with its content. In fact, it is precisely this type of trigger-happy opinionising that pushes the bogan's buttons most of all. But no news story, documentary or opinion piece — no matter how painstakingly researched, nuanced or entirely factual in nature — has any chance of passing through the bogan's bias detector if the bogan doesn't like what it is saying. In short, any opinion or fact that doesn't have the telltale flavour of the Kraken's syrup is deemed irrevocably biased.

This argumentative tic is a consequence of the bogan's lack of curiosity and fear of the unknown. The Trashmedia caters to the bogan's indolence by providing a self-contained ecosystem of news and views. The bogan's misappropriation of 'bias' demonstrates that anything external to that ecosystem is treated with immediate suspicion. In a phenomenal sleight of hand performed in order to appear impartial (and, thus, credible) to the bogan, Trashmedia appendages — whether they be TV news programs, papers or magazines — must side with the bogan at all times. The appropriate strategy for achieving this is a complicated dance in which the Trashmedia takes the lead but must constantly make an estimation of bogan opinion to ensure no toes are trodden on.

Although the bogan believes that the Trashmedia represents precisely the nature of things in 'the world', what results from this serpentine news tango is a thoroughly compromised, blinkered picture of the universe. And as this purportedly 'unbiased' melange of parochial populism and inch-deep analysis comes to occupy the space of the 'real world' in the bogan's mind, it leaves scant room for a truly deep understanding of the actual nature of things.

One of the many cleverly disguised appendages of the Kraken.

In fact, it breeds in the bogan a hostility towards insightful analysis and thorough investigative reporting. Most importantly, it prompts animosity towards things the bogan doesn't already know. To avoid inadvertently being on the receiving end of this hostility, the Trashmedia must employ Apparent Learnings.

Apparent Learnings

Although the bogan has an innate distrust of intellectuals, it enjoys holding the impression that it is informed about things. The Trashmedia is both a key enabler and a primary beneficiary of this mind-set. The bogan is unwilling to dedicate time to studying things in anything but the most cursory detail, and the Trashmedia knows this. This is why the Kraken provides a shortcut: Apparent Learnings. The Trashmedia drip-feeds bogans a solution rich in Apparent Learnings, which are items of pseudo knowledge that are either bleedingly obvious or examples of firmly established, yet erroneous, conventional wisdom. Some Apparent Learnings are true; some are not. Some are close to being correct but are too simplistic to be completely right, or do not provide the proper context to allow a meaningful understanding of the issue they address.

What all Apparent Learnings have in common is that they have no actual new knowledge to impart — except, perhaps, to the thickest bogan. Apparent Learnings act as reminders of things the bogan already believes, mostly as the result of previous Apparent Learnings. The result is a feedback loop of unquestioned idiocy. The Trashmedia Kraken doesn't often secrete genuine learnings, and this has proven intoxicating for the intrinsically anti-learning bogan. Apparent Learnings are preferable, because they make the bogan feel smart, informed and thoroughly in command of a world in which they can only ever be a stupefied and ignorant passenger. In turn, this is highly convenient for the Trashmedia establishment, which can peddle Apparent Learnings instead of the more taxing, and potentially embarrassing, Actual Learnings.

Table 6.1 Examples of Apparent Learnings

Foreigners are not to be trusted.
Corporate fat cats are greedy.
Celebrities are better than the rest of us.
Journalists are involved in a mighty quest to hold great powers accountable to the masses.
Journalists are irredeemably biased and base proponents of Political Correctness Gone Mad.
Tradespeople are dodgy.

The PCGM channels

Apparent Learnings allow the bogan to feel smart without the need to throw itself into a potentially humiliating confrontation with Actual Learnings. The Trashmedia's soothing reiteration of familiar topics and stories has instilled in the bogan an appetite for more Trashmedia programming and engendered a deep hostility for non-Trashmedia programming. Neither the Trashmedia nor the bogan are willing to make substantive alterations to the agreed-upon reality, which represents a symbiotic dance of mutual laziness, with the bogan condemning and forgiving on cue, and the Trashmedia working off a familiar and proven script in order to garner bogan approval and loyalty. These resulting, mutually convenient fallacies are often held up by shaky reasoning, holes in which are either patched over or ignored. Such a precarious edifice is easily toppled, which explains why the bogan is so quick to anger when it is shown a different perspective on the world.

For this reason the primarily public-funded broadcasters ABC and SBS and their digital offshoots, known collectively here as the Political Correctness Gone Mad (PCGM) channels, are not popular with the bogan. In terms of in-depth, investigative reporting, the PCGM stations' current affairs offerings are without peer in Australia. But the PCGM channels focus on considerably weightier issues than the bogan cares to think about, particularly events taking place overseas. The bogan has little interest in the goings-on in countries it has never heard of, such as Eritrea or Barbados or Egypt, unless those goings-on involve a fellow bogan.

Similarly, the bogan has no interest in musings on foreign affairs, just as it has very little time for charming little food/travel documentaries presented by old foreign gourmands. In fact, in between World Cups and apart from the small amount of *Iron Chef* that compels the bogan to impersonate a Japanese citizen every time it orders its beef and black bean, the bogan has little use for the PCGM channels. Perhaps if these networks pointed their journalists' attentions towards shifty guttering installers or drunk local politicians mouthing off in restaurants, they could gain more bogan exposure. But thanks in part to them having guaranteed income from the public purse (much to the bogan's chagrin), the PCGM channels are able to conduct their business more or less exempt from the imperative of bogan ratings.

When the bogan inadvertently strays onto a PCGM channel, particularly during news or documentary programming, its responses bear evidence of its intensive training by the Trashmedia Kraken. In addition to identifying the material as Politically Correct (the bogan knows to use this as a catch-all pejorative), the bogan will proclaim that the material it is watching was produced under the influence of a mysterious and dangerous substance: the Latte.

The Latte threat

The Latte — not to be mistaken for the Italian word meaning 'milk' — is a substance which causes immense trepidation in the bogan. Despite the bogan's well-documented love for drinks containing stimulants — including the Latte's active ingredient, caffeine — no substance known to the bogan is more likely to endanger its sense of identity than the Latte. And although the bogan may indeed drink coffee with milk regularly, the bogan loathes the Latte and everything it stands for. This is made readily apparent by the frequency with which the Latte is blamed for analysis that directly contradicts the bogan's sense of order in the world (that is to say, the Trashmedia's take on things).

It is understood that the Latte was first concocted by a malevolent French barista to send the intelligentsia of Paris insane with smug self-congratulation and blind them to the true nature of the 'real world'. It is rumoured that in those early days Political Correctness — after some period of teetering on the edge of sanity — actually went mad after being offered a Latte by a shabby artist on the Rive Gauche. Since then, and especially in the mind of the bogan, drinking Lattes has become essential to the inner city, professional, elitist experience and the bogan is quick to identify the influence of Latte whenever it encounters a point of view which it believes represents this frame of reference.

Table 6.2 Energy drink vs Latte

	Energy drink	Latte
Active ingredients	Caffeine, guarana, ginseng, taurine, sugar, bubbles	Caffeine, milk, froth
Known effects	Awesomeness, maxtremity, erectile maxfunction, road rage (awesome variety), turning Jagermeister into incendiary device	Smugness, elitism, pedantry, political correctness (mad variety), wrongness about things, living in inner city, becoming homosexual
Average cost	$5.50	$3.20
Dignity cost	$4000	$3.20

While the bogan remains ever diligent of the Latte threat, it remains unaware of the Latte sipping that goes on under its very nose. Unbeknownst to the bogan, many Trashmedia operatives —

from journalists and subeditors to TV presenters, ad representatives and executive management — are themselves fuelled by this malfeasant beverage. In fact, a Latte habit is also known to be the secret shame at the root of one particular, well-known right-wing columnist's intense anger at the world. However, such is the analgesic effect of Trashmedia content that the bogan has not yet gotten wind of this fact.

Talkback Radio

As codified under Article 19 of the *Universal Declaration of Human Rights*, the concept of free speech promises ordinary citizens the freedom to express their feelings and beliefs without censorship. Although the bogan is either indifferent or actively hostile towards the rights of others, it is adamant about the rights of itself — and the bogan is a staunch defender of its right to freedom of speech. The bogan particularly likes this right because freedom of speech allows it to express its ill-defined yet fiercely held opinions in every tone of bleating indifference its voicebox can afford. And because the bogan believes its own opinion on everything to

Bogan nirvana: Alan Jones with André Rieu.

be the most important one, it is no stranger to exercising this right. The resultant cacophony of nasal voices is raised up in the cumulative dissonant whine best known as Talkback Radio.

Talkback Radio, however, doesn't only afford the bogan the opportunity to express its freedom to bleat — it also gives the bogan an audience. So instead of complaining to its bogan mates at the pub about the cyclist who got mouthy after nearly being made paraplegic by the bogan's erratic driving, it can voice that complaint to many thousands of other bogans simultaneously. Talkback Radio gives the bogan the opportunity to spend around thirty seconds being a star — and not just any star: a star of complaining. It has the power to make the bogan believe that itself and its opinions are at the absolute centre of the universe. In this, Talkback Radio is similar to reality TV, but the advantage is that the bogan doesn't have to go through a series of auditions — or be young and good looking — to take part.

Talkback Radio allows the bogan to be part of the Trashmedia construction process, and many bogans have proven themselves to be naturals at this. It has allowed some bogan savants to fully embrace the process of fabricating and distorting facts, and, like wonky reactionaries in training, use the dissemination of these false facts as a launching pad for their own clumsily constructed opinionising.

Talkback Radio has become an essential means for Trashmedia broadcasters to monitor, court, cajole and bait bogan opinion, creating bogue-primed content high in outrage while obviating any legal liability for the rumours and far-fetched fantasies that consequently circulate in public. Sometimes, this manner of idiocy can wind up causing genuine (and often maxtreme) consequences. Talkback Radio has thus become Australia's home of scandal and earned the dubious accolade of having whipped up angry Sydney bogans into creating what is arguably racist Australia's longest moment in the sun of international news reportage: the Cronulla race riots.

While the bogan is terminally prone to displays of aggression against co-bogans and non-bogans alike, it is not known for its organisational capacity. As a result, bogan violence is often localised and without any overarching structure or discernible purpose. But in the case of the Cronulla riots, Talkback Radio provided the bogan with a potent megaphone for airing its beach-related grievances to other like-minded bogans. And thanks to Alan Jones's legally circumspect but morally reprehensible prodding, the bogan discovered a means by which to arrange for an enormous, writhing orgy of racially motivated violence.

Righteous fury, glowing pride

Perhaps second only to the bogan's greed, the bogan's righteous fury is a primary driving force of Australian politics today. But, as discussed earlier, the bogan's fury is not entirely its own. Granted, bogan anger is the leading cause of road rage, shopping-trolley rage, pram rage and airport check-in rage in this country, but these forms of bogan anger tend to be localised and comparatively unimportant on the national stage. With the Trashmedia's prompting, however, the bogan's righteous fury can very easily go national. And because politicians require bogan approval to remain in office, the profession richly rewards those who excel at averting, ducking or mitigating bogan fury.

Perhaps it is in acknowledgement of this power that the Trashmedia customarily steers bogan rage towards smaller targets: the overcharging plasterer, the slovenly public-housing tenant, the immigrant mother in a burqa. Thus modulated, the bogan's rage is ready to be deployed strategically to enact the Kraken's devious schemes and provide spectacle for its dark amusement. The Kraken has an innate understanding of the bogan's hot buttons and has learned that, when pressed correctly, it will never fail to engage maxtreme rage in the bogan population.

The bogan has a counterpoint to its righteous fury, however. The bogan's soft centre is its fondness for Ordinary Aussies; the bogan's heart swells with pride at the mention of them. Despite thinking that it is a remarkable, unique snowflake and mere weeks away from worldwide celebrity, the bogan also believes that it is itself an Ordinary Aussie. So when the Trashmedia wants the bogan to identify with a character in one of its reports, it will deploy this phrase and, in an instant, the bogan's abstract and unwieldy rage is anchored to its soft and spongy heart. Suddenly, immigrants aren't just taking some guy's job — they're taking the bogan's job. Dodgy decking contractors aren't just leaving a mess in some guy's backyard — they're creating a potential twisted ankle at the bogan's own family barbecue.

When the Trashmedia wishes to draw the bogan's attention to things happening outside of Australia, it often needs to conduct a frantic search for an Ordinary Aussie caught up in the fray. The Trashmedia knows that the bogan is uninterested in the trials and tribulations of the locals as their lives are uprooted by a momentous event, but the bogan will be reliably aquiver when Ordinary Aussies can't get an immediate flight out and have to sleep on the airport floor. So a Trashmedia camera crew will interview an Aussie reclining on its luggage, and if it manages to crack a smile the bogan will marvel at the resilience of the Aussie spirit.

Thanks to years of the Trashmedia's merciless button pushing and heartstrings pulling, the bogan has come to identify every positive human characteristic as something that is uniquely Australian. After the segment the bogan — suitably reassured that other places in the world are in serious deep shit but at least Aussies are all right — can be returned safely to local programming about overcharging driveway contractors. The only other sure-fire way to get a bogan to care about a world event is to throw a benefit concert featuring Powderfinger, Midnight Oil and John Butler.

Event journalism

There are very few things that are more likely to bring about a benefit concert featuring Powderfinger, Midnight Oil and John Butler than a natural disaster — especially one that takes place locally or manages to ensnare a large quantity of Ordinary Aussies. Particularly in the case of natural disasters, the local residents' life-shattering tragedy is the Trashmedia's fortunate and unexpected windfall. When one of these scenarios looms on the horizon emergency services workers and volunteers prepare for the worst, and local residents either hunker down or grab what they can and flee the area. As this takes place, Trashmedia operatives scramble to their extensive archives of sentimental music, cloying clichés and hero-narrative templates, and set about collecting footage for emotive montages. If the event is maxtreme enough, the Trashmedia could be feeding off it for weeks.

In times of extreme stress, and especially in moments of great shared danger, human beings have a remarkable capacity for generosity, self-sacrifice and service. Communities of people who had previously barely noticed each other in the street band together against the shared threat. It is in these moments that the loftiest ideals of ancient thinkers transform from miasmic ponderings into concrete, lived reality, and individuals put aside the things that have been holding them inside of themselves and address the needs of their fellow man. In those moments, Trashmedia operatives lurk amongst the wreckage, hoping to obtain footage to put alongside a Foo Fighters song.

When a home-grown news event takes place the Trashmedia will earmark large swathes of broadcasting time and dedicate its efforts towards looking at that event from every possible angle, recruiting all its talking heads to the task and leaving scant space for other programming. As bogans throughout the nation attach themselves to the box, hoping to learn everything they can about an unfolding event of this type, each channel gleefully competes for their custom, throwing gimmick after cheap gimmick at the disaster, hoping to arrest the bogan's attention and thus derive massive amounts of advertisers' cash. Maxtreme events are explained with the help of expensive-looking computer-generated animations, intellectual experts are briefly given a reprieve from being macheted for their Latte-sipping ways and brought into the studio to help explain events; correspondents are helicoptered in to stricken regions to interview stricken residents, then helicoptered out again, leaving the stricken residents just as stricken as they were before (or perhaps just filmed in the helicopter on the landing pad of the local television station, implying they were flying over or near a stricken region without having to pay the petrol costs). In the 24-hour-a-day coverage that results, the networks give countless shoddy landscapers a free pass, such is their fervour to squeeze as many ratings points as possible out of the event.

A disaster of this type can also mark the making or breaking of those in the public eye, particularly politicians. The Trashmedia is the primary conduit through which public figures' performance in crises is judged. And when the pressure is on there is very little that can help those for whom the Trashmedia already has a negative predisposition. In these moments public officials — especially those who could be held directly responsible for disaster preparedness or response — fear the Kraken more than the disaster itself. Because after maxtreme events cause loss of life, hundreds of millions of dollars of damage and Celine Dion montages, someone will have to be sacrificed to the Kraken; after this long stretch of saccharine sentimentality has momentarily filled the bogan with empathy for other humans, the bogan will be out for blood.

Sports Section Creep

The bogan is known for its love of sports. Indeed, sportspeople are to bogan culture as the members of indie supergroup Broken Social Scene are to hipsters. This is why the Trashmedia will use any opportunity it can to mention sport. This has resulted in the phenomenon of Sports Section Creep, in which sports-related stories break the banks of the designated sports segment, or dedicated program, and begin to flood into the regular news reporting, and even the weather. It must be noted that the traffic rarely, if ever, goes the other way. The Trashmedia has learned that, given sportspeople's celebrity status, news content can be generated about even the most mundane events in their lives. As such, sportsperson-related reportage represents the shortest possible route between no story and story.

Sports Section Creep happens in response to a number of things. If a sportsperson stops playing sport, it can creep. If a sportsperson stops playing one sport and starts playing another, it can creep. If a sportsperson acts like a bit of a bogan on a night out, it can creep. If the sportsperson has sex with someone he or she is not supposed to, it can creep — in fact, the sportsperson sex scandal is perhaps the archetypal justification for Sports Section Creep. This manner of material appeals to the bogan due to its presenting to the bogan dual and equally irresistible fantasies: that of being a celebrity and thus being instantaneously desirable to the opposite sex, and that of having sex with a celebrity, thereby becoming involved in her or his glamorous life and possibly destroying her or his marriage.

Thanks to the immense bogue appeal of stories about the lives of sportspeople and the ease with which this material can be thrown together, the Trashmedia treats sportspeople with a sweet–sour mix of tenderness and savagery. The Trashmedia is willing to give sportspeople a chance to defend themselves, and provides an almost limitless supply of get-out-of-jail-free cards, on the proviso that the Trashmedia has the right to inhumanely invade the sportspeople's lives at any moment and air their dirty laundry in the national spotlight.

The benefit to the Trashmedia is twofold. First, the Trashmedia is afforded the chance to report occurrences which, when happening to a normal person, would barely be worthy of a Facebook status update. Second, such a scenario allows for an ever-scintillating, never-changing commentary game to commence. The order of play is as follows:

1. First, one commentator experiences grotesque enlargement of their outrage gland and eviscerates the sportsperson, the sport they play and, indeed, sport in general for this behaviour. This occurs even when the behaviour is the simplest boganesque indiscretion, such as urinating in public — something that happens tens of thousands of times in Australia on any given Friday or Saturday night. Nonetheless, the opening salvo of this commentary game is always the same: because of this sportsperson's idiotic action, sportspeople, sports — nay, *society* — are irrevocably damaged.

2. A commentator more sympathetic with sportspeople will leap to their defence. Even when the indiscretion is significantly more serious than illicit bladder emptying — for instance, sexual assault of a minor — this action is everyone's fault but the sportsperson's. Justifications will range from the 'boys will be boys' argument to the more nuanced appeal that people be sympathetic to the pressures sportspeople are under, casually blaming the victim (be it glassing, scrapping, forced intercourse or being urinated upon). Customarily, commentators will also make a plea for sportspeople's right to privacy. Clearly this is disingenuous, because the Trashmedia operatives' very livelihood depends on being able to engage in this type of speculation.

In this situation, the bogan is likely to side with the sportsperson, although in some cases the bogan finds itself siding against them. However, if it does side against the sportsperson — even in the case of someone like Wayne Carey — it is always able to be cajoled into forgiving the sportsperson at some future point. This sets up the sportsperson for another round of the sports-scandal commentary game in the future. An emotional

In the bogan's mind, what better to cheer up an accused glasser than hanging with a chick in bunny ears.

rollercoaster of this sort only serves to further bind the bogan to the Trashmedia.

It is important to note that the legality of sportspeople's behaviour has no bearing on how the bogan feels about that behaviour. In fact, the bogan has no problem with illegal behaviour if it is suitably maxtreme and bogan approved. But, as will be shown, there is no guarantee that the truly maxtreme will win the bogan's approval; in fact, the system of bogan justice bears very little resemblance to conventional law.

Heroes and villains

Reliant on bogan bucks, and often dealing with issues of law and order, the Trashmedia must be keyed in to the bogan view of justice. The bogan has a long and complicated history with crime, both personally and within its own cultural imaginings. Some criminals are demonised by the bogan and others idolised. Similarly, members of the constabulary occupy the space of either hero or villain in the bogan's pantheon of archetypes. This reflects the true order of things: there are indeed bad cops and good crooks, as of course there are good people who do bad things and bad people who do good things.

We live in a post-Aristotelian world where good and bad are neither absolute nor constant, and morality is a matter tied to conceptions of self, and codified into unwritten law as much as it is indelibly inscribed into our society's legal tomes. In fact, despite the old world's not inconsiderable injustices, many conservative thinkers point to the breakdown of agreed-upon morality as a principal source of the modern world's ills. For these thinkers, regarding the serious business of morality with such flim-flammery is a pernicious and dangerous habit. They posit that the modern mischief finds a hiding place for itself in the type of thinking that regards morals as relative and not absolute.

The bogan, despite its marked unsophistication, is, above all, a creature of modern times and it must itself navigate the modern world's murky moral waters, however feebly. Here is a brief rundown of how the bogan negotiates an ambiguous universe, as it pertains to the law and those who transgress it.

OUTLAW HEROES
- Chopper Read
- The entire cast of *Underbelly*, and max gangsters generally
- Pranksters and those who evade the law in a highly publicised manner
- Hoons
- Aussies locked up for breaking the laws of other countries, no matter how immoral or idiotic (this excludes David Hicks and other known or alleged terrorists)

OUTLAW VILLAINS

- Rapists (except sportspeople and other celebrities who can't be guilty of rape because they're totally hot)
- Terrorists*
- Non–gang related murderers (for bogans, revenge, psychosis or boredom are not valid reasons for murder. However, control of illicit drug supply is)
- Ethnic gang activity (unlike the bogan's maxtreme criminal heroes in the cast of *Underbelly*, ethnic gangs engaged in the exact same industry in real life are undoubtedly villains. Not only are they bloodthirsty criminals peddling dangerous substances to the nation's youth, but they're also taking jobs from hard-working Australians)
- Corporate fat cats and fraudsters
- Guttering installation contractors who overcharge
- Charities that conduct marketing activities
- People smugglers
- Asylum seekers (all Muslims, therefore terrorists)
- Environmental activists (terrorists, and also Latte-fuelled PCGM warriors)
- Meddling scientists and their so-called 'quest for knowledge'

GOOD COP

- Quarantine/border protection (keeping terrorists out)
- Cops with cool jobs (helicopter pilots, motorcycle cops and any SWAT-style rappelling police person. Police in pursuit vehicles are loved because of their high-powered vehicles, right up until they catch the bogan speeding — see 'Fun Police')
- Maxine McKew (rhymes with maxtreme)

- Speed camera operators (revenue raisers)
- Booze bus/breathalyser operators (revenue raisers, and also Fun Police)
- Fun Police (any cop who tries to stop a bogan from doing something idiotic. This includes cops who confiscate the bogan's drugs at music festivals and cops who eject rowdy and drunken bogans from sporting events, especially the MCG's bay 13)
- Any police involved in arresting one of the bogan's max gangster heroes

* *A quick note about terrorists:* In the addled brain of the bogan, all Arabs are Muslims and all Muslims are terrorists. The bogan considers Muslim women to be innocent victims of their own belief system and, more importantly, their husbands, who are twice cursed for being terrorists and also kidnappers. The bogan believes there can be no love between Muslim couples, only Stockholm syndrome. Any contradiction of these convictions is clearly an example of Political Correctness Gone Mad.

The war against law enforcement

So we have established that the bogan's own system of rules doesn't correlate with society's at large. Indeed, the bogan's internally inconsistent values mean that bogans are the most likely subset of society to run into trouble with the law. Many bogans evade getting into trouble with the law either through pure luck, the pettiness of their law-breaking, pity on the part of the authorities or themselves being a member of the police force. But often, the bogan's lack of critical thinking skills, skewed value system, lack of relevant immunity and daily pursuit of the maxtreme at all costs, will put it on a direct collision course with the law.

The most common way in which this will take place is via the bogan's vehicular behaviour. Although the bogan is largely aware of the concept of speed limits, it doesn't appreciate being limited in anything it does. So even while driving a stock 1992 Hyundai Excel with flat front tyres and frangipani stickers on the rear window, the bogan imagines itself to be a maxtreme stunt driver. It will perform what it believes to be precise manoeuvring in and out of traffic, in order to progress approximately 5 metres ahead of where it would otherwise be were it not so inclined to endanger the lives of everyone around it in this recklessly selfish and idiotic way.

The bogan considers its ability to depress the accelerator pedal on its vehicle until it exceeds the speed limit as proof that it is an excellent driver. So when the bogan receives a letter in the mail implying that its driving does not meet the approval of the authorities, it becomes angry. This presents an opportunity for the Trashmedia to offer its help. The Kraken — not too ashamed to stoop to snivelling sycophancy in order to further ingratiate itself with the bogan — is willing to give the appearance of being able to protect the bogan from the consequences of its own actions in this crucial, bogan-sensitive area.

The Kraken responds to the bogan's anguish and is quick to give the source of this pain an evil name: 'revenue raising'. The bogan — although deeply in love with the taxpayer's largesse — absolutely hates tax, so by characterising speeding fines in such a way, the Trashmedia Kraken reclassifies punitive measures aimed at discouraging dangerous and illegal activities as an unfair new tax, one aimed directly at bogankind.

In defence of the bogan's perceived right to drive like an idiot, endangering itself and anyone in its proximity without consequences or remorse, the Trashmedia concocted a marvellous stratagem. It would reveal to the bogan the exact location of every single speeding camera, going so far as to give it regular updates throughout the day. Thus it can provide the bogan with fair warning of when to momentarily observe the road laws, before careening off into the distance. In what is a testament to the bogan's impulsiveness and endemic stupidity, the speeding fines continue to appear in its letterbox.

The bogan perseveres, however, and in the morning — after it finishes memorising all the speed cameras on its route to work — it flicks to the next page of the newspaper. It sees an opinion piece condemning hoon driving. Above this is a table comparing this year's death toll on the roads to the previous year's. The bogan registers no awareness of the paradox.

Research outsourcing

During the course of their work, Trashmedia operatives often find themselves in the position of having to find something to write about and, therefore, being forced to engage in some manner of research. Operatives in this position are faced with a choice: perform genuine journalistic work and produce good journalism, or do as little as possible and produce Trashmedia. Thankfully for the operatives, the Kraken has worked tirelessly in order to clear the way for the latter.

After years spent developing a taste for the Kraken's sugared gloop, the bogan doesn't recognise good journalism and, therefore, doesn't expect good journalism. In fact, as discussed earlier in this chapter, if the bogan accidentally chances across good journalism, it will react as if it's reached its hand into a lolly jar, pulled something out and placed it in its mouth, salivating in anticipation of something particularly sweet, only to find itself sucking on a lemon. So Trashmedia operatives have become used to having their laziness rewarded, and over the years they have become simultaneously lazier and better at their jobs.

Every few months a social and market research firm, increasingly cognisant of the Trashmedia's laziness, will release a study into something familiar to the bogan. These organisations — which have formed like limpets on the Kraken's thick and irriguous tentacles — have become increasingly adept at picking bogan-friendly topics, conducting a limited amount of research based around a foregone conclusion and packaging the findings in a format which best allows Trashmedia operatives to painlessly paraphrase it into news content.

The Trashmedia has found great success in outsourcing its research in this way. Attitudinal surveys provide a fantastic way for its operatives to draw broad conclusions about the nature of society, allowing for even broader and far more sensational articles. For instance, if a survey discovers that 15 per cent of younger female respondents can cook a meatloaf as opposed to 60 per cent of older female respondents, the article can speculate offensively about the lack of old-fashioned family values in modern society.

Outrage trolling and the war against social cohesion

The manner of speculation detailed above has a phenomenally pronounced effect on the bogan's outrage gland. First, it allows sexist bogans to use this fatal deficit of meatloaf-based knowledge as justification for their view that 'feminism has gone too far'. Second, it allows for another article to be written pointing out the idiocy and offensiveness of the first article's conclusion. Many bogans will nod furiously in agreement with the second article, not realising that, once again, they have been unwilling dupes in one of the Kraken's many ruses.

This process, known as 'outrage trolling', situates the bogan on a continuum of opinion, manufactured in such a way as to ensure that outrage and rhetoric flourish but any perspective remains permanently obscured. Outrage trolling generally presents a dualism that allows for a potentially endless war of words in which, although individual participants may find momentary catharsis, neither side can hope to gain any real ground. Here are some examples of the two sides to some popular outrage-trolling coins:

Table 6.3 Outrage-trolling topics

Women	Men
Cyclists	Motorists
Generation X	Baby boomers
Renters	Landlords

This technique is particularly popular on interactive Trashmedia such as Talkback Radio, and news websites and blogs which have a function allowing users to comment. Believing that the force of its opinion on a given topic will make a dent in the rigidly drawn battlelines of the debate, the bogan will participate with an unholy fury it usually reserves for activities like finding a car park or masturbating.

The Trashmedia has learned that the bogan will continue to find this illicit surge of excitement in being outraged about the same things again and again. This allows outrage-trolling topics to be reused endlessly. Because no matter how much the bogan wants what it already believes to be true to be continually reaffirmed, the opposite will do just fine as long as it also gives the bogan the opportunity to disagree vociferously and clumsily.

Current affairs

After the regular news, sport and weather, Trashmedia channels like to offer bogans a little bit extra. Much like the non-news sections of major newspapers, current affairs programs like *Today Tonight* and *A Current Affair* simply slot onto regular news programming like clip-on sunglass lenses over a pair of prescription bifocals. Customarily, current affairs programs are intended to provide extra context, analysis and discussion of issues and stories that appear in the news broadcast, and also provide a platform for investigative reports. As such, they are meant to give viewers a more detailed and in-depth perspective of the world we live in than the shorter news bulletins are capable of doing.

In the past, current affairs broadcasting was many a would-be journalist's dream career. These types of programs have been the launching pad for some highly memorable investigative reporting, a powerful medium that has the potential to awaken the passion for truth lying dormant in many. Well-regarded journalists have used the format to combine killer instinct with painstaking research and often heroic self-endangerment in order to uncover skulduggery and shine a light on some of the lesser-seen parts of our society. Indeed, current affairs journalism is often regarded as a force for positive change in our society — striking fear into corrupt officials, exploitative businesses and organised crime alike, and speeding up the process of justice for causes that had long since fallen from the attention of legal authorities. This legacy has allowed current affairs journalism to hold a reputation as being the news bulletin's deeper, sexier, more dangerous older sister.

However, in reality Trashmedia current affairs is even more shallow than the news broadcast it follows. Due to the sustained fact-fatigue that the bogan's brain exhibits after 30 minutes or more of news, the Trashmedia's current affairs offerings swap deep analysis for shallow, populist infotainment. Much like a lazy chef adding salt to a meal to make up for a lack of flavour, Trashmedia operatives adulterate their thin journalistic broth with knee-jerk outrage, parochial character pieces, celebrity ephemera and advertisements-as-advisory. This allows them to hold on to the bogan's attention long enough to take advantage of crucial prime-time advertising dollars, and ensure that the bogan's TV dinner is accompanied by lashings of the Kraken's coded malevolence.

Indeed, nothing defines the bogan's worldview — as disseminated by the Trashmedia — quite as succinctly as the current affairs format. Here, like nowhere else within the Trashmedia ecosystem, bogan heroes and villains are made and unmade, and the myopic frame of reference the bogan is best known for is fostered, coddled and exploited for commercial gain. Each night these programs give the bogan the ability to jack its cerebellum directly into the Kraken's gloop-giving tentacle. As the weeks, months and years stretch into one, the bogan's dependence on these nightly feedings of Trashmedia protein grows. The bogan becomes ever more superstitious, racked with fear of the outside, and resolved to guard itself against the various chimeras the Trashmedia conjures in its mind. This fortress mentality is exactly what brings the bogan back to the current affairs program night after night; as the numbers of those a bogan thinks it can trust dwindle, the bogan's need for the Trashmedia grows. But, like an opium addict, the bogan does not feel trapped by the Trashmedia: it feels enlightened, protected and liberated.

The Trashmedia's current affairs offerings can be split into the following categories:

NEIGHBOURLY RELATIONS

These segments provide the bogan with in-depth analysis of various small, localised occurrences that take place somewhere in Australia's vast and anonymous suburbia. As such, they tend to involve bogans fighting with other bogans, bogans fighting with non-bogans and, often, bogans' stoushes with the local, state or federal government, or big business. The aim of these stories is to remind the bogan that its own petty inter-bogan squabbles are important enough to potentially garner nationwide coverage, and that its grievances with authority can be aired, and increasingly mended, by the Kraken's semi-random, vengeful thrashing. As such, Trashmedia current affairs have come to be used as a sort of de facto legal service by bogans searching for maxtreme justice — or, simply, some negative attention from strangers. The Kraken uses these types of stories to provide assurances that it is on the bogan's side, and that the formless rage that it feels is okay.

Neighbourly relations stories can be created from as little as tensions flaring over a shabby and dilapidated fence. If the Trashmedia operative is particularly lucky a confrontation scene

The Trashmedia Kraken likes nothing better than busting scams and giving airtime to bankrupted bogans.

will develop, especially when these stories involve neighbours in co-boganity. And a good Trashmedia operative will be able to pick subjects willing to showcase their hostility.

Ethnic undertones, always lurking in the background of Trashmedia current affairs, can also be added to neighbourly relations stories. The 'Islamic school does not fit with local character' story pits racist bogans and non-bogans alike against not only an institution but a foreign value system, often framed as an incursion deep into bogan territory. This situates the often abstract concepts of immigration, globalisation and multiculturalism in the bogan's domain and presents them as a fight, which is something the bogan understands intuitively.

'Public housing tenants — your taxpayer dollars at work' is another particularly popular plot line which ties together fights, bad neighbours and another bogan hot button: perceived squandering of public funds. Targeting public housing tenants also allows the Trashmedia to harness the bogan's class anxieties to best effect. But strugglers often appear as heroes in Trashmedia current affairs narratives — for instance, when a shady landlord refuses to cough up for urgent repairs.

CONSUMER AFFAIRS

The bogan likes to buy things. Marketers know this, and on their behalf the Trashmedia is only too happy to point bogans towards things that can be bought. In fact, the Trashmedia holds the bogan in such thrall that it is able to make the bogan line up overnight to purchase something, simply by running a story on the fact that there are people lining up overnight to purchase something. The Trashmedia's consumer-affairs segments provide marketers with a less-than-subtle inroad into the bogan's wallet, by encouraging the bogan to believe that it is being given practical advice that will save it money and allow it to make better purchases.

As purchasing things is so important to the bogan, it is happy watching another set of advertisements between ad breaks, so long as the advertisements are thinly disguised as consumer advice. Over time, marketers and Trashmedia operatives hope to train the bogan into a state where it is neither able nor willing to distinguish between the advertisement and programmed content, and is consequently actively suspicious of anything that isn't related to something it can spend money on.

There's really nothing we can add to this picture.

Paradoxically, these segments often use the saving of money as a lure for the bogan, with supermarket prices a recurring theme. But while the bogan is absorbing information on how to fill its basket for less, it is also seeing a number of regularly consumed, branded household products flash across its screen. Like a checkout scanner, the bogan registers the product and its price, visualising itself purchasing each supermarket item in turn. This powerful programming tool enables the bogan to associate the concept of saving money with the concept of spending money.

Recruiting a celebrity is another method the Trashmedia Kraken uses to activate the bogan's spending glands. Sometimes the celebrities correlate with the products, such as when elite sportspeople are deployed to road-test athletic products, and sometimes the products and the celebrities are unconnected, such as when Delta Goodrem is brought in to hawk fishing line. This type of segment compels the bogan to connect the celebrity's vitality and good-hearted banter with the products, and associate the attainment of good looks, prosperity and fame with purchasing the various products on offer.

However, often the products reviewed are so obviously questionable that the Trashmedia can run a segment exposing them. These plot lines, which are similar to the classic 'dodgy driveway contractors — we chase them down the street' story, aim to impress upon the bogan the scientific certitude and journalistic bravery of the Trashmedia and its reliability as a source for advice regarding which products to buy. The Trashmedia is also able to bring forward the ever-present racial undercurrent while simultaneously appearing to be asking the tough questions of big business: 'Imported toys from China — are your children at risk?'

HEALTH AND WELLNESS

The bogan, aware that almost all celebrities are fit and attractive, longs to also be fit and attractive. Trashmedia operatives know this and will periodically remind out-of-shape bogans of their slovenly selves by way of spruiking fad diets, exercise gimmicks and crazes. The bogan is shamed by the implication that it is not doing enough to take care of itself, and will regard this as sage and timely advice. This leaves the way open for the Trashmedia to throw in scaremongering about the pitfalls of these same procedures and techniques in the future, should they prove to be ineffective or potentially fatal. The bogan will have forgotten that the Trashmedia was singing the praises of the same diet or fitness product a few weeks previously, and, as it sits slumped on the couch, tucking into its microwave dinner, it will think about getting fit.

A Trashmedia current affairs program's flagship fitness segment purports to reveal to the bogan a newly developed weight loss 'miracle'. Although the standard format will aim to paint this fad diet in the most favourable light possible, occasionally these segments will eschew spruiking the latest dieting innovation to 'expose' the pitfalls of one which the program had previously trumpeted the virtues of, and the bogan will learn that the cinnamon scroll detox is a bad idea. At the end of the fad diet exposé, the Trashmedia may come to the correct conclusion that the best way to become fit and healthy is to observe a sensible diet and engage in regular exercise. However, in a startling illustration of the Trashmedia's short memory, drawing this conclusion at the end of one segment provides no obstacle to the program jumping on the next fad diet craze with unbroken fervour.

Often these segments will provide the opportunity for the Trashmedia to wheel out a celebrity. These opportunities are rarely passed up, and because the bogan has learned to associate celebrity with everything it could ever desire, it will pay closer attention to a celebrity's dieting and fitness tips than to those of a leading nutritionist, physician or personal trainer. The one exception is when the suffix 'to the stars' is added to these professionals' titles, all their other qualifications thereby being rendered irrelevant to the bogan.

We'd ridicule Lisa Oldfield, but feel the damage was already done when her husband aligned himself with Pauline Hanson.

The Trashmedia is aware, however, that despite its health and fitness advice — or, perhaps, due to it — many bogans remain unhealthy and unfit. These bogans are reminded of their state constantly, as lithe celebrities and sportspeople cavort across their screens and diets are exposed as fraudulent. The bogan's TV projects endless streams of images of fitness and health which are cruelly juxtaposed with images of sumptuous desserts, gourmet getaways and fast-food-feasts-that-feed-the-family. Marketers know that the bogan's impulsiveness is a thoroughly reliable commodity, and that the road from slovenly bogan to svelte and fit bogan requires extended periods of dedication and self-sacrifice. This is why the bogan is generally pleased when the option of plastic surgery is brought up.

MORAL HAZARD

Moral hazard reporting represents the Trashmedia current affairs programs' contribution to the bogan's view on political life. These segments seldom aim to instil a greater understanding of our society but instead act to reinforce the bogan's most closely held misconceptions, and to reassure the bogan about its basest prejudices. The last thing the Trashmedia wants to do is alienate the bogan by teaching it something it doesn't know about an issue it believes itself expert in. In this vein the Trashmedia seeks out stories that reassure the bogan that its gut prejudices are valid and justified, and actively avoids stories which challenge or contradict them.

Because the bogan spends its time in the cultural bubble that contains its workplace, its vehicle and its home (at which most of its attention is absorbed by its television), it remains deeply ignorant about things that exist on the outside of that bubble. The Trashmedia is anxious to convince the bogan that its self-imposed isolation has been a wise choice because the outside world is filled with potential danger. Despite Australia being a very safe place to live in, the bogan has become convinced of a litany of reasons never to venture far from its front door. The Trashmedia has played a central role in this.

Indeed, even though the bogan rarely ventures from its habitual meanderings, it believes that it is uniquely cognisant of the ways of the world, precisely because it believes the Trashmedia's services are entirely sufficient in informing it. These programs aim to confirm the bogan's limited perspective on events. The bogan is rarely surprised by the stories that current affairs programs tell, and will offer this as evidence that it is savvy and understands the 'real world' as well as ever.

Despite its largely comfortable, suburban landscape — low in crime, corruption and conflict — Trashmedia current affairs programs paint a picture of urban Australia as an arena in which the crooks run wild. For decades the Trashmedia has ignored the consistently falling rates of violent crime, and has thus been able to convince bogans that the country is getting more and more dangerous. This has skewed society's crucial dialogues about law enforcement dangerously towards collusion with fantasy. One of the key recipients of the Trashmedia's blame for the ills of this concocted reality is the Courts.

In the Trashmedia world violent criminals are turned loose due to lenient sentences, free to offend again. This is the case with the 'dangerous criminals turned loose by crooked courts — is your suburb at risk?' plot line. The legal system is presented as a soft and compromised bureaucracy that has turned its back on the hardworking, law-abiding bogan, and is willing to allow pandemonium on the streets. Reticent to work over the complicated and morally murky terrain of rehabilitation outcomes, and the specifics of sentencing guidelines under which judges operate, the Trashmedia instead seeks easy answers to irrelevant questions. The purported cause of this particular moral hazard is the legal profession's infantile and naive subscription to outmoded and unrealistic conceptions of human rights. Indeed, the Courts are perhaps the location at which political correctness is deemed by Trashmedia and bogan alike to be at its maddest.

Ethnic Australians also regularly appear on current affairs programs, exemplified by the 'ethnic gangs in your neighbourhood' story. The bogan believes that ethnically homogenous criminal gangs roam the streets in increasing numbers. Stories on ethnic gangs press the requisite bogan panic buttons about increasing violent crime, and also allow the Trashmedia to validate bogans' intrinsic fear of ethnic minorities.

Indeed, ethnic groups are never discussed in the Trashmedia outside of a context in which they can be made to appear a threat, whether as gang members or as refugees 'invading' the country by sea. Generally the Trashmedia avoids approaching the issue of multiculturalism from the perspective of a member of a minority ethnicity in Australia. When ethnic perspectives are utilised it is customarily only when a member of an ethnic group is doing something suitably bogan or novel, to be accepted by bogan viewers as one of their own, something of a novelty, or both.

Usually the Trashmedia reports on ethnic groups by way of providing warnings about potential infiltrators into the bogan way of life. A benign story on a non-bogan doing non-bogan things is considered to be something best left to the PCGM channels. But if a non-bogan doing non-bogan things can be presented within the narrative 'foreigners don't respect the Australian way of life', it may be able to be turned into good Trashmedia. This effort to increase the bogan's moral outrage and fear of the outside world will customarily need to be modulated by a softer story.

CELEBRITIES

The bogan loves celebrities and considers them to be part of the family. The Trashmedia's perennial fall-backs — stories on the lives of entertainers — are sure-fire winners with an audience of bogans. And since the lives of entertainers continue to happen day after day, the Trashmedia will never run out of material. Even when entertainers cease to be famous, it is only a decade before the 'Where are they now?' specials can commence.

For example, current affairs programs provide a convenient vehicle for celebrities to come clean or atone for a particular scandal.

Wilkins ushers in the *Twilight* of entertainment reporting.

Generally presented in an interview format, the celebrity will appear under studio lighting for a 'candid' prepared and stage-managed interview, and will be asked variously about its family life and career before the interviewer will choose a moment to ask a pointed question about a recent and scandalous event in the celebrity's life, usually one covered in excruciating detail by the Trashmedia over the preceding few months. Customarily the celebrity will respond in a good-natured but apologetic, self-effacing way, and the interview will proceed promptly to other topics. This will allow the bogan to feel that the celebrity has done the appropriate penance for their actions and allow all to be forgiven.

Sometimes the celebrity interview is a way for a visiting actor to conduct promotional activities for his or her latest film, and it is often packaged as an 'exclusive' preview feature. The bogan intrinsically likes things that are exclusive, especially if they involve celebrities, and particularly if they can be accessed by simply watching free-to-air television. These features purport to bring the velvet ropes and red carpets of a Hollywood film premiere directly into the bogan's home. In reality they are thinly veiled commercials for Hollywood films that have done poorly in America, and which must resort to current-affairs-program special features in the hope of doing better in the Australian market.

SPECIAL EVENTS

In certain limited situations, Trashmedia current affairs programs actually discuss current affairs. Occasionally the course of events conspires to force their hand in this regard, and a news event, such as a natural disaster, becomes so large that a Trashmedia channel would be endangering its market share by ignoring it. Other special events are not so important yet are highly entertaining to the bogan.

Also included in the special events category are the times when a current affairs program picks a fight with another, identical, current affairs program. This carefully orchestrated event draws both programs into a mutually beneficial embrace of feigned animosity.

As such, it is arguably the most meaningless of all current affairs stories, and the most mindlessly entertaining. For this reason, the 'feigned animosity with other current affairs program' storyline is regarded as the defining creation of Trashmedia current affairs.

Trash magazines and the behavioural celebritisation of the bogan

The lives of celebrities present a fantastic opportunity for current affairs programs to conduct minimal news-making activities and still come up with hours upon hours of content. And current affairs programs are far from the worst culprit when it comes to drawing blood from a celebrity stone. The proliferation of weekly trash magazines, filled to the brim with celebrity reportage, attest to the gargantuan volume of copy that can be generated in the pursuit of this type of ephemera.

The Hollywood ecosystem need only continue to exist, and celebrity news will be created; as the stars and starlets go about their daily business, an army of Trashmedia operatives and mercenary photographers follow closely behind. A celebrity only has to spill its frappuccino on Rodeo Drive for a Trashmedia operative to leap upon this event and promptly convert it into news copy. Speculation will then proceed thus: *Is her new role putting her under too much pressure? Is she taking drugs (or, to use appropriate nomenclature, is she in the midst of a drug hell)? Is she pregnant? And who is that guy she's having coffee with anyway? Is she being unfaithful to her boyfriend? Quick, get a photo of them embracing goodbye.* In this way a single, seemingly innocuous, event can provide months upon months of potential coverage.

The Trashmedia Kraken follows this type of trivia because it has learned that the bogan wants to hear about things it can relate to — so the lives of celebrities are of intense interest to the bogan only insofar as those lives can be brought into a context the bogan can understand. The Trashmedia, aware of this fact, doesn't focus on celebrities' work or what makes them unique; it is not concerned with what work an actor did to help her understand her character or what it felt like to finally nail that pivotal scene; it is not interested in which '60s garage bootleg a musician stole most of his hit song from. But it is intensely concerned with getting a satisfactory photograph of the two tongue-kissing. The focus is on entertainers' social calendars, their sex lives, their haircuts, how many drinks they have, what they name their babies, the fluctuations in their BMI. In short, the Trashmedia focuses on what makes celebrities like the bogan, and not what sets them apart.

This type of speculation is profoundly popular because it presents a tantalising mix of fantasy, voyeurism and fandom, a hook upon which the bogan can hang its imaginings and move them from one celebrity to another, thereby sharing in an entertainer's ascendency, swooning at their love interests and being captivated by the everyday intrigue of their personal lives. However, the bogan must be quick to detach itself from a celebrity when it falls out of favour, so it can savour the *schadenfreude* of

A fine example of the Kraken's manufacturing prowess.

watching the celebrity squirm helplessly under the Trashmedia's microscope as he or she is prodded, examined and goaded into throwing a potentially entertaining temper tantrum. But after the appropriate shaming period is concluded with a candid interview or two, the bogan is then ready to forgive the celebrity and share in his or her recuperation and eventual triumph. Corresponding with the Trashmedia magazine's speculative extrapolation on what are generally only blurry photos and some hearsay from an unnamed source 'close to' the celebrity in question, the bogan dutifully idolises, judges, condemns and forgives on cue.

The Trashmedia Kraken has a deeper motive for submerging the bogan in this type of reporting. As the bogan learns about the events of celebrities' lives it is also absorbing information about how it should feel about those events, what is worthy of praise and what else is worthy of judgement. This instructive element of Trashmedia reportage comes to permeate inter-bogan and extra-bogan relations, colouring and guiding the bogan's own social discourse. So the types of celebrity behaviour the bogan is compelled by the Trashmedia to praise are exactly the types of behaviour it finds itself praising in others, and emulating itself. And as the value system of the bogan is directly informed by current affairs programs, it is more obliquely programmed by speculative musings on the lives of entertainers.

Further to the Trashmedia's subliminal instruction in bogan values comes one of desire and goal alignment. Over the years the bogan's dependency on receiving news about the lives of celebrities grows more chronic, and the idea that these people are intrinsically remarkable and interesting gets embedded deeper and deeper in the bogan's psyche. Although celebrities' poor choices are, on the surface, criticised, the magazines themselves represent a thinly veiled celebration of this behaviour and the barely earned, seemingly bottomless font of money and adoration from which it springs. Soon the bogan comes to understand the celebrity way of life as the ultimate lifestyle, and being rich and adored becomes an end in itself. From this point on the bogan will do anything within its limited power to emulate Trashmedia-approved entertainers. Thankfully, Trashmedia magazines also contain ample advice on how best to achieve this.

The other side of the celebrity reportage coin is beauty and fashion advice. This varies from cosmetics tutorials and dieting advice to fashion feature articles and holiday giveaway/advertorial segments. A favourite is the celebrity fashion how-to. Alongside pictures of flawless celebrities swanning down the red carpet in $3000 gowns, Trashmedia operatives place a cheaper version of this gown, what make-up to apply to achieve a similar effect and what accessories will complete the look. These articles will often provide prices and point bogans towards particular retailers that will assist them to impersonate the celebrity in question.

Although the bogan will regard it as useful advice, it is clear to the non-bogan that this type of content occupies the ethical twilight zone between advertising and advisory. And although stockists may not pay directly for this type of coverage, a promotional relationship of this sort demonstrates the considerable symbiosis that exists between advertisers and Trashmedia magazines. These advertisement-as-consumer-advisory articles also demonstrate the increasingly blurry line that exists between advertising and actual content in trash magazines. And on top of this, Trashmedia magazines are also crammed with earmarked promotional segments, competitions, product giveaways and special offers, all competing with the 70 per cent of page space that is taken up by traditional advertisements, which is precisely why the bogan is entirely at home ensconced in the midst of multiple prominent advertisements.

This explains satisfactorily a number of telltale bogan behaviours: Why, day and night, the bogan shrouds itself in clothing bearing loud and prominent branding. Why it attached a visibility-obscuring sticker proudly proclaiming its car's manufacturer on its rear window, despite the car having gone on sale with prominently located badges already affixed for this purpose. Why it named its daughter Mercedes and its cat Prada.

How to dress for your body shape

Another example of Trashmedia magazine sleight of hand is the ever-popular 'How to Dress for Your Body Shape' article. At any given time there are roughly fifteen versions of this story on the newsstands. On its surface this type of article appears to be both helpful and liberating. As photos of fit, skinny bodies take up approximately 85 per cent of the Trashmedia magazines' page space, it at first appears charitable that they would provide a small article giving fashion advice for the vast majority of people who have less-than-ideal physiques. However, the Kraken's malevolence is often cloaked by the appearance of altruism, and a deeper look here will reveal a darker motive at play.

The purpose of the 'How to Dress for Your Body Shape' article is to give fashion marketers the power to make bogan women feel simultaneously fat and deeply dissatisfied with their wardrobes. This double whammy of self-loathing and spending lust has proven highly lucrative for fashion retailers. Much like a bitchy older sister, the supposedly good-natured advice deals out a barely concealed cargo of shame and dangles the proposed solution tantalisingly: the bogan must spend more money on clothes to fix the situation. To rub salt into this already smarting wound, other parts of the magazine helpfully hand out celebrity diet secrets, fad workouts and advice on exercise gadgets. These will induce the bogan to spend up big in the hope of changing its body shape, potentially leaving the way open for further shape-specific fashion purchases down the line.

This maze-like game is typical of the many tortuous trials through which the Kraken leads the bogan. First, a solution is offered to one of the bogan's perceived problems — and, invariably, this solution is a product or service the bogan can purchase.

Second, the solution itself activates a brand-new problem. This cycle continues perpetually throughout the bogan's life.

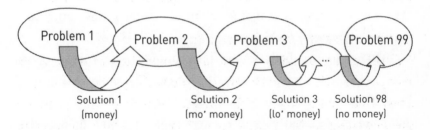

Figure 6.2 The Mo' Money, Mo' Problems paradox: a notorious dilemma

But perhaps the Kraken's most circuitous method to induce the femme-bogue to feel terrible about their body is through judicious use of celebrity body-shame photography.

Celebrity body-shame photography

The celebrity body-shame photography segment is one of the Trashmedia magazines' perennial favourites. It is made up of photographs of celebrities that are taken at inopportune moments and unflattering angles, giving the impression that the celebs are not the epitome of beauty suggested elsewhere in the magazine. The same image-altering touch-up software that is used to enhance these entertainers' looks elsewhere in the magazine is now turned upon them and cruelly used to accentuate any scant evidence of wrinkles, subcutaneous fat, discoloured skin or blemishes already visible on their bodies.

On the surface this appears quite benign — indeed, one could even be excused for seeing it as a potential ego boost for a bogan whose sense of self-worth takes a regular battering from daily viewings of airbrushed models, features on fitness bootcamps, diets and cosmetic procedures, and updates on the scintillating sex lives of celebs with genetically fortunate and intensively maintained physiques. But while body-shame photography appears initially to be a welcome attempt to bring celebrities down a peg, as if to say, 'It's okay, we all have bad days', closer inspection reveals the real forces at work. In fact, it is a good rule of thumb that if it appears as if the Kraken is doing something altruistically, the reality is that it is going about its usual malevolence in a particularly sneaky fashion.

What celebrity body-shame photography does to the bogan is to remind it that no matter how many Trashmedia-approved beauty tips and tricks it employs, or how body-shape-specific its jeans are, it will still be vulnerable to the ever-present potential for criticism. Indeed, the closer it gets to attaining the impossible heights of a totes celeb body, the closer its appearance will be scrutinised and criticised by its peers and potential mates. So, far from giving the bogan an ego boost, celebrity body-shame photography brings it as close to an existential crisis as a bogan is likely to come.

At times the bogan can become disillusioned with the Trashmedia Kraken. It will only take a new celebrity wardrobe malfunction or a football player's appearance on *A Current Affair* to reveal the details of his sordid sex scandal to remedy any reluctance to engage. But silence is not golden to the bogan, so should they turn off the television and step away from their smartphone they still need noise to distract them from boring stuff. So the bogan reaches for the iPod Nano and turns up the volume.

7
MUSIC

While the bogan primarily defines itself by the tangible goods it can advertise visually to its neighbours, particularly those that demonstrate their expense, it occasionally needs cultural touchstones around with which to bond with other bogans. While reality television and 3D movies assist in this a great deal, they share a commonality. They are done in silence. They are done while watching a screen and not engaging with others. They do not allow the easy use of finger-guns. The bogan's choice in music, however, is a demonstration of its love of mad party stylz. The bogan likes this very much.

What kind of music does the bogan like?

A dull and unimaginative herd animal that is easily spooked, the bogan values safety in numbers when navigating the cultural and leisure-activity landscape. It prefers the peaceful pastures of conformity to the barren minefield of potential faux pas and ostracism that is independent thought. This pack mentality largely crowds out any organic development of likes and dislikes at the individual level. As a result, the individual bogan does not have any of its own tastes and opinions beyond those that are instinctive.

Thus, when it comes to the bogan's musical tastes, it is not the objective quality of the music that matters so much as the need for the herd as a whole to approve of it — the bogan's reasoning being that if so many others like something, it must be good. While this kind of shallow analysis is likely to prompt scepticism and further questions from a reasonable person, the bogan — who is anything but reasonable — is entirely happy with this conclusion and has no further questions. In fact, the ability to come to conclusions based on paper-thin, surface-level analysis, and then believe in those conclusions absolutely, is one of the key traits that make the bogan the creature it is. Lacking the self-awareness to realise that it is a member of a group of individuals who are uniformly following the group as a whole, the bogan fails to ask itself this: if everybody is following the herd, who is steering it?

Who is steering the herd?

Two groups have influence over the bogan's musical habits: the largely benevolent and oblivious early adopter, from whom the late-adopting bogan takes cultural cues; and the strictly malevolent and manipulative music recording industry, against whose marketing techniques the bogan is powerless. This dichotomy has developed over time amid the simultaneous growth of the bogan population and increase in size, concentration, power and sheer omnipresence of the music industry. Prior to this it was the early adopter who was all-powerful, driving music trends which then trickled through to the masses.

This was a time before auto-tune, the 'big four' record labels and the superstar DJ era. Back then the market for music was characterised largely by a market-pull mechanism, whereby consumers rewarded the supplier (musician) who created the product (music) that best fit their tastes. The music industry acted primarily as an intermediary between artists and consumers, responsible mainly for financing and managing the process of recording, manufacturing and distribution of the product to a market that already existed, while having little to do with the creation of the music. The early adopter's defiant insistence on thinking independently and critically sees this side of the market continue to operate in a similar manner today. In contrast, the bogan's staunch insistence that such thinking is 'for poofs' has seen its musical tastes become increasingly dictated by the marketing push of the professional bogan shepherds of the modern music recording industry.

Why does the recording industry care what music the bogan likes?

As music recording and playback technology became affordable to the average consumer, there emerged a growing consumer market for recorded music. Entrepreneurial types saw a business opportunity in facilitating aspects of the production and distribution of music from artists to this market. These innovators were the beginning of the modern music recording industry. For the industry to grow, people had to consume more recorded music. And the most obvious way to get people to consume more recorded music was to supply more of what the people wanted.

So the recording industry operated largely in this market-pull manner, scouring the globe for talented artists with the potential for commercial success. But after a while a large number of record labels had sprung up and the industry had uncovered and monetised virtually all the commercially viable talent; as fast as they discovered a new act, an old one would flame out. Unless something changed, the size of the market for recorded music would hit a ceiling. Thus, marketing became more of a focus as the industry tried to sell each artist to a wider audience to sustain growth.

From here, it would become apparent that the marketing of an artist's image and 'brand' could have as much influence on their popularity and sales as the quality of their musical output. One of the earliest examples of this knowledge being put to use occurred in the mid 1960s, when a couple of film producers created the fictional pop quartet The Monkees, in an image reminiscent of The Beatles, for a television sitcom centred on the 'band'. The television studio retained the rights to the recordings and used the popularity derived from the television program to drive record sales.

Again, the growth in music consumption began to plateau as the marginal benefit from each additional dollar of marketing

P!nk is a goddess to the Antipodean bogan: she has tatts, rides motorbikes and loves V8s. The bogan male is especially impressed.

spend on an artist approached zero. As the bulk of the marketing cost is in getting the artist established, each subsequent release after the first album requires substantially less marketing spend and, given similar sales, will therefore be more profitable. So the focus turned to getting a greater quantity out of each artist. This meant rushing out an album a year, releasing seven singles off each album (P!nk, *Funhouse*, 2008), putting out a greatest-hits compilation while the artist is still active (P!nk, *Greatest Hits ... So Far!!!*, 2010), and prolonging artists' careers well past their prime (P!nk, post 2000).

The industry also became more involved in the creative process, to make sure it happened quickly and that the artist kept churning out music that fit with the image that had been so carefully constructed and heavily invested in. Naturally, quality suffered — but it mattered little. For every early-adopter dollar lost as they got bored and sought out original, independent music, multiple bogan dollars were gained as the bogan followed the herd, which followed the marketers. The industry had come to realise that it could make more money by cheaply and quickly churning out generic, derivative music at a rapid rate, and spending big on marketing to sell it to bogans, than it could by simply letting the market decide what music it likes and producing as much of that as possible.

How does the industry do it?

Bribes? Physical intimidation? Being threatened with spending a year on a raft with only Richard Wilkins for company? Some kind of elaborate mind control device? Close. Over the years, marketers have become intimately acquainted with the bogan hivemind. The bogan's herd behaviour and short attention span, its love of celebrity, its fear of the unknown and its more-is-more, bigger-is-better, my-wide-screen-is-bigger-than-yours consumptive attitude are by now well known and equally well exploited. Those in the music industry have played on this knowledge to sculpt their product and accompanying marketing strategy into a masterpiece of bogan bait.

One key challenge for the industry has been finding a way to continually introduce new artists to the fearful-of-the-unknown-and-resistant-to-change bogan in an increasingly rapid manner, in

The bogan would very much like to glass this person.

order to harvest ever more wads of bogan cash. The second album — or single — is generally a relatively easy sell once the artist has gained herd approval, provided it is similar enough to the first. It is gaining that initial foothold that is the difficult part, for the bogan likes things that are familiar and safe — like the ten songs played by the cover band Princes of Neon every Saturday night at the local glassing barn, which the bogan knows will never change.

The bogan's desire for safety stems from the fact that it uses the things it consumes to augment its personality and, in turn, to clearly signal its position within the fat part of the normal curve. One wrong move, therefore, and the bogan worries that it might find itself on the outer alongside the very worst of society, like paedophiles, murderers and emos. New things must therefore be carefully and strategically introduced so as not to spook the skittish bogan and provoke a defensive response.

A common strategy used by marketers when trying to sell the bogan new things is to make those new things variations on old, familiar things. Making things larger is almost always a winner, as is increasing the number of acronyms, like HD, LCD, LED, HDMI, WTF. Making things shinier and more attention-grabbing rarely fails either. Lately, increasing the number of dimensions in which things can be experienced has been a popular tactic employed by the entertainment industry, with the marginal benefits of moving to the third dimension arguably greater than any dimension that has gone before.

In the music sphere, one of the prime strategies used to massage the bogan's familiarity gland until cash spurts out of its credit card has been to maximise the degree to which an artist sounds like U2. This is a strategy that has recently been perfected by the royal family themselves, the Kings of Leon. Quite successful in the indie scene when they sounded like Creedence Clearwater Revival, the band soon realised their mistake and, upon shifting to a sound more reminiscent of U2, and trimming their hair and beards (the bogan's aversion to beards is discussed in the

Fashion chapter), instantly cracked the infinitely more lucrative bogan market. The path from indie phenomenon to chart-topping, stadium-filling status via the U2 sound was, in fact, well trodden by the time the Kings of Leon charged down it, though, having been worn by the likes of Coldplay and Snow Patrol before them. The Kings of Leon transformation was merely a textbook execution of the indie-to-sell-outie play.

This U2-soundalike manoeuvre relies on the fact that, despite dismissing most of the early adopter's music collection as being for 'weirdos', 'pansies' or 'emos', the bogan covets the early adopter's perceived trendsetter status and the exclusivity of picking a winner and getting in on the ground floor ahead of its peers. As a result, a trickle effect emerges in which a gradual uptake of a fraction of the early adopter's most inoffensive music eventually reaches a critical mass, at which point the rest of the thundering bogan herd follows instinctively.

A recent example of this was Mumford & Sons, who shot to bogan fame when they clinched the number one spot on the Triple J Hottest 100 in 2009, two years after the indie-folk movement had reached its zenith with Fleet Foxes. A relatively inoffensive and watered-down serving of indie-folk, Mumford & Sons offered a veritable tasting plate for the bogan, for whom listening to Fleet Foxes would have been akin to devouring a fiery beef vindaloo. But the play only works for a handful of the most bogan-friendly indie artists each year. Consequently it is also necessary to bring new artists directly to the bogan, bypassing the early adopter.

The challenge in taking a new artist straight to the bogan market is to make them appear safe and accepted as quickly as possible. As alluded to, the bogan is not one to go out on a limb, and without the trickle-down effect from the early adopter to gradually project herd approval upon an artist, other strategies are required to manufacture credibility for the artist in the mind of the bogan. The most effective tactic is to focus on building the artist's image into that of a celebrity, rather than just a musician.

The team behind Lady Gaga have demonstrated this admirably in recent times with various publicity stunts — the highlight being their perpetuation of rumours that she is a hermaphrodite — along with social-media saturation. Basically, anything that allows the bogan to judge the book by its cover is the goal, allowing the metaphorical book to be left largely devoid of content (unless said book is about horny teen vampires or was already a major motion picture starring Tom Hanks).

Of course, it is of immense benefit if the artist has some brand awareness in the marketplace before ever releasing a song. This is the aforementioned Monkees strategy, which is now being exemplified with television programs like *Idol* and *The X Factor*, as well as teen televisual phenomena like *High School Musical*, *Glee* and *Hannah Montana*. The success of the *Glee* soundtrack, in particular, is an astonishing example of cynical marketing genius. It combines the Monkees television-to-music-sales strategy with the familiarity play to take music that the bogan already liked and had previously bought, have it reproduced by television show characters in a manner that is competent yet cold and devoid of all feeling, and sell it to the bogan — again.

The popularity of the *Glee* soundtrack is also reflective of the recent bogan love for covers, as perpetrated by the likes of Michael Bublé, André Rieu and André Rieu's hair. After discovering the ease with which it was able to sell the bogan music that sounded almost exactly like the music it already owned, the recording industry took this a step further by selling the bogan music that actually *is* exactly like the music it already owns.

Behind all of this is the bogan's desire to appear unique and cutting edge, but not *too* 'out there', because 'out there' is lonely and scary. Accordingly, the bogan doesn't want to hear 'New York, New York' performed by some crusty old crooner — it wants to hear it performed by a young, handsome Canadian man; this is 'classy' and 'sophisticated', yet 'modern' and 'fresh'. The bogan doesn't want to hear 'What About Me?' performed by some mulleted

Bogans love Michael Bublé — even fake bogans are partial to the Canadian crooner.

'80s bogan; it wants to hear it performed by some twenty-first century flavour saver-ed bogan. And the bogan certainly doesn't want to listen to an orchestra perform classical music, which is for intellectual poofs. It wants to hear an orchestra perform 'Tie Me Kangaroo Down' and the *Neighbours* theme song. The success of Human Nature's Motown cover albums and Guy Sebastian's Memphis cover album stand testament to the power of the cover, along with the disproportionate number of covers that have reached number one in the singles charts over the years.

The bogan's recorded music consumption

The bogan knows that it should like music. It sees others deriving pleasure from, and bonding over, music and seeks that for itself. It sees the smugness projected by the hipster because it was into Grizzly Bear way before they made it 'big' and wants that smugness for itself. It sees other people with things, and it desires those things. For the bogan hates to be on the outer; it must colonise all physical and cultural spaces. And music represents yet another way for the bogan to signpost its membership to the 'in' group via consumption. Particular artists or styles of music are secondary issues to be determined by the herd — the bogan simply needs to appear to be into music in general.

Commercial radio

The bogan's music consumption begins at commercial radio, which acts largely as an extension of the recording industry's vast bogan mind-control arsenal. In a symbiotic, tail-chasing relationship, commercial radio playlists are based on sales charts to attract the best ratings, and commercial radio airplay drives sales. The bogan uses commercial radio as a filter, in order to limit the music to which it is exposed to that which sounds as near as possible to the music it already likes. Commercial radio broadcasters are only too happy to oblige so they can gain the easily influenced bogan audience that their advertisers are desperate to target. As a result, the typical commercial pop station's programming during the day consists of endless repetition of the songs currently in the Top 40 in the singles charts; perhaps in the evening there will be a listener-request-based program during which bogans request songs that are currently in the Top 40 in the singles charts, or a Top-40 singles charts countdown-based program. 'Variety' is achieved by occasionally throwing in an old Michael Jackson, Powderfinger or AC/DC hit. This is, of course, interspersed with painfully frequent, excruciatingly jingle-heavy advertisements to which the bogan sings along happily, barely noticing when a song ends and an ad starts. And then there are the hosts, whose banter ranges from the previous night's commercial television programs to discussion of celebrity gossip from that week's trash magazines, along with the occasional replay of a telephone interview with Kim

Kardashian. And throughout all of this — omnipresent in every song, advertisement, station promo fill and minute of mindless talk-show-host banter — is the Bogan Buzz.

The Bogan Buzz is the highly sampled, computerised drum-and-crunchy-bumblebee-synth-bass rhythm section that barely changes across almost every song on commercial radio. It is as if the producers of commercial music created some kind of computer program which would sample all of the bogan's existing favourite songs and spit out an instant rhythm section for the bogan's new favourite song. Then, over time, those new songs were fed back into the machine and re-sampled, creating a feedback loop resulting in convergence towards the Bogan Buzz.

Once the generator fires out its instant rhythm section, all that is needed is the addition of hooks and empty lyrics and, presto, the sixth single for the new Katy Perry album is born. Add slightly more guitar and make the lyrics and vocal hooks more aggressive yet equally meaningless and you've got a P!nk hit instead. Turn up the Bogan Buzz volume, add the words 'Feat. [name of notable producer/DJ]' and some squiggly, bleepy sounds and you've got a remix. When George Orwell peered into the future from 1949 through the prism of his classic novel *Nineteen Eighty-Four*, he described a future in which the task of making popular music had been handed over to a machine called a 'Versificator', with no human intervention whatsoever. It was a remarkably accurate vision, the only differences being that it took a couple of decades longer and that the machine is called a 'David Guetta'.

On commercial radio the Bogan Buzz even seems to linger in the background when the hosts speak, as well as forming the basis of every program intro, station promo fill and advertising jingle. It almost never stops and, combined with the inane babble of the hosts and extreme repetition of songs and ads, seems to have an almost hypnotic effect on the bogan. This is perhaps part of the reason behind the bogan's tendency to engage in bouts of extreme road rage to the soundtrack of Austereo and DMG network radio stations. When some idiot attempts to merge and forces the bogan to slow slightly, not only is the bogan inconvenienced in an unacceptable way, it is also snapped out of its Bogan Buzz trance, causing it to act like a chicken.

The evolution of the Bogan Buzz has seen the sound of much of the popular music heard on commercial radio today edge noticeably closer to the sound of the remixed music that would traditionally be heard in dance clubs. This is largely due to the fact that the bogan wishes to feel like it is in the club at all times. The club is to the bogan as the jungle is to the mountain gorilla, and when the bogan listens to music it likes to picture itself as king or queen of its domain. For the man-bogue this is achieved by physically intimidating the other males and, as a result, gaining the attention of the female; for the femme-bogue: being provocative yet elusive, stirring lust among the males and envy among the other females. The manifestations of these visualisations can be observed in many places, but perhaps most notably in clothing stores and gyms, which tend to have mirrors and blast commercial radio or playlists of Bogan Buzz based music. In these places the bogan can often be seen pouting at itself in the mirror, posing/flexing while somewhat subtly bopping along to the bass thump, imagining itself dominating the club with its sick new outfit or slightly greater (male) or lower (female) body mass.

Singles

There are two groups of people who buy singles: children and bogans. Children tend to buy singles because their developing minds lack the attention span required for full-length albums, and singles are cheaper than albums. Bogans tend to buy singles because their meandering minds lack the attention span for full-length albums. The advent of digital music downloads has greatly enhanced the bogan's ability to procure a handful of singles from its favourite artists. Indeed, the bogan's iPod is recognisable for its 5000 songs and six albums.

Case Study 7.1: Analysing the bogan's influence on Australian singles sales charts over time

Figure 7.1 tracks the level of the boganic music index (BMI) over time. The index is calculated by, first, taking the number one selling single at a given time as a proxy for the level of boganity at that time; then, with all the number one songs from a given year forming a sample, the average annual level of boganity is calculated by taking into account time spent at number one and total sales for each song. This annual average represents the level of the BMI for that particular year.

A tipping point — or what traders refer to as a 'breakout' — seemed to occur in the latter stages of the 1970s: where the early '70s had seen pioneering artists such as former members of The Beatles, The Rolling Stones and Led Zeppelin as mainstays at the pointy end of the Australian charts, some of their successors in the latter half of the decade were decidedly more boganic. Suddenly novelty songs and soundtracks from popular films began appearing not just in the charts but atop them; ABBA had a string of hits and songs from the *Grease* soundtrack polled well. This was tempered, however, by Queen's 'Bohemian Rhapsody' along with brief appearances by Gerry Rafferty and Kate Bush.

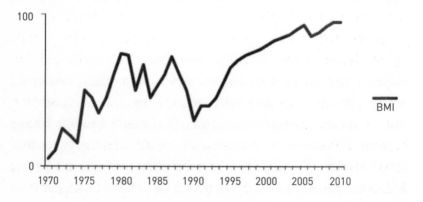

Figure 7.1 The boganic music index (BMI) over time

Perhaps the most ominous sign of impending boganity was when Joe Dolce's 'Shaddap You Face' spent eight weeks at the top of the Australian singles charts in late 1980. In fact, the song went to number one in no less than eleven countries, making boganity Australia's chief export in the 1980–81 financial year.

After the Joe Dolce-induced spike in 1980–81, things settled down a little aside from a blip in 1983 when a comedy piece by Austen Tayshus entitled *Australiana* reached the number one position. Moderate growth in the BMI then occurred through the mid '80s, driven by the likes of Wham! and Bananarama, but offset somewhat by appearances by Midnight Oil and Models. A surge then occurred in 1987 as Kylie Minogue's 'Loco-motion' and Rick Astley's 'Never Gonna Give You Up' hit in quick succession.

Things steadied through the late 1980s, although the period did see success for future cover band favourite 'I'm Gonna Be (500 miles)' by The Proclaimers, and the bogan's favourite neighbour, Kylie Minogue. The bogan then seemed to go into its shell for a while in the early 1990s, perhaps unsure whether to follow the plastic pop trend or the heavy metal mania that the late '80s had thrown up, or clamber aboard the rapidly expanding grunge bandwagon. Consequently, the period saw decidedly un-bogan bands like Faith No More and Ratcat hit the head of the charts, although they were accompanied during the period by hits from Bon Jovi along with school disco favourite 'Grease Megamix'.

It was the mid '90s when the BMI started tracking sharply uphill. This was the period of boy bands, girl bands and two different 'Macarenae', the volume of which completely overwhelmed a brief patriotic fascination with teen grunge prodigies Silverchair. Even a sneaky appearance at the top of the charts by Britpop superstars Oasis, with 'Wonderwall', merely reflected a case of bogan bandwagon jumping, with other Britpop acts like Blur and Radiohead failing to gain the bogan's attention.

The latter stages of the 1990s and the early 2000s saw the bogan become infatuated with teen pop starlets such as Britney

Spears, Christina Aguilera and Mandy Moore, while the movie *Titanic* was the best thing to ever happen to Celine Dion and the worst thing to ever happen to anyone unfortunate enough to be subject to commercial radio during that time. The bogan also discovered a new band called The Offspring, who had only released four albums over the best part of a decade before capturing the bogan's attention with their worst yet, and the worst song from it, 'Pretty Fly (For a White Guy)'. The bogan proceeded to make Lou Bega's highly irritating 'Mambo No. 5' the top-selling single of 1999, while the new millennium brought the same old bogan staples to the top of the charts: novelty songs — Chris Franklin's 'Bloke', as well as 'Who Let the Dogs Out' and 'The Ketchup Song'; and covers — Madonna's insipid take on 'American Pie', and Alien Ant Farm's maximum tough version of 'Smooth Criminal'. The early 2000s also offered an ominous glimpse into the future as P!nk first appeared atop the charts along with the first reality-TV-generated 'stars', while 2002 was significant for having number one singles from three separate former *Neighbours* starlets. If you were an Australian artist during this period, you pretty much

Holly Valance: Soap star. Pop starlet. Hollywood aspirant. Bogan wet dream.

needed to have been on TV to get anywhere near the top of the charts.

It was basically all up, up, up for the BMI through the mid- and late noughties. As an indication of the sheer level of euphoric boganity that had been reached, the slight dip in the BMI in 2006 was largely due to Youth Group's 'Forever Young', a folksy take on Alphaville's 1984 synthpop anthem; the fact that a cover was able to cause a *decrease* in the BMI was an indication that the market was exhibiting bubble-like characteristics. Yet the BMI continued to soldier on. As famed economist John Maynard Keynes (see Chapter 3, Economics) once quipped, 'The market can remain irrational longer than you can remain solvent.' If alive today, he would surely say, 'The market can remain irrational as long as the bogan can remain solvent.' In fact it is largely through Keynesian theories of economic management — rather than any market acumen on the part of the bogan — that the BMI has proven resilient to the global financial crisis. Around the onset of the subprime mortgage crisis in 2007, and again in 2009, the central musical authority, the Ministry of Sound (MoS), injected liquidity into the market by printing vast quantities of the global bogan reserve currency — the Guetta — in order to avoid any potentially catastrophic nightclub remix shortfalls. The bogan, needing little encouragement to keep buying things, responded positively, sustaining the BMI at its historically high level.

Reflecting the ongoing strength of the BMI, the second half of the noughties decade saw number one songs come from a procession of *Idol* contestants, R&B and pop starlets with increasingly vocoded robot voices, P!nk, remixes, and people 'Feat.' other people (predominantly it is David Guetta being featured or doing the featuring). As mentioned, the prominence of these highly produced songs and remixes and generally Bogan Buzzed music atop the charts reflects the bogan's need to feel like it is in the club at all times.

The bogan's live music consumption

The bogan views its recorded music consumption — consisting largely of commercial radio, singles and individual song downloads played back with judicious use of the 'repeat' button (aka the 'press here if you are a bogan' button) — as generally providing a satisfactory soundtrack to its day-to-day goings-on. But for its more maxtreme goings-on — of the type that tend to happen at night-time and on weekends, and which involve lengthy periods standing behind velvet ropes, excessive drinking, fighting, excessive drug taking, fighting, yelling and fighting — the bogan prefers the greater thrill of a live performance as accompaniment.

Unfortunately for the bogan, its list of approved artists consists largely of big-name international acts of the type which rarely find time to venture to the antipodes — and Powderfinger. After witnessing P!nk defile its nearest high-capacity sporting stadium on an average of seventeen nights per year, the bogan is still left with a large deficit in its annual live music requirements. The summer festival season goes some way towards filling the gap (more on that later), as do rare arena tours by the five rock acts that the bogan is willing to subject its ears to: U2, Green Day, Kings of Leon, Coldplay and Nickelback (plus maybe the Foo Fighters). But their scarcity leaves a substantial void, into which must step the cover band.

Cover bands

The cover band is a group of four people who peaked in high school and now exist solely to play familiar songs to the bogan live at the local pub. Found nationally in all good glassing barns, a good cover band has the ability to distract the bogan from its usual arguing, glassing, groping and leering just long enough for it to prematurely jump into the chorus of 'Blister in the Sun'. A strictly regulated product, the cover band's mandated set-list is determined by a powerful computer utilising a complex mathematical model which takes into account the following variables:

X1 = the most repeated songs on the bogan's iPod

X2 = the number of opportunities within a given song for the bogan to yell 'Whoooah-oh!'

X3 = the number of opportunities within a given song for the bogan to yell 'Yeeeaaah!'

X4 = the number of opportunities within a given song for the bogan to stomp the floor/clap its hands

X5 = the number of opportunities within a given song for the bogan to engage in fist pumps

X6 = the number of opportunities within a given song for the bogan to engage in finger guns

X7 = the number of opportunities within a given song for the bogan to adjust the lyrics to refer to its own life (for example, to nostalgically refer to a summer during which it was 'alive', or to covet the girlfriend of a person other than Jessie).

Once all factors are computed the following set-list is devised.

Jessie's Girl; 500 Miles; Summer of '69; Livin' on a Prayer; Sex on Fire; Betterman; My Sharona; Sweet Home Alabama; Venus; Tainted Love; We Will Rock You; You Shook Me All Night Long; Khe Sanh; Holy Grail; Good Riddance (Time of Your Life); Better (by the Screaming Jets); Drops of Jupiter; Love Shack; Shimmer; Blister in the Sun; Angels; and Wonderwall.

The bogan in the club

The bogan is convinced that it likes house music. The term 'house' dates back to sometime around the late 1970s or early 1980s and is thought to have emerged through some combination of reference to Chicago nightclub The Warehouse and the fact that it tended to be based on the soul, funk, disco and R&B records that its young proponents could find at home in their parents' record collections.

The bogan does not like soul, funk, disco and R&B from the 1970s and earlier. House music was initially a counter-culture movement emanating from the hard-scrabble urban environs of America's big cities and, in particular, the gay, African-American and Latino-American communities therein. The bogan is suspicious of these groups, and of counter-cultures. It also dislikes hard-scrabble urban environs because these days they tend to be filled either with Latte-sipping intellectuals or people who are legitimately dangerous — in contrast to the bogan, who has merely spent hundreds of dollars on skull/fire/heart/dagger/fierce animal/aggressive-font-related apparel in an attempt to look dangerous.

Yet, when asked what kind of music it likes, the bogan replies quickly and firmly: 'Oh, you know, a bit of everything … mainly house.' The bogan, it seems, has liked house music ever since the Ministry of Sound and its army of superstar DJs invented it in the 1990s — it was around this time that the bogan discovered that people it did not like had been attending secret warehouse parties and bush raves that it was not aware of, and dancing to something called 'house'. This caused the bogan to feel left out and stoked its instinct to colonise. But the bogan found the world of house to be vast and confusing, consisting of a seemingly endless variety of subgenres. This left the bogan vulnerable to influence, and for every vulnerable bogan there exists an equal and opposite entrepreneurial conglomerate waiting to relieve the bogan of its money.

Since its roots back in the primitive days of the tape-splicing house pioneers, the edifice of modern dance music has been built upon simulacra. It has remained original despite its habit of sampling and re-sampling its old material. New sounds are constantly being built out of old. Like a musical version of the human centipede, today's dance DJs still play sounds that were once played live by soul '70s, funk, disco and R&B bands but which have since been filtered, squelched, sliced and diced by generation after generation of music producers.

Music nerds who hoard metric tonnes of rare vinyl in their mum's garage make a sport out of being able to recognise drum fills, bass lines and horn breaks from these old recordings, as they peer through the opaque gauze of filters and vocoders, making use of their encyclopaedic knowledge of really cheesy music from the pre-AIDS era. The bogan is not a music snob, and could never engage in this level of trainspotting. But the bogan *can* recognise the chorus of 'When Love Takes Over', and will, on command, put up its hands for declining American industrial cities. Bogan-savvy DJs became aware of this and, using the commercial remix and the producer-crafted club 'banger', are now monetising the bogan night out with more fervour than a nineteen-year-old homeboy with a backpack full of green Mitsubishis.

Choose your own bogan nightclub adventure

For this exercise the reader must put themself in the bogan's shoes.

You step onto the footpath outside 'ViperSnake' nightclub. It is 11.30 p.m. on a Saturday evening and you have spent the previous few hours at the local pub, consuming a range of sugary and caffeine-enhanced alcoholic beverages and wailing along with poor timing to all the *Whoooa-ohs* and the *Yeeeeah-eeaahs* of the resident cover band. Those remaining acquaintances who have not already become overly intoxicated/embroiled in fights or forced to go home/to the hospital/to the police station join you at the club.

1. Upon arrival at the club's entrance you are greeted with a long line, at the head of which stands a very enticing velvet rope. You are more important than the average person because your cousin's ex-boyfriend's sister knows someone who was once on *Big Brother*, and this level of celebrity entitles you to jump the queue as you are probably on 'the list'. **If you wish to: slum it with the regular folk for a change, go to part 2; push in, go to part 3.**

2. A lengthy spell spent peering around those in front of you in order to catch a glimpse of the velvet rope has left you thirsty and impatient. You head to the bar for refreshments only to find yet another queue, this one without a velvet rope to encourage orderly behaviour. **If you are: sick of waiting in lines, go to part 3; willing to wait your turn, go to part 4.**

3. You have picked the wrong person to push in on: another, larger bogan. Yelling quickly turns to posturing, and then grill-getting-up-in. Your flight-or-fight response is heavily weighted toward fight at the best of times, let alone after a few drinks. The larger bogan easily accounts for you in an emotionless display of violence. You end up sprawled, semiconscious, on the footpath. **Game over. You lose.**

4. After repeatedly waving a $50 note under the barperson's nose eventually proves an effective method of gaining their attention, you order a round of Jägerbombs. You consume yours in a heroic manner, punctuating this with a hearty *Whooo-hooo* while raising your glass aloft triumphantly. But then, as you look around the venue, an anxious feeling suddenly comes over you. This place seems pretty good, but you begin to question whether or not, maybe, the people are more celeb, the beats sicker and the drinks more explosive at some other club. You fear you are not having the most maxtreme time possible. **If you wish to: leave and seek greener pastures, go to part 1; stay, go to part 5.**

5. You decide to cut a lap of the place to check things out. It is extremely crowded, requiring you to push your way through the crowd, thereby inconveniencing the entire patronage of the club. You persist, regardless of the fact that you're not going anywhere

in particular. As you conclude your lap a stranger offers you a random blue pill at the low cost of $40. **If you wish to: take it, go to part 6; politely decline, go to part 7.**

6. You soon lose control of your bodily functions. You end up sprawled, semiconscious, on the footpath. **Game over. You lose.**

7. Having decided to stick to the liquor, you head back to the bar and conquer another Jägerbomb before going to check out the DJ. The DJ's booth is sectioned off with velvet rope. You spend a few minutes peering beyond the rope, wondering what it would be like to be on the other side. Then the DJ starts playing a song that you don't recognise from any Ministry of Sound compilations. That anxious feeling comes over you again. **If you want to: leave this club and seek greener pastures, go to part 1; go out for a cigarette, go to part 8.**

8. You head out the door you so recently waited in line to enter. You see someone smoking and ask to bum a cigarette ... and a light. You have neither, because you only smoke when you're 'out'. You scoff at a few sad losers sprawled on the footpath, obviously either unable to handle their liquor or handle themselves in a fight. You are feeling pretty wasted and tired yourself by now. **Do you: hop in a cab and call it a night, go to part 9; persist, go to part 10.**

9. Conveniently, you see a cab pulling up. As you step to its door, someone else has the same idea. You want this cab, and you go for it. **Go to part 3.**

10. Persistence is the key to success, you tell yourself. More Jägerbombs sees you thoroughly intoxicated. **Go to part 6.**

Festivals

Music festivals are an example of economies of scale. Organisers reduce the average overhead cost per artist by bringing many artists together on the same bill. By doing this they are able to offer low prices on a per-artist basis, ultimately allowing music fans to witness multiple live performances in one hit for a fraction of what it would cost to attend those artists' gigs individually.

Economies of scale have nothing to do with why the bogan attends music festivals, despite the plague-like scale on which it swarms them. The bogan is typically aware of a fraction of the artists on the bill of any festival it attends, and is genuinely interested in seeing even fewer. This means that, rather than benefiting from economies of scale, music festivals mostly just represent a more expensive way for the bogan to do exactly the same things it would normally do — become intoxicated and make a nuisance of itself — in a slightly different locational context.

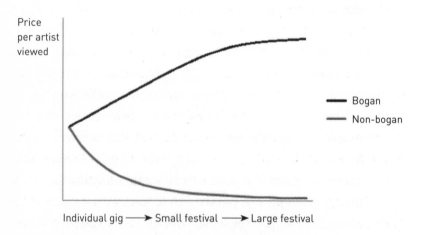

Figure 7.2 Number of artists on bill vs. price per artist viewed, bogan & non-bogan

Figure 7.2 illustrates the economics of festival attendance for the bogan in comparison to the non-bogan. Because the non-bogan typically opts to attend festivals featuring a high proportion of artists that it is interested in seeing, it benefits from festivals' economies of scale; although a larger festival will have a higher admission cost, the marginal increase in cost diminishes as the size of the festival increases, bringing the price per artist down. In contrast, the number of artists that the bogan is interested in seeing at any festival is effectively constant, being strictly limited to bands it has heard on commercial radio. This means that as the size of the festival increases, the admission cost faced by the bogan rises while the number of artists it wishes to see remains constant, resulting in an upward-sloping price-per-artist curve.

The way in which the bogan consumes music festivals suggest that it views them as a commodity good for which there is little differentiation across suppliers. This is perhaps influenced to some extent by section 23.4 of the *Trade Practices Act*, which dictates that all Australian music festivals are uniformly required to feature Paul Kelly in their line-ups. Nonetheless, whether it is a festival based around rock music, dance music or something else, as long as it features notable artists and attracts a large crowd, the bogan displays the same level of interest: maxtreme.

Not driven by value for money or by any intense attraction to the music beyond maybe one or two headline acts — which are often included in the line-up specifically to act as bogan bait — the motivation for the bogan's rabid music festival consumption is, instead, thus: the bogan seeks to use the fact that most festivals revolve around somewhat 'alternative' or 'independent' music as a way to associate itself with desirable characteristics like individuality and edginess. Rather than actually possessing those qualities, the bogan sees music festivals as a chance to purchase them for the price of admission.

It was as the turn of the millennium approached and the commodities boom began to gain momentum that the bogan discovered vast deposits of music festivals in parklands and showgrounds in Sydney, Melbourne, Adelaide, Perth, the Gold Coast and Auckland. Prior to this, these festivals had largely been frequented by native hipsters and early adopters who had named them the 'Big Day Out'. When the bogan arrived, the traditional owners were quickly overrun and forced into subjugation. Reflecting the new world order, the Blink-182 craze of the late 1990s and early 2000s saw them headline in 2000, while Limp Bizkit were the major drawcard the following year. Then, at the height of their fame, Limp Bizkit soon wished they had never heard of the bogan and its Big Day Out, after the death of a crowd member during their Sydney performance and subsequent criticism from the coroner for their part in it.

The arrival of the bogan at festivals such as the Big Day Out and Lorne's Falls Festival saw many of those events' original attendees become disenfranchised by the increasingly commercial line-ups which catered to the bogan, along with the bogan's frequently unsavoury behaviour and the resultant tightening of rules and regulations. Voting with their feet, these displaced souls then wandered the desert searching for a festival which the bogan was not yet aware of, many ending up spread across a range of smaller second-tier festivals such as Meredith. Meanwhile, a crop of new festivals, such as Splendour in the Grass and St Jerome's Laneway Festival, sprouted. The displaced had variously found refuge and naively believed that their ordeal was over; all they needed to do was keep these festivals secret from the bogan. The wily bogan, however, had by that time thoroughly colonised Triple J and learned how to use Google, making the keeping of this secret an all but impossible task.

Compared to the big-city, mega-festival nature of the Big Day Out, the more disparate cluster of smaller events worked in the festival refugees' favour. With these festivals it wasn't the case that every bogan in the country could suddenly rock up to the local leg sometime around Australia Day with an Australian-flag cape, and a pocket full of pills, and lay claim to the territory in the name of national pride. This time it would take several years for the bogan to catch up, but it would happen. In contrast to

Bikini-clad girls, shirtless guys with Southern Cross tattoos, pricey alcohol, this year's designer drug, queues for everything, large plastic ball with Australian flag motif … Oh, and those pesky bands.

the bogan blitzkrieg on the Big Day Out, it was more by stealth infiltration — or 'bogan creep' — that the second-tier group of festivals came under increasing bogan occupation.

This prompted yet another round of hipster flight, to yet smaller festivals in yet more obscure locations with less descriptive names such as Playground Weekender and Boogie, in an attempt to throw the bogan off the scent once more. (For example, the bogan is yet to discover that the Golden Plains Festival is an event that is put on by the Meredith organisers and is exactly the same as Meredith in almost every way, right down to being held in the same location.) But the bogan will continue to colonise, causing the hipster to flee again, and the bogan to give chase again, and this cat-and-mouse game will go on for all eternity.

The retro 'it' band

As well as driving hipsters to attend increasingly secretive and more intimate musical gatherings, the bogan's colonisation of the music festival season has seen it caught up in another curious phenomenon: the seasonal retro 'it' band. Every year or two a band that was initially successful fifteen to 30 years ago will return to the festival/touring circuit to cash in on their retro cred when their style of music completes another lap of the fashion merry-go-round, a new generation waiting to greet it as it swings to the front. This has, in recent years, seen the bogan clamouring to the radio request line, music retailers, iTunes and sellers of tickets to gigs and festivals to conspicuously broadcast their love for 'that sick new band Daft Punk'. In addition to Daft Punk in 2007, recent examples include Devo in 2008, which saw the bogan sporting flowerpot hats at every dress-up party it could find, and The Prodigy in 2009, which saw the bogan confused as to whether it should be dancing or fighting.

The bogan considers Devo to be a one-hit wonder. This is because the bogan has only heard one Devo song.

In conclusion

After studying this chapter, the reader should possess a strong grasp of the bogan's musical habits and, more importantly, what drives them. To this end, it is important to understand in a broader context both the ways of the bogan and the workings of the music industry and how the two feed off one another: the bogan's unquenchable desire for consumable products with which to augment its personality and signpost its position within the fat part of the normal curve, and the industry's evolution from a mere facilitator of recorded music production and distribution to an all-powerful, omnipresent bogan puppet master.

Activity

Compose an essay discussing whether commercial music evolved into its current state to meet the demands of the bogan or, instead, if it was the music industry's manipulative ways that shepherded the bogan's tastes into their current state. That is, if you like, did the bogan cause David Guetta, or did David Guetta cause the bogan?

8
TELEVISION

After accounting for full-time work hours and a good night's sleep, there remains around 72 hours in the average bogan's week for activities that are largely of its choosing. Some of these hours are chewed up by necessary evils like commuting to and from inconveniently located McMansions, running around after children and doing housework. Of the remaining time that is available purely for dedication to personal and leisure activities, by far the largest chunk is dedicated to watching television.

Sure, the bogan's leisure activities extend to socialising and other forms of entertainment such as music, Facebook and occasionally reading self-help books when instructed to by Oprah Winfrey. But in terms of time dedicated, the television is dominant. The average Australian watches over 21 hours of television per week, and when you consider that this average is dragged down by hipsters who are 'post-TV' and the tech savvy who get their television content through the intertubes, it is safe to assume that the figure is even higher for the average bogan.

It can therefore be said that television forms a central part of the bogan's life. For one thing, the bogan is kept informed, alert and alarmed through the transmission of infotainment supplied by the televisual arm of the Trashmedia Kraken, as discussed in the chapter of this book thusly named. In addition to this, television also provides the bogan with programming that is entirely for entertainment purposes, rather than just mostly for entertainment purposes; this includes the bogan's favourite sitcoms, dramas, reality and variety shows. The focus of this chapter will be on the 'just for entertainment' side of the bogan's televisual life. Of course, there are also the ads which the bogan will tell you that it doesn't watch as it steps into its limited edition Toyota RAV4 Altitude to head down to KFC to grab a Zinger Tower Combo, $7.95, available for a limited time only.

A brief history

While the first television broadcasts began in the 1920s, it wasn't until 1956 that the widespread broadcasting of television to the public began in Australia. Things had developed at a faster rate in the US and Europe, albeit on divergent paths. Much of Europe had adopted a public broadcasting model, under which state-funded media broadcast content that was deemed to be in the public interest. The US, on the other hand, had opted largely for commercial broadcasting under private ownership, funded by advertising. When television began in Australia, it was decided that both paths would be taken. Today, the ABC and SBS stand at the head of the first path, pursuing the broadcasting of content that is at least tangentially in the public interest and reflective of Australia's cultural diversity. On the other path lie the commercial networks, which exist solely as a medium by which advertisers and the Trashmedia pursue control of the bogan's mind and, in turn, its spending and voting habits.

The public interest which the public broadcasters try to stand up for tends to be somewhat intangible and unimmediate, and is therefore of little to no interest to the bogan. Only on rare occasions — such as when SBS deems that foreign breasts are an important reflection of Australia's multicultural society — do the bogan's interests appear to intersect with those of the public that SBS envisages. The commercial networks, on the other hand, have little use for people who think about the public interest or who fall within a cultural minority. Those people's interests and values tend to be many and varied, making them hard to target and influence en masse, which means that they don't bring in the max advertising cash. The commercial networks focus instead on the highly malleable, congealed beige Play-Doh of humanity that falls within the big-spending, small-thinking fat part of the normal curve that the advertisers love: the bogan. In an enduring symbiotic relationship, the bogan peers down the tube seeking mindless validation and commercial television broadcasters provide it in exchange for the bogan's mindless witnessing of advertisements.

The television as an object

Beyond the house and car, the television is among the next most important items that signal the bogan's position in society. If the bogan wishes to move up the pecking order, it is vitally important that its television ownership be on a scale at least as large as its neighbours'. All else being equal, the bogan views more television as signifying more wealth. With apparent wealth being one of the bogan's key priorities in life, the size and number of televisions possessed by the bogan is directly proportional to its sense of self-worth. Reflecting this, the number of televisions required by the bogan can be represented by the simple equation: $y = n + 1$, where y is the number of televisions desired and n is the number currently possessed.

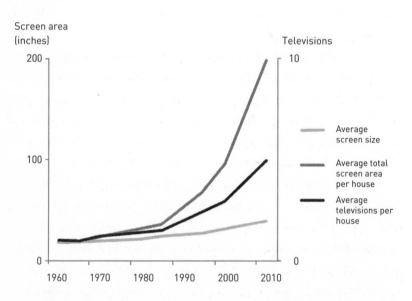

Figure 8.1 Televisions per house, screen size and total screen area

Figure 8.1 tracks over time the average number of televisions per house on the right axis, and average screen size on the left. The product of these two variables gives the average total television screen area per house. Growth in this key measure has been on an exponential path since the 1990s. Since that time, the bogan has been receiving increasingly frequent visits from a crusty, ageing stork named Harvey, who has been bringing the bogan ever larger and more prolifically acronymed and dimensioned bundles of joy.

Televisual life validation

Televisions not only act as status symbols — they also have practical applications that are extremely useful to the bogan. For one thing, they make a highly effective argument mediator. Any time the bogan is losing an argument, it is able to turn up the volume and fixate on the screen, transporting itself to a place where nobody can argue back except Charlie Sheen. Or the television can be an avenue for the referral of unresolved disputes to a higher power, such as Dr Phil or Carrie from *Sex and the City*. The television also represents the shimmering façade of one of the Trashmedia Kraken's many slimy, bile-filled, bogan-nourishing tentacles, via which all of the bogan's opinions are implanted into its brain. However, arguably the most important application of the television is the transmission of purely pleasure-oriented content that allows the bogan to be entertained in the absence of conscious thought. And commercial television networks know that the bogan is most entertained by things that validate its life.

In order to provide max appeal to the bogan and get it to tune in week after week, commercial television networks must ensure that their programs speak to the bogan's deep-seated beliefs and desires. This is, of course, in addition to explosions, car chases, guns, sex and the like. Every bogan-friendly television show targets the validation of one or more aspects of the bogan's psyche via characters and storylines that reflect and reiterate the bogan's worldview, with different genres tending to target particular aspects of the bogan's life and dreams for validation.

Dominating at life

The bogan's goal in life is to become inexplicably wealthy and notable. It wants to look down upon others, to have others look up to it and to receive things without earning them. The creators of *Two And A Half Men* (*TAAHM*) know this all too well, which is why they created Charlie Sheen's character, Charlie, as a vessel through which to titillate the male bogan by acting out all of its selfish and shallow fantasies. Via a vague jingle-writing career which occurs entirely off screen — and which, given the high proportion of time that the show is on screen, appears to entail very little jingle writing — Charlie has grown rich enough to live a life of luxurious leisure and debauchery from his Malibu beach house. Tall, handsome and confident, Charlie finds that women throw themselves at him constantly. The show's other protagonist is Charlie's brother, Alan. A hapless, divorced father of one, Alan

Charlie Sheen represents everything the bogan wants but can't have.

is the polar opposite of Charlie. Small, feeble, neurotic, broke and particularly awkward when it comes to women, Alan is portrayed as wholly unsuccessful despite being a chiropractic doctor. The male bogan is Charlie. Other men are Alan.

Along similar lines to Charlie is the Barney Stinson character appearing on *TAAHM*'s CBS stablemate, *How I Met Your Mother* (*HIMYM*). Barney is a similarly inexplicably wealthy Peter Pan character, and a similarly staunch and highly successful bachelor who, like *TAAHM*'s Charlie, exists to act out the male bogan's lecherous fantasies. However, the bogan likes *TAAHM* far more than it likes *HIMYM*. The reasons for this are twofold. First, the canned laugh track on *TAAHM* is multiple times more boisterous than that of *HIMYM*, leaving the bogan in no doubt as to when, and to what extent, something is funny (this, incidentally, is 'always' and 'very', if the laugh track is to be believed). Second, there are two meaningful female characters on *HIMYM*, compared to zero on *TAAHM*, where the female characters are strictly sideline in nature. Running the numbers, *TAAHM* has two and a half characters: Charlie (1), Alan (1) and the entire female cast plus the kid (0.5). Despite this, there does exist a *TAAHM* character that the female bogan identifies with: the string of Charlie's casual hook-ups, who represent his instant, unearned access to money and celebrity. To this end, Sheen's character appears designed to be half Charlie Harper, fictional jingle writer, and half Charlie Sheen, real-life actor and celebrity. The bogan does not question this. The female bogan is Charlie's girls. Other women are the vindictive ex, the crazy stalker or the sexually ambiguous, overweight housekeeper.

In early 2011 the crossover between Charlie the character and Charlie the actor became so great that it resulted in a warping of time–space around the Los Angeles area. This saw artificial Charlie somehow leapfrog actual Charlie, resulting in the emergence of hypermax Charlie, an enthrallingly magnified version of television character Charlie whose real-life exploits necessitated the scrapping of the show's filming schedule for the 2011 season and the replacement of Charlie Sheen with Ashton Kutcher, who incidentally has pulled a cougar with a hot body in real life. Things bode well for *TAAHM* but not so well for hypermax Charlie.

The female bogan is better catered to by *Sex and the City (SATC)*. A show about four 30-or-40-something New York City women who are simultaneously successful, independent and indolent, *SATC* has multiple characters who represent the female bogan's dream life. Purportedly reflective of female empowerment, the women are rarely seen working but are frequently seen coveting and consuming ultra-expensive brands, and vying for and receiving the attention and gifts of wealthy men. For example, the lead character and narrator, Carrie Bradshaw, appears to write one newspaper column per week yet lives on Manhattan's Upper East Side and is routinely seen purchasing and/or wearing expensive designer apparel. This is the kind of empowerment that the female bogan will fight for.

Looking down

The bogan is wholly unable to consider its life in absolute terms. To the bogan's largely unconscious mind, everything becomes relative, which is why it will always describe itself as happy, content, et cetera when asked yet simultaneously display immense status anxiety. Relative to people whom the bogan considers itself better than, the bogan is happy. But relative to people better off than it, the bogan could be happier. For example, the intense pride felt upon taking ownership of a new 84-inch television soon gives way to anxious envy of those with larger, or more, televisions.

There is always *someone* better off than the bogan, and there is always someone worse off. This is a large part of the reason why the bogan is highly susceptible to advertising. Like a hamster in a wheel, the bogan constantly feels as if it is one purchase away from joining those at a higher level of happiness.

The existence of people who are further away than the bogan from that higher level of happiness makes the bogan feel closer, boosting its self-esteem and encouraging it to continue its pursuit.

The bogan therefore likes to be reminded of the people that it deems itself better than in some way. And so downward-looking reality television was created, to highlight the flaws of other bogans for the viewing bogan's entertainment. This type of program has the power to transform the viewing bogan sitting on its couch, watching other bogans on television, into an aristocrat sitting atop a mighty pedestal of virtue watching the savages compete for the scraps of its attention. Like the Roman gladiators who risked their lives for the amusement of the patrician elite, these marginalised bogans put their dignity on the line for the entertainment of the couch-going bogan, itself often in only slightly better shape than those it derides.

Foremost among this category of reality television is *The Biggest Loser*, which pits overweight adults against one another in a weight-losing contest that is akin to a grown-up version of forcing the fat kids to fight each other in the schoolyard. The viewing bogan is able to look down upon the contestants, who are in relatively poorer shape, and thus feel closer to having the body of a sports star, actor or other attractive person — perhaps,

The variety of bogan *schadenfreude* that doesn't involve Jagermeister.

in fact, only one purchase of a Fat Magnet away from that dream body, or a tub of Yoplait, a Vodafone mobile phone or a Domino's pizza away from bliss. These are just some of the brands that sponsor the show in an attempt to help the bogan trim the fat from its wallet. Rather than identifying with the contestants, the bogan sees itself in the place of the 'celebrity' personal trainers, rescuing the hapless fatties from themselves and showing them how to be relatively more healthy — like the bogan.

Along similar *schadenfreude* lines is *Ladette to Lady*, which sees bogans who are slightly more bogan than the average bogan (the ladettes) attempt to become slightly less bogan by attending a finishing school. Teachers at the school attempt to teach the ladettes outdated high-society customs while largely ignoring more pressing concerns such as their complete inability to exercise anything resembling self-control. Again, the bogan naturally identifies upwards — with the teachers rather than the ladettes.

It is the same story in the early stages of reality television talent-search programs such as *X Factor*, *Idol* and *So You Think You Can Dance*. The bogan takes great pleasure in the misguided audition attempts made by other bogans, all the while harbouring the belief that it will one day receive an unsolicited offer to become a celebrity when a scout recognises its singing talent at a karaoke bar or its epic moves on the nightclub dance floor. The idea that people can become celebrities for being less than mediocre is highly appealing to the bogan, as it lowers the benchmark to a point even lower than the bogan's.

Looking in the mirror

Perceiving itself to be a veritable well of potential waiting to be tapped, the bogan harbours the belief that simply being its awesome self will soon carry it to fame and fortune. As has been the theme throughout this chapter, the bogan's television viewership is best captured by programs that validate such fantastical beliefs. Television executives began to realise the power of the fame dream in the 1990s, when the first programs that turned regular people with, at best, moderate talent, into instant celebrities emerged. 'Regular' and 'instant' are key words here, in a similar way that 'working families' and 'a fair go' are important phrases in political campaigning. In each case they are respectively code for 'the bogan' and 'receiving things without having had to earn them'.

It started in Australia in 1992 with a program called *Sylvania Waters*, which tracked a real-life family of newly cashed-up bogans as they spent and bickered their way through six months of existence. The format then took a while to take off, only gaining significant momentum towards the turn of the millennium. At this point two crucial reality television concepts gained substantial traction: the public talent-search and humans-in-captivity observational studies. The former caters to the bogan's desire to believe in the existence of an avenue to becoming a famous singer, dancer, model, chef or similar that doesn't require a lifetime of hard work and sacrifice; the latter encourages the bogan's belief that its life is so outstanding as to warrant the 24-hour-a-day attention of the general populace.

Not only did these types of reality shows attain strong ratings as bogan viewers imagined themselves in the position of successful contestants, bogans also clambered over each other to appear on the programs free of charge to take their shot at faux celebrity status. In the case of *Big Brother*, for which there was no talent requirement whatsoever, the shows' producers were only too happy to select a cast of the most boganesque bogan specimens they could get their hands on. They knew that unlike regular people appearing on national television, these bogans' complete lack of self-awareness would render them entirely unable to regulate their behaviour, thus giving the show maximum zoo-like quality.

Programs that document the lives of successful famous people have, of course, existed for much longer than reality television has been making mediocre people famous for the excitement of viewing bogans. Known as biographical documentaries, these programs tend to prove unpopular with the bogan, who has little interest in stories

Kim Kardashian is from the Paris Hilton School of Celebrity — not unlike the Ponds Institute but you need a sex tape to enrol.

about people toiling away in obscurity for years, working their way slowly up the ranks in their field before arriving at a point where they are accomplished enough to warrant the attention of the general public. The words 'toiling', 'working' and 'slowly' are highly repulsive to the bogan. Like watching a sausage being made, the bogan finds the end product — fame — highly appealing but finds the process by which it is generally achieved to be less than desirable. Television executives realised this, creating reality television to provide the bogan with the belief that it can subvert the process. Kim Kardashian and Paris Hilton never had to toil or work to achieve celebrity status, so the bogan shouldn't have to either.

Catching the bad guy

The Trashmedia frequently reminds the bogan that there are people who are poorer than it, and that it needs to be protected from these people. The bogan believes that people poorer than it are likely to suicide-bomb its local megamall, otherwise physically harm itself or its family, or steal its belongings or job. People poorer than the bogan include foreign people, disorganised criminals and people whom the bogan considers to be bogans. Reflecting this, television networks ply the bogan with programs — both reality and scripted — in which the bad guy is caught, humiliated and punished on the bogan's behalf, over and over again, every week. The core requirement for these programs is that they clearly distinguish between the good guys and the bad guys, and to ensure that the good guys resemble the bogan and that the bad guys do not. As a result, the bad guys invariably tend to be clearly painted as one of the following: mentally deranged; foreign; poor; rich, greedy and immoral; cowardly; grotesquely selfish; some combination of the above. The good guys, on the other hand, are uniformly moral, brave and stoic. The bogan is able to easily identify the winning team.

Chief among these victory-for-the-virtuous programs is Channel Seven's *Border Security: Australia's Front Line*, a reality show which documents the work of Australia's customs, quarantine and immigration officials (the good guys) as they protect the bogan from foreigners (the bad guys). *Border Security*'s Channel Nine clone, *Customs*, documents basically the same thing. Notably, in fact, both are portentously hosted/narrated by recognised and trustworthy former *Blue Heelers* (Mt Thomas's Front Line) good guys. The bogan is comforted by the fact that we have our best men on the case.

The editing of these shows suggests that their chief objective is to report instances in which foreign persons from regions with a lower standard of living than Australia are prevented from moving about in Australia in the manner in which they hope to. Each of these instances is a victory for Australia and, therefore, for the bogan. Under the guise of national security, the shows appeal to the bogan's desire to wall itself off from the outside world, protecting its habitat from people whom its steadfast refusal to understand leads it to imagine are uniformly dangerous and immoral.

There is particular focus on trafficking of illicit substances, reflecting the bogan's commitment to the war on drugs and

Vietnamese fish sauce. The bogan exists separately to the drug-trafficking trade and any social issues related to substance abuse, because it only uses party drugs casually and gets them from a friend with connections, rather than from the anus of a shifty-looking south-east Asian person. The other key priority of the program is to document cases in which immigration laws are upheld. This allows the bogan to feel like the person in charge of the velvet rope at an exclusive club, deciding who gets in and who doesn't based largely on their appearance.

On the fictional side is the plethora of police procedurals such as the *Law & Order* and *CSI* franchises, which repeat variations of the same story every week. A heinous crime is committed; cops arrive on the scene and investigate a few incorrect angles before eventually catching and prosecuting the bad guy. The bogan observes from its moral high horse, ending each show relieved that another murderous paedophile Colombian drug lord is off the street.

Just as much as the main storyline, the subplots along the way also get the bogan's juices flowing. Included here are plots such as: *the cop with the hunch who no one believes but who ends up being right all along; the cop who lets it get 'personal', initially making bad choices but in the end making up for it by catching the bad guy; the ostracised cop who appears to be corrupt but ends up actually being on a renegade undercover mission/being blackmailed, and who eventually proves everyone wrong by catching the bad guy; and the ordinary citizen forced to take the law into their own hands to prevent a tragedy.* The bogan sees itself in the shoes of the person upholding justice at all costs, imposing their own personal values in place of the law, and being the only one who was right all along.

Being the bad guy

While the bogan takes great pleasure in seeing many bad guys caught and punished, there are some whom the bogan, from the comfort of its living room, instead idolises and likes to fantasise about emulating. Particularly worthy of role-model status is the bad guy who is a bit of a larrikin, and who can be thought of as a kind of maxtreme business person and Robin Hood–type character, stealing from the rich/bad and perpetrating crimes that can be perceived as victimless. This type of bad guy combines 'street smarts' with measured brutality, to outflank its more primitive rivals, and 'book smart' law enforcement, on the way to gaining immense wealth and notoriety in a quick and easy fashion. This is enormously appealing to the bogan, who is unable to resist a good short cut and who is convinced of the value of its extensive knowledge of the 'real world'. In essence, bad guys who resemble the bogan and commit crimes against those who do not resemble the bogan are to be idolised. Bad guys who do not resemble the bogan, on the other hand, should be caught and punished/deported back where they came from.

Catering to the bogan's crime kingpin fantasy are shows like *Underbelly* and its various sequels, spin-offs and hurriedly cobbled-together crime family documentaries, which dramatise and re-enact the goings-on in the world of organised crime. Not included in this category, however, are other programs that feature questionable characters, like *The Sopranos*, *Dexter* and *Breaking Bad*. These shows have a key difference in that they highlight the difficulties in making an easy living through crime, and challenge the viewer to make their own judgements on morally murky issues by positioning their protagonists in a conflicted middle ground between right and wrong. The uncertainty does not sit well with the bogan, who likes to focus only on the potential riches of crime and prefers clear instruction as to whom to cheer for and whom to cheer against — that is, which characters represent it and which do not. That is not to say, though, that the bogan won't watch *Dexter* or *The Sopranos*: it enjoys *Dexter* for the violence and its Miami setting, and *The Sopranos* for its violence, sex, swearing and mobster stereotyping of Italian-Americans. The bogan is, however, entirely oblivious to the shows' underlying social and philosophical commentaries.

Underbelly and the like studiously avoid such depth, instead focusing on the glitz, glamour, riches and, most importantly, notoriety of being a major organised-crime player. This is much more appealing to the bogan, whose dream it is to dominate notable city nightclub strips while dressed in garishly flashy attire, and to be simultaneously feared as a ruthless crime boss and revered as a local celeb. While *Underbelly*'s bad guys are frequently portrayed doing bad things, a bogan caveat is always present in that their deeds are carried out in the name of family, loyalty, honour, respect or control of illicit-substance supply chains. This is facilitated by the bogan's tendency to focus on events in isolation and to be oblivious to the bigger picture. In this line of thinking, tit-for-tat acts of revenge and subsequent counter-revenge do not seem at all futile to the bogan. Similarly, the bogan's staunch belief that two wrongs make a right is reflected in *Underbelly*'s obligatory portrayal of dirty cops, which, in the bogan's mind, acts to validate any and all illegal behaviour.

The poorly suited pantheon of Boganic Gods.

Being funny

Despite lacking the insight, nuance and timing of a comedian, the bogan believes that in a given room or group, its role is to be 'the funny one'. While this is clearly misguided and contradictory, the fact that the bogan is unburdened by wit is the very thing that facilitates this belief, by shielding the bogan from awareness of its malnourished humour gland. As is often the case, television assists the bogan to paper over this particular crack in its character. Alongside movie comedies, joke books written by Kochie and funny things other people have said on the Internet, the bogan uses content from television comedies to supplement its comedic deficiency. In particular, it is comedy catchphrases that the bogan commandeers and repeats ad nauseam in pursuit of 'LOLs' from everyone within a 100-metre radius of wherever it happens to be at the time, along with everyone connected to its Facebook and Twitter feeds.

In the television sphere, no program in recent years has played to this more than *Little Britain*, which the bogan has adopted as its catchphrase generator *du jour*, parroting truly hilarious lines like 'Computer says noooo' and 'I want that one' anytime they can be feasibly shoehorned into a conversation or situation, and often even when they can't.

In addition to its catchphrases, *Little Britain*'s arsenal of additional never-fail bogan laughter bait includes middle-aged men dressed as women, middle-aged men dressed as elderly women, middle-aged men dressed as babies, middle-aged men dressed as teenage girls, middle-aged men mocking the handicapped and middle-aged men mocking gay people. The fact that one of the writers is gay and that he himself mocks and stereotypes homosexuals allows the bogan to feel it has carte blanche to do the same, just as having an Asian friend or colleague leaves the bogan free to make racist jokes. *Little Britain* also has the advantage of assisting in the bogan's quest to paint itself as a higher-order being for liking British comedy, despite its interest being mostly limited to catchphrases and middle-aged men playing characters other than middle-aged men.

One of the few instances in which the bogan finds humour in a male actor portraying a male character of similar age who is not over-the-top flamboyantly homosexual or disabled is when the character is what the bogan would consider a bogan — i.e. an old-school bogan (OSB) — with commensurate catchphrases. The outrageous bogan love for comedian Heath Franklin's impersonation of Eric Bana impersonating Mark 'Chopper' Read is testament to this. Read — the earless baby boomer ex-convict turned celebrity — is the textbook OSB, with his tough-guy attitude, home-style tattoos and ultimate handlebar moustache. The multi-stage Chinese whispers process ending at Franklin, however, distilled the 'Chopper' character down to the barest of bogan memes, with the surviving caricature retaining some theoretical capacity to commit crimes but ending up primarily a stammering pastiche of pitch-shifted dumbed-down quips of indeterminate origin, designed to extract low-hanging bogan laughs in 90-second parcels.

Neighbours meets *Little Britain*: **quite a confusing moment for the bogan.**

Indeed, the bogan's *modus operandi* when it comes to comedies is to extract the catchphrases, slapstick and toilet humour while leaving any irony or social commentary entirely undisturbed. This is perhaps best evidenced by the bogan's interactions with animated TV shows *The Simpsons* and *South Park*. The statement that perhaps best sums this up is that Bart is the bogan's favourite *Simpsons* character. With his many catchphrases, pranks and rebellious attitude, Bart's humour is pitched precisely at the level of the bogan, who is oblivious to the fact that these gags are incidental to wider commentary on issues such as family and society. On a similar plane is the bogan's enjoyment of *South Park*, another show that cleverly uses two levels of humour to appeal to viewers at both ends of the spectrum. The bogan is taken in by the crude language of the young characters and the gross-out humour; all the while, as with *The Simpsons*, the fact that the rude jokes and storylines are merely an avenue by which to comment on broader social and philosophical themes is entirely lost on the bogan.

Even more television

As the total area of television screen in the bogan's home began its rapid expansion in the 1990s, the bogan realised that it not only wanted more screen but more things *on* its screen. Your typical garden-variety cynical entrepreneur is able to detect the sound of the bogan desiring something in a manner similar to the way in which whales communicate via sonar, and thus soon there did indeed exist a way for the bogan to achieve a greater rate of things-per-screen in the form of pay television.

Pay television

In contrast to commercial television — which funds its broadcasts with payments from advertisers, allowing it to provide the content to the viewer for free — the pay-television model sees advertising largely eschewed and broadcasting instead subsidised by viewer subscription fees. Australia's first pay television service, Galaxy, was launched on Australia Day 1995. While Galaxy initially only had two channels, it contained the letter X, and therefore bogans began to sign up. Soon Galaxy was joined by Optus Vision, which had a bigger budget but fewer Xs. In October 1995 the key player entered the fray. Foxtel had an even bigger budget, allowing it to offer twenty channels, *and* its name contained the letter X. From this point onwards the story of pay television in Australia effectively became the story of the bogan's love for Foxtel.

Foxtel was bound to succeed. Initially a 50-50 joint venture between Telstra and bogan svengali News Corporation, 25 per cent of the company was subsequently transferred to PBL, then owner of such bogan treasures as Crown Casino, Burswood Casino and Richard Wilkins. Like numerous other truly clever bogan-cash-harvesting undertakings, Foxtel has never really given the bogan something it didn't already have. Instead Foxtel has mainly just offered more of the same, reinforcing to the bogan that more is better and, therefore, worth paying more for. Or, in this case, worth paying something for, rather than nothing. Indeed, pay television can be seen as the bottled water of home entertainment.

This is not to say that the bogan doesn't derive an enormous amount of value from having Foxtel. The mere act of signing up for channels such as National Geographic and Discovery Channel serves as a big boost to the bogan's estimation of itself as a sophisticate, even if its occasional encounters with those two channels are largely confined to watching large animals killing things and seeing tribal boobs, respectively. A recently watched documentary allows the bogan to proudly recite a couple of obscure factual details from the program, before they permanently exit its memory 48 hours later.

Other channels allow the bogan to view movies it would never have paid money for at a video store, or spend hours per week watching obscure sports that it does not understand. Foxtel's consistent growth in average revenue per user, to more than double the cost of a basic 'starter' package, is a shining tribute to the company's ability to sell the bogan ever more add-ons that it didn't know it wanted.

The recent advent of digital television in Australia has allowed the free-to-air networks to finally strike back, offering the bogan more: more things that were too dismal to screen when each network only had one channel. Now the bogan is torn between watching the thrills of a Bhutan v Senegal test match on Fox Sports 3 or another exciting rerun of *Murder, She Wrote* on Gem. While this choice can be confusing, one thing that does not confuse the bogan is its ongoing need for more television.

In conclusion

After studying this chapter, the reader should recognise the multiple roles of the television in the bogan's life: the television itself as a status symbol; the content broadcast by commercial networks as entertainment in the form of life validation; and the infotainment spewed forth by the televisual arm of the Trashmedia Kraken as a means to furnish the bogan with its opinions, as further discussed in the chapter of this book thusly named. With television occupying the bogan for more time than any other leisure activity, it should be understood that it is one of the aspirational bogan's primary goals in life to possess a greater total area of television screen than its neighbours and, beyond that, to have the ability to make more things appear on a given screen. The reader should also possess a comprehensive understanding of the way in which the bogan's need to have its life and views constantly validated, combined with the commercial television networks' need to gain the marketing-malleable bogan audience in order to attract maximum advertising cash, resulted in the downward spiral that saw Shane Warne briefly hosting his own talk show.

9
FASHION

Oscar Wilde once said 'Fashion is a form of ugliness so intolerable that we have to alter it every six months'. Existentially fleeting, fashion has been on the move since the dawn of civilisation. It has appalled, shocked, flattered, aroused, disgusted and inspired the masses for centuries, as they consumed the sartorial whims of the bourgeois in an attempt to vicariously escape their drudgery.

The bogan of the twenty-first century has much in common with the plague-infested townsfolk of the sixteenth century in that it is contagious and uncomfortably aspirational. Yet the nouveau bogan has acquired the financial means to physically mimic the celebrity-endorsed fashions of the day which has resolutely come to define its existence. Politely swayed by the Trashmedia Kraken's nourishing appendages, the bogan is only too happy to abandon any sense of self and be guided into the fashionable arms of someone or something that is 'couture'. A human billboard, the bogan proudly advertises its affiliations to brands and people that help it construct a sense of meaning in its life. Whatever the attraction, a powerful undercurrent in the bogan's fashion universe is the need to be loud and garish, and proclaim to the world that it paid large sums of money in order to look like somebody else.

Goaded by these sweeping tides of conformity, the non-bogan population has sought refuge in the fashions of music, literature and art. Not to be left out, the bogan also demanded to be herded into the perfumed atmosphere of acceptance where it could satiate itself with the knowledge that everyone is unique while still being exactly the same. This has proved enormously helpful for anyone looking to extract maximum bogan bucks: as long as something was seen as fashionable due to being validated by the opinions of others, the bogan was ready to pay for it.

Fashion fads can last anywhere between a week and a year, but the bogan is inevitably late to the show. This perhaps explains why bogans embrace recently deceased trends with such profane vehemence. The once beloved Ralph Lauren Polo shirt is a fine example of a product that now firmly resides in the purgatory of boganic fashion. A key aspect to understanding bogan fashion is to therefore abandon any sense of the subtle or classic, and instead dwell in its vivid fluorescence.

In order to properly appreciate the bogan's erosion of self, it is useful to look towards its ancestors. The bogan of yore, as mentioned earlier in this book, was a self-actualised individual who cared little for celebrity and had no use for hair gel. It was remarkably resistant to the poisons of the Trashmedia, preferring instead to adopt a simple, functional approach to its fashions. The passage of time has, however, witnessed some unsavoury changes. The nouveau bogan's fragmented sense of identity lies splayed across trashy magazines, television and Facebook, resulting in a morass of imitation and idolatry. Any sense of originality or class is now veering precariously on the fringes of extinction.

Branding

Sociologist Thorstein Veblen argued that life is not driven by notions of value, but by social vestiges from prehistoric times. He also introduced the concept of conspicuous consumption, which he saw as an utter waste of money and resources. Some 112 years later, it would seem that Veblen was onto something. The Longman American dictionary defines conspicuous consumption as 'the act of buying a lot of things, especially expensive things that are not necessary, in a way that people notice'. Research has also found that this act takes up at least 70 per cent of the bogan's cerebral activity on any given day, making branding — the thing that other people are meant to notice — a crucial part of its protozoan existence.

The importance of branding in bogan fashion cannot be overstated. From a marketing perspective, brands define the personality of a product, service or person relative to their counterparts. While the idea of endowing watches, for example, with personality may seem odd in some circles, marketers have found it to be the most successful method of distinction. From the bogan's standpoint, brands are the single best way to tell the world who or what it stands for. They represent everything that the bogan doesn't have to say, write or sing, because nothing can justifiably capture its nuanced worldview like four letters that almost spell FUCK. Furthermore, brands make it impossibly easy for bogans to spot fellow members of their tribe. While the bogan wishes to be the stalwart of cool, it craves the recognition of its peers. And few things are more flattering to the bogan than imitation.

Luckily for the bogan, its elixir of life comes in many forms. Ranging from T-shirts to cans, its 'personality' may be manifested by a number of unique brands that capably distil its essence. Of course, some products are better than others in their ability to play the part of 'brand-as-person': clothes, watches, shoes, cars and others that lend themselves to a high degree of social visibility. People in white lab coats (unbranded, to the casual observer) have long maintained that social identification is a part of the normal evolutionary cycle. Even non-bogans have seen the need for socialisation, although their version tends to involve *people* rather than *things* as a means of social bonding.

A critical aspect of bogan branding lies in understanding the psychology of the bogan's needs. Similar to the dynamics of war, group identity is terribly salient to the bogan and has therefore become the dominant paradigm through which it views itself. This is perhaps testament to the fact that collective validation is the oxygen that allows the bogan's inimitability to breathe.

For the purposes of furthering the threshold of boganic knowledge, this chapter will deal with fashion in its myriad manifestations, ranging from tattoos to exercise-themed clothing. It will attempt to analyse the motivations of boganic consumption and explore the reasons for its stark differences. It will seek to elucidate the power of celebrity and the meagre contribution of taste to the bogan's sense of fashion.

The power of couture

The bogan knows not what 'haute couture' means; in fact, it doesn't really know what either 'haute' or 'couture' mean, but it doesn't care. However, the bogan definitely knows it wants both of these things immediately. What began as a French term to describe the creation of exclusive, bespoke clothing in the nineteenth century has today devolved to simply mean 'better'. For the bogan female the term conveys many desirable qualities which it knows it deserves, invoking lucid fantasies of mingling with Parisian aristocracy or being Jennifer Hawkins. For the male bogan it simply brings to mind the great American mixed-martial artist and Greco-Roman champion Randy Couture, beating people

Bogans love a powerful message. They love it even more on a T-shirt.

to a bloody pulp. Either way, the bogan knows that this couture stuff is expensive, exclusive and celebrities have it. Consequently, the bogan must also have it.

However, should the bogan witness *actual* haute couture on fashion runways, it will quickly dismiss it as 'stupid' and observantly remark, 'As if anybody will actually wear that!' Until, of course, it spots a safe variation of a once-outrageous Givenchy gown on sale at Supré for $28.99. The female bogan is also particularly susceptible to the couture-isms displayed on the red carpet. Award ceremonies such as the Logies, where celebrities parade their extravagant wares, are ripe with juicy fashion ideas for the bogan to imitate. If Megan Gale's scandalous frontless, backless, strapless, crotchless black dress makes the femme-bogue's significant other tremble with lust, she knows that she simply must have it. She will thus promptly march into Sass & Bide the following morning and happily part with $2000, all the while dreaming about being a famous, well-heeled vixen commanding legions of salivating men.

Despite the femme-bogan being only too happy to pay lots of money to look like someone else, it is not averse to the idea of paying less while still pilfering the cachet of couture. The Stella McCartney couture range, which was exclusive to discount variety retailer Target, was the only time the upwardly mobile bogan ever admitted going into such a place. This was because its feeble conscience allowed it this one indiscretion, and it could not resist the temptation to look like a celebrity on the cheap.

The male bogan doesn't really care for couture unless it is extreme in some fashion. For example, it knows that exercising, fighting and killing things are extreme pastimes that require clothing explicitly made for such activities. Marketers, being acutely attuned cash extractors, have sensed this need in the bogan and introduced appropriately themed clothing for its various endeavours. Such clothing may be classified in the following way: fight-branded clothing; exercise-themed clothing; numerical clothing; extreme sports clothing; and absence of clothing.

The advent of this Themed Activity-Based clothing (TAB) revolutionised the bogan's wardrobe as it simplified its decision-making process by around 675 per cent. No longer are its pre-club hours spent racking its brain, pondering whether bright green and bright orange are compatible. Now it can simply refer to the fight-branded aisle of its walk-in cupboard and choose a suitably mean number for its nighttime activities. The creative bogan micro-minority has sometimes been known to combine different themes, such as the numerical-fight-exercise combination, which has allowed it to count the number of repetitions during its kickboxing training sessions.

Such is the power of couture that the term has been appropriated for products other than clothing. Fragrances, cosmetics, watches, jewellery and accessories all bear this label, stripping away any semblance of relevance or meaning from the original term. It is, indeed, a powerful reminder that the bogan is decidedly indifferent about what it has been sold, and is purely driven by the idea of a product being 'better' because it is marketed in a particular manner.

The life cycle of bogan fashion

A fad-following troglodyte, the bogan is content to sit passively at the table while the lazy Susan of fashion whirls dizzyingly before its eyes.

It all begins with early-adopting cool kids who concoct (or, in some cases, copy) an eventual trend while sipping Lattes and being concerned about the plight of trees. At this stage only a select hundred thousand people 'in the know' are privy to the future style of millions. Sales, while growing, are minimal, with the trend only available in a handful of independent stores located in alleyways that are only accessible via other alleyways. The bogan is unaware that at any given time a trend that it will eventually demolish is being propagated by people it hates.

In phase two, celebrities, being the fashion savants that they are, catch wind of the trend which has been developed by the cool kids. They are then paid obscene amounts of money by astute designers to road-test the trend. This is done in order to evaluate whether enough bogans are sufficiently enamoured of the trend to warrant immediate, low-cost, large-scale production in a country that does not recognise minimum-wage laws. In this phase it is crucial that celebrities play the role of fashion guinea pigs, because the bogan considers celebrities to be the best and most credible representation of humanity possible.

Phase three is contingent on the success of its predecessor, and involves the rapid penetration of the trend into the succulent heart of the mainstream. Shopping malls and franchises are particularly important channels, as the bogan doesn't trust unbranded independent stores (because they are filled with Latte-sipping flora sympathisers). Large amounts of cash money are imminent, with marketers readying their proboscides in anticipation. The Trashmedia ably informs its faithful vassals about the imminent arrival of the trend. As a result the bogan community is giddy with excitement, awaiting the opportunity to saturate the world with its new-found fashions.

In phase four, the Trashmedia Kraken finally deems the trend permissible for the bogan hordes. Within a matter of weeks the rate of boganic adoption is so furious that it blinds the general population and causes irrevocable retinal scorching. Any semblance of style or taste has been hacked to death in a consumptive orgy of ugliness. By this phase the cool kids have long since abandoned their affiliation with the trend, contenting themselves with boutique cider and contemplating a move to the coniferous forests of northern Russia. Sales of the trend peak and then fall rapidly, as even the bogan suffers a fatigue from overexposure to the fad rays of the day, resulting in large-scale diagnoses of sartorial melanomas.

Some 20 to 25 years later, when memories of the trend have abated amongst the collective populace, a bunch of caffeinated cool kids will bring it back in the name of irony. Thus, the lazy

Susan of boganic fashion comes full circle, beginning with freshly steamed dumplings and leaving the bogan with cold and congealed remnants. But the bogan doesn't care. It remains stationed, like a dog without hobbies, adjacent to the sartorial dinner table. There it eagerly awaits any and all scraps that tumble down from the feast taking place above its head.

Dress codes

Dress codes refer to commonly accepted rules of dress, established to signal the appropriate level and manner of formality required at a place or occasion. They evolved from ancient Greek sumptuary laws, which attempted to regulate the consumption habits of commoners.

The bogan detests commoners and being regulated, and therefore does not heed regulation of any stripe, least of all sartorially. Instead it has adopted its own dress code, one that captures its unique ability to blend a lime green suit with gleaming white crocodile leather shoes and a novelty tie. Like non-bogans, the bogan's outfit also varies with occasion, except that it has the propensity to confuse marriages with funerals and supermarkets with Mediterranean supper clubs. It is also not uncommon for the female bogan to profess its love for 'men in uniform', which has prompted many a male bogan to seriously consider becoming a fireman or policeman — but it is more likely that it will simply purchase a uniformed costume for attendance at a dress-up party.

It is now worth examining the dynamic nature of the bogan dress code, as preferred for each occasion.

Table 9.1 Bogan dress code

Occasion	Male Dress Code	Female Dress Code
Pub	Depending on the weather, the bogan's typical pub apparel will include a (TAB) T-shirt (fight, exercise or numerical-based themes are most popular), coupled with ill-fitting though expensive jeans that may or may not bear stylised paint stains. Jackets are banned, because the male bogan is impervious to cold. Thongs, brightly coloured pointed leather shoes or brightly coloured sneakers are all fair game. Cargo pants or shorts are also an option, irrespective of season.	The femme-bogue's idea of fashion may be expressed in three words: less is more. It is acutely aware that nothing appeals to the male of its species more than the gratuitous display of flesh. Its favourite pub wear will thus involve some variation of tight denim shorts and a plunging blouse. Platform shoes/high heels or Roman sandals add the critical 'bondage' appeal to finish off the classy ensemble. Accessories include seventeen Pandora bracelets, four shiny wristbands spruiking worthy causes and six cubic zirconia rings.
Club	The club is a sacred institution in the bogan's quest for spirituality. It therefore demands that the bogan be immaculately dressed in order to find sexual salvation. The fundamental ethos of club wear is that brighter is better. TAB clothing is a must and jackets are still banned, with the only main difference being that shoes are mandatory. The male bogan is also prone to bringing glowsticks, which it will fashion into hats, antennae and gifts solemnly conferred to female bogans it wishes to mount.	Again, the less the better. For the female the club is like a giant sperm bank, teeming with potential fluid exchangers. It therefore must become a walking mirrorball in order to attract a mate. Extremely tight jeans/micro-mini skirt, a suffocating low-cut top and broad, shiny black platform shoes complete its ensemble-as-mating-call. Accessories include seventeen Pandora bracelets, four shiny wristbands spruiking worthy causes, two glowsticks and six cubic zirconia rings.

Occasion	Male Dress Code	Female Dress Code
Bar	Bogan bar clothing is a wonky combination of pub and club styling; it is likely that the bogan will wear a leather jacket in winter because it once saw the movie *Cocktail* and confused it for *Top Gun*. The bogan is regularly out of its comfort zone in the confines of a small bar, and is therefore likely to be wearing a furrowed brow due to the lack of remixes, dance floors, and glassings.	See male dress code, only add spraytan and miniskirt.
Beach	The beach provides the bogan with many absence-of-apparel options. In most cases, however, a brightly coloured, loudly branded pair of board shorts will work to glamorously frame the bogan's oddly toned physique. Singlets are popular but are quickly discarded on arrival and rarely make an appearance for the rest of the visit. Shoes are banned and large towels are optional, as is sunscreen. The beach offers an excellent opportunity for the bogan male to don its flag cape.	There is no more relevant occasion for the female bogan to capitalise on the less-is-more tactic than the beach. Bikinis with Australian flags are a safe bet as they offer the dual benefits of overexposed boob and patriotism. Thongs with the Australian flag further add to the spectacle. Female bogans who catch the eye of a male may be offered the opportunity to wear a flag cape for a short time. In return, sex is expected.
The races	A landmark event in the boganic social calendar, the races are the raison d'être for the bogan's ownership of a suit. Never conservative or understated, its brightly coloured or striped 'good' suit is mandatory. Accessories are crucial because it is here that the bogan can distinguish itself in order to catch the booze-blurred eye of a female. Diamante-studded designer sunglasses, dagger-like leather shoes, lavender ties and magenta wristbands are some of its favoured garnishes.	The races offer the female bogan an excellent opportunity to experiment with taste. Unfortunately, it nearly always fails. The formula of elongated gowns, fascinators, super-high heels and cheap bubbly proves too difficult for it to master. At the end of the day it can usually be found slumped over a male, like a tube sock on a clothesline, carrying its shoes and being stoically whisked away to be taken advantage of.

Occasion	Male Dress Code	Female Dress Code
Weddings	The bogan's wedding suit has been known to sometimes exhibit aspects of normalcy. Largely driven by societal and parental pressure, the bogan may renege on its primordial urges and wear something demure. The black suit, dark tie, white shirt and black shoes combination is a common formal choice for heads of state, style icons and other non-bogans. On its special day the bogan is likely to wear a combination of the above, while retaining a striking hue of its individuality. The black-suit ensemble will be modified to include a bright element, such as tie or shoes, or a poorly chosen hat. Flowers are banned because they are for poofs, but thongs are okay if the wedding is anywhere in the vicinity of a beach.	The bogan female has long known what it will wear for its wedding day. It has intricately fantasised about its day in the sun for at least 65 per cent of its life. As with everything, celebrities are the primary source of inspiration, and the bogan will hungrily scour trash magazines for ideas. In the end, after immense stress and multiple thousands of dollars, it will settle on a long white dress with lots of frills, paired with the shiniest jewellery it can source.
Funerals	See Races.	See Club.
Formal Occasions (other than the races and weddings)	Not applicable to bogans.	Not applicable to bogans.
Music Festivals	See Beach.	See Beach.

Tattoos

Tattooing has been practised for centuries across the world; some date it to the Neolithic era. Tattoos have been used to symbolise many significant occurrences in an individual's life, such as rites of passage, marks of status and rank, religious and spiritual devotion, pledges of love and punishment, and a host of others. They have served as cultural landmarks in mapping the anthropology of human civilisation, offering revealing insights into the distant past.

For the bogan, tattoos provide an opportunity to display to the world that it has successfully procreated and is vaguely literate. Additionally, they are an indelible reminder that the bogan is simultaneously caring, sensitive, worldly, literate, fertile, brutal and sexually pliable. Tattoos offer the bogan a unique and unrivalled ability to express its intricate facets. Never before, for instance, has it been able to combine its affection for family nomenclature with its love for exothermic reactions to form a heroic display of its creative prowess.

The location of the tattoo is just as important as the tattoo itself. For it is utterly useless to the bogan if its tattoo cannot be witnessed with amazement by the world, thus providing a chilling insight into its favoured sports team and residential postcode.

Tattoos can take many forms and tend to vary in size according to the bogan's ability to lift slabs of concrete, bench press four times its weight or evade prison. Essentially, the bigger the bogan, the more space it has for covering itself in clumsy scribbles. Most bogans, however, tend to settle for a stock-standard set of symbols representing a stock-standard set of attributes that the bogan wishes to convey. The bogan's tattoos are a garish kaleidoscope of pictures, symbols, letters and numbers that act as its existential narrative and capture its essence as a human. Each symbol has a commonly accepted meaning which the bogan will take very seriously in explaining the reasons for its many tattoos. For example, the picture of a rose is a symbol of passion, chastity and purity, even amongst non-bogans. The boganic rose tattoo, however, will never simply be a rose; it will inevitably be merged with a dagger or thorns, or a wonky scroll that bears a misspelt name. By engaging in this manner of inspired expression, the bogan can claim that it 'designed' the picture itself and tell the world it is both passionate and brutal.

The bogan has a limited set of predefined meanings attached to a limited set of predefined images, from which it rarely veers. Let us look at some of the popular options and their associations:

DOLPHINS — PLAYFUL, UNPREDICTABLE, MAMMALIAN, INTELLIGENT, MATERNAL

A favourite with the femme-bogue — a medium-sized picture of the cute aquatic mammal allows it to convey to a prospective suitor that it is playful and unpredictable, while also suggesting that it will be a nurturing and caring mother someday. Zoologists have often posited that dolphins are the second most intelligent creature on earth, behind humans. The bogan — aspirational as it is — selects this animal for a tattoo to represent its desire to overtake the dolphin and secure second place for itself. Common locations for the dolphin, relative to its prevalence in the Yangtze River, are the ankles, bellybutton, neck, webbing between index finger and thumb, or lower back of the bogan female.

ROSES/FLORAL DESIGNS — PASSION, ROMANCE, FEMININITY, FIERY, SEXUALLY CHARGED, LOVE, VITALITY

A tattooed image of a flower tells the world that the bogan is a passionate, pretty being. Roses, lilies, petunias and sunflowers are all popular choices, with each flower bearing a detailed communiqué of the bogan's intentions. Essentially, flowers symbolise femininity and grace but, when combined with tribal designs, also signify the bogan's ability to break limbs when required. Floral tattoos are found all over the body, but are particularly suggestive when worn on the feet, behind the shoulder, below the bellybutton, between breasts and on the loins.

SKULLS — BRUTALITY, DANGER, CAPACITY TO END LIVES, PROTECTOR

Nothing conveys danger, strength and brutality like the picture of a human skull etched onto one's body. A favourite of the seasoned warrior, skull tattoos have long denoted machismo and bravery in order to intimidate the bogan's many enemies. By sporting a burning skull on its tricep, the bogan displays a stern warning to those who would do wrong to it that it is ready and willing to end their lives. On the male, skulls may be found decorated with tribal patterns, fire, barbed wire or other impaling devices. On the female, skulls are adorned with flowers, wings, hearts or stars in order to ineffectually retain femininity. They are usually found wherever large tracts of skin may be displayed without compromising the bogan's sensibilities, which is to say, anywhere.

FLAMES — HEAT, PRESENT ON HOT RODS, DESTRUCTION, HELL

Flames or fiery motifs are meant to convey destruction, sin, temptation, lust and other vice-related attributes. The bogan is an impulsive beast, capable of combusting spontaneously. Flames are also found on the sides of maxtreme automobiles such as motorbikes and hot rods, thereby associating the flame-tattoo wearer with similarly maxtreme ideals of speed and petrol consumption. The flame imagery is almost always used in conjunction with other bogan tattoo staples, in order to add the necessary maxtremity to an otherwise staid picture of a skull juxtaposed with a butterfly. Also found where large areas of skin real estate are available for public display.

DRAGON — FIRE, UNTAMED, MYSTERIOUS, MYTHOLOGICAL
In Eastern mythology the dragon is seen as a benevolent creature, a protector of life, fertility and good fortune. The bogan, however, simply sees the dragon as an evil creature that must be killed because it destroys villages and guards vast amounts of treasure. Either way, bogans love dragon tattoos — and the bigger the better. One of the best-selling books in recent years homed in on this obsession; *The Girl With the Dragon Tattoo* was never going to fail. The bogan male also finds appeal in the idea of conquering a flaming dragon in order to save a femme-bogue in distress, even though the male's romantic intentions for the female are likely to cause more distress than the dragon ever would have — more flames, more sharp fangs, more wings. Dragons are a simple and effective means to tell the world that the bogan is both spiritual and demonic, and does not hesitate to unsheath its sword.

BUTTERFLY — SOFT, DELICATE, GENTLE, CARING, GRACEFUL
While the sight of insects may, from time to time, send the femme-bogue into shrill fits of screaming, butterflies are an exception. One of the most popular tattoo designs for female bogans, butterflies are meant to be profound symbols of life, fragility and transformation. This lofty image of transformation into something beautiful is generally not manifested in the bogan's actual behaviour, for the bogan is a bogan due to its lack of willpower to work at being anything else. Despite this, it is common to see shoulders, ankles, backs, hips and other revealing areas plastered with multicoloured cutesy doodles of butterflies. By engaging in this manner of expression, the female says that it is indeed ready to suck the nectar from a male stamen at any given moment.

TRIBAL — WARRIOR, MAXTREMITY, GANGSTER, BATTLE READINESS

The bogan wants to be a gladiator, warrior, gangster, rapper and small-time thug. The tribal tattoo offers it the opportunity to combine all of these desired characteristics into a chaotic, disorganised swirl of razor-sharp lines. The tribal tattoo is arguably the bogan's favourite design, evidenced by its imposing presence in many of the bogan's other tattoos. In the recorded history of bogan tribals there is yet to be a single instance where the bogan has not designed its own tattoo, proving beyond doubt that it is indeed a visionary artist.

**FOREIGN LANGUAGE — WORLDLY, COSMOPOLITAN,
PROFOUND, MYSTERIOUS**

Notwithstanding its hatred of things it hasn't attempted to understand, the bogan loves the idea of being inked up in a foreign language — preferably an Asian language, because they offer a

dizzying array of squiggles and pointy bits that better convey the idea of worldly mystique. Japanese, Thai and Chinese characters are tested bogan favourites due to their ease of availability in Jetstar-approved destinations. Roman alphabet languages such as French, Spanish or Italian are rare because the bogan does not trust its Balinese tattoo artist's knowledge of romance languages. Furthermore, it also risks being unable to provide a lengthy explanation of the word *amour* when quizzed about its meaning. Foreign-language tattoos are best suited to spacious areas such as the forearm, spine, across the posterior of the neck or horizontally along the bogan's calf.

STARS/ASTRONOMY — NATIONALISTIC, PRETTY, SMART, PATRIOTIC
Rounding off the bogan's tattoo preferences is its love for astronomical objects. It does not, however, care for planets, moons or satellites; it is solely concerned with stars: little stars, big stars, tribal stars, floral stars, tiger stars or even foreign stars. The bogan will try to explain that a star symbolises its hopes and aspirations, but it is lying. It loves stars for one reason: they can be clumsily arranged in order to resemble the smallest of the eighty-eight constellations — the Southern Cross. By wearing a constellation that is visible in over 50 countries, the bogan feels such an intense rush of national pride that it allows itself the right to be racially intolerant. Other forms of stars are also popular, with designs such as the hexagram, septagram and other pointed patterns currying boganic favour. The ankle, lower back, hips, shoulder and clavicle are some popular locations for its starry-eyed endeavours.

Celebrities and endorsements

As discussed previously, celebrities play a pivotal role in moulding the fashions of the bogan. They are the teat from which the bogan suckles ideas in order to remain sartorially nourished. This is largely due to celebrities being perceived as better humans than the bogan, ones that it aspires to ape in every way. The bogan is, therefore, highly receptive to most things that celebrities endorse. It will usually take a little piece of each celebrity-endorsed titbit and assemble them into an elaborate existential jigsaw puzzle. Endorsements are an enormously lucrative side project for celebrities, who get paid copious amounts of money to convince the bogan that it is now allergic to dairy and must switch to soy milk, before being cruelly and confusingly marketed skim milk by a different celebrity on the payroll of some other company. Often a celebrity will sell products that have little relevance to their own field of expertise. But the bogan doesn't care — it only requires the validation afforded by the celebrity's fame and popularity. The bogan is singularly driven by the need to consume, steered by the safe, honeyed tones of a celebrity who will tell it what to buy. Table 9.2 offers some amusing examples of products that various celebrities have convinced the bogan it needs.

Table 9.2 Celebrity-endorsed products that bogans need

Product	Celebrity endorser	Features
Power Balance bands	Brendon Fevola, Michael Clarke, Shaquille O'Neal	• Promises 500 per cent more power, flexibility and strength through an embedded hologram • Designed to work with the body's natural flow and increase strength, endurance, balance and flexibility • The special hologram has been treated with energy waves at specific positive frequencies
In an amazing display of celebrity prowess, the bogan has been convinced that it will be able to perform at the level of an elite athlete simply by wearing a $60 rubber wristband adorned with shiny holograms. The bogan is convinced that the product is scientifically robust because the advertisement contained a celebrity saying the phrase 'energy waves'.		

Product	Celebrity endorser	Features
Soy milk, Wii-Fit, Nintendo DS Brain Training, shampoo, skin-care cream, music magazines and Australia	Delta Goodrem	• Intelligence • Fitness • High protein • Soft skin • Soft hair • Enhances musical taste • Opportunity to get sunburnt
Delta Goodrem is arguably the country's most credible bogan celebrity. In one fell swoop she has convinced the bogan that: it is allergic to dairy; it can get smarter by solving second-grade puzzles; it can become fitter by standing still and watching television; its hair is frizzy and unmanageable; its skin is infested with acne; Australia is the luckiest country in the world. The bogan agrees.		
Phiten	Lleyton Hewitt	• Exclusive processes enhance the body's energy-management system • Increases capacity of every cell • Aqua-titanium technology • Micro-titan nanoparticles
Australia's foremost tennis bogan — who married that chick from the telly — also possesses hypnotic powers. He has convinced the bogan that in addition to owning many Power Balance bands, it must also purchase many Phiten bands if it is serious about its 'health'. What the Phiten lacks in shiny holograms it makes up for in sciency-sounding appendages such as the Aqua Titan Micro Nano ball. Essentially it promises to help the bogan be better at things in a faster, stronger fashion.		
Nicotine gum, hair regeneration laser therapy	Shane Warne	• Celebrity-approved quitting formula • Eases cigarette cravings by up to 250 per cent • Activates the pleasure molecule in a slow and peaceful manner • Regenerate one's own hair without the pain of sticking in somebody else's • Capacity to acquire Liz Hurley
Australia's best cricket bogan is so believable that he convinced the bogan of the power of nicotine gum to help it quit smoking while secretly choking down durries himself. Warne also told the balding bogan that it should invest in a laser-based treatment that magically grows its hair back or it will never get laid ever again. The bogan promptly did as it was told.		

Product	Celebrity endorser	Features
Chewing gum	Alisa Camplin	• Fresh breath • Strong teeth • No cavities

In a glorious example of the bogan brain's ductility, it has been convinced that an Olympic aerial skier is a trustworthy source of dental advice. One can only infer that the connection between snow and dental hygiene lies in the fact that, in both cases, the whiter, the better. Wielding a broad interpretation of freshness, the bogan is happy to concede that someone who spends a large amount of her time around snow is best qualified to tell it that it has bad breath and needs a chewy. More recently Camplin has been elected to the board of the Collingwood Football Club, despite possessing sketchy credentials for such a role aside from the trust of the bogan.

Face fashion

Psychologist Robert Pellegrini once said that 'the male beard communicates a heroic image of the independent, sturdy, and resourceful pioneer; ready, willing and able to do manly things'. The bogan, while aspiring to many of these virtues, dislikes full beards because it associates them with feral, leaf-eating eco-terrorists (hippies) or inner-city, Latte-sipping poofters (hipsters). It also knows that beards convey a certain level of smugness that may be mistaken for intellectualism because a maths teacher it once hated also had a beard. Further adding to the bogan's distrust of beards is the fact that a great many foreign people whom it believes to be actual terrorists also wear full beards. Unlike hair, there are also very few branded products that a bogan can buy for a beard. The hair on the head can receive bleach, gel, wax, trucker caps and a swivelled pair of Oakleys, but a beard does not help the bogan to consume things at all.

Instead, the bogan prefers to be clean shaven or to sport a designer stubble, both of which allow it to purchase branded products such as shaving razors with too many blades or celebrity-endorsed aftershave. Alternatively it will opt for a small patch of facial hair located just below the lower lip but above the chin. Colloquially known as the 'flavour saver' or 'soul patch', this style of facial strip came to bogan prominence through *Australian Idol* finalist and ultra-bogan Shannon Noll. The bogan can also use the soul patch to make crass jokes about its ability to retain the flavour of vagina after a shabby cunnilingus performance.

The George David, which traces a finely sculpted line along the jaw (named after its inventors, George Michael and Craig David), is another bogan-preferred facial hair style. While the George David allows the bogan to feel like an R&B star at all times, it is unable to conceal the scars caused by the overeager use of the nine-blade extra super-max razor that it purchased because all of its favourite sports stars told it to.

While the bogan dabbles in a few variations of facial hair, nothing appeals to it more than the opportunity to sport a moustache for Movember. The irresistible 'Movember' portmanteau, combined with celebrity-approved fundraising opportunities, has seen the bogan transform a noble cause into a seedy gimmick. Having a moustache allows it to act like a smut merchant and make endless jokes about being some manner of tradesperson, offering people — mostly women — its pool-cleaning services. The bogan female is unlikely to make advances towards a moustachioed male in any ordinary circumstance, but will make an exception during the hirsute month of Movember. For exactly 30 days the bogan female is willing to shed its reservations about the fact that it will be mounted by someone whose facial aesthetics it normally associates with paedophilia. The bogan male will take full advantage of this narrow window of tolerance, seeking to bed as many women as possible using poorly constructed porn dialogues. At the end of the stipulated period proceedings will return to normal, with the bogan male shedding its lip fur and huddling back into its familiar pit of rejection.

10
FOOD AND DRINK

Just as its tastes in clothing, music and television have changed over the past twenty or so years, the bogan's culinary habits have come a long way since the 1980s. The bogan of yore cared not for *MasterChef*, peri-peri sauce or massive cans of energy drink. In its day a home-cooked meal meant meat and three veg, while Sunday night meant roast dinner (which, by extension, meant only lamb and beef). Dining out meant a counter meal, and takeaway meant fish and chips or pizza. Meals were served, not 'plated up', the only person that could tell it what to cook was its mother or Peter Russell-Clarke, and the only thing it wanted 'a little bit fancy' was the odd prawn alongside snags and chops on the barbie.

Back then, the national beverage was strictly beer. Drinkers were fiercely parochial and divided along state lines, with VB the only exception to the rule. Beer was served cold or icy cold, came in cans or brown stubbies, and bore no mention of carbohydrates, calories, infusions of lime or German purity laws. A publican who put a slice of lemon in a beer could have expected a punch in the face. Red wine was consumed largely by posh folk, white wine meant goon, mention of a Jägerbomb would have sent its father ducking for cover, and 'sex on the beach' meant just that.

Today, the bogan has more sophisticated tastes. Well travelled and exotic, the bogan has embraced international cuisine — or, at least, its own limited and confused version of this. Its culinary repertoire now includes mild curries, taco night, and beef and black bean, though it will still racially insult the Indian waiter when he walks away. It spends much more on food than it used to, paying top dollar for 'premiumised' or more convenient versions of the same products it used to purchase, much to the delight of food producers and cafe owners. What it drinks must be expensive, imported and very, very conspicuous. And although the bogan's diet is more unbalanced and unhealthy than ever, hours of watching celebrities and reality-television contestants in the kitchen have turned it into a food critic, convinced of the fact that it too can cook.

FOOD OF THE WORLD

The bogan is generally wary of foreigners. It strongly believes its inability to afford a nine-room McMansion with swimming pool, tennis court and outdoor entertaining area less than 30 kilometres from the CBD is the fault of Chinese property investors, rather than of its own hopelessly unrealistic expectations, the chronic undersupply of housing in Australia or our favourable negative-gearing rules. It knows that those boats Tony Abbott keeps talking about are not filled with refugees displaced by war in Afghanistan — they are full of dodgy foreigners coming to take their jobs and steal their children's university places. And the bogan is pretty sure Asians are to blame for rising petrol prices, the Queensland floods and the 5.36 train to Flinders Street being delayed by ten minutes this morning. But that doesn't mean the bogan doesn't have global tastes. Oh, no.

Since Jetstar starting ferrying planeloads of bogans to the exotic countries like Bali, Patong and Koh Samui (and it subsequently saw a guy on *MasterChef* make a crab curry or something), the bogan has broadened its palate and embraced a new world of international tastes and flavours. But just like the fat guy from *Kenny* being roped into hosting the Australian version of *Top Gear*, the bogan's idea of international cuisine is a pale imitation of the real deal. Typically, this involves taking the blandest dishes from a particular country's cuisine and diluting them further, resulting in a banal, boganised interpretation of a nation's fare, usually unrecognisable by its own citizens.

The bogan's intercontinental degustation might contain some of the following:

Indian — Besides cheating at cricket, taxiing the bogan home after a night of Jägerbombs and being an excellent source of Slurpees, the bogan now realises that Indian people can also cook. Every Saturday night the local Tandoori Palace will be inundated with overweight bogans, eager to spice up their life. While the typical Indian menu contains over 50 dishes, the bogan will always choose either tandoori chicken, butter chicken or chicken korma. All curries are served with a garlic naan and ordered mild, and vegetarian options are never considered.

Thai — Since Jetstar and Magda Szubanski alerted the bogan to the former kingdom of Siam's existence, planeloads of bogans have been heading to Patong Beach, Koh Samui and that full moon place to drink out of buckets, get tattoos and find wives. Weeks spent in beach resorts eating spring rolls have also opened the bogan's eyes to the exotic world of Thai cuisine. But don't expect to find the bogan processing its own curry paste: it will only eat at Thai restaurants with stupid pun names like Thai-riffic, Thai-tanic, Bow-Thai and Thai-Me-Up. Favourite dishes include spring rolls, pad thai and red chicken curry served extra mild.

Japanese — Without being fully aware of it, the bogan has long driven cars, played video games and watched pornography from the land of the rising sun. Japanese cuisine, however, has proven a longer bamboo bridge to cross for bogan tastebuds. Until, that is, it discovered the California roll. About as authentically Japanese as Tom Cruise in *The Last Samurai*, the California roll appeals to the bogan not only due to its fairly bland taste, price and convenience, but because it makes the bogan think of the magical land where celebrities come from (just don't tell it the roll contains imitation crab stick). The bogan's like of shopping centre sushi will occasionally cause it to try a Japanese restaurant, where it will order chicken teriyaki or more sushi (to the bewilderment of Japanese, for whom sushi is snack food). The bogan will not try miso, anything containing the word 'tofu' or anything it believes to be 'raw fish'.

Chinese — One of the best examples of the boganisation of international cuisines, Chinese has long been a favourite for midweek takeaway or discount dining. Chinese cuisine is one of the most varied and complex on the planet, encompassing dozens of distinct regional styles including Sichuan, Guangdong, Jiangsu and Shandong, to name a few, each with their own unique ingredients, cooking techniques and dishes. All of this means little to the bogan, for whom Chinese food constitutes the following: fried rice, beef and black bean, sweet and sour pork, beef and black bean, lemon chicken, beef and black bean, dim sims (which it expects to resemble the same dim sims from a fish-and-chip shop) and spring rolls (which it will joke the cook uses cats in, when in truth it is Tibetans). The bogan will scoff when offered green tea and will complain that its food tastes like 'there is MGMT in it.' It will only eat at Chinese restaurants frequented by non-Asian people. The presence of 'real' Asians will lead it to believe the restaurant is cheap and, therefore, non-premium.

Italian — Another of the world's great cuisines to be bastardised by the bogan hordes. While a typical Italian meal

Until recent years, the bogan would have considered sushi to be bait.

consists of *aperitivo, antipasto, primo, secondo, contorno, dolce, formaggio e frutta, caffè* and *digestivo*, to the bogan, Italian equates strictly to pasta or pizza. Pasta is routinely eaten at La Porchetta or its upmarket cousin, Sofia, and comes in spaghetti bolognese, lasagne or fettuccine carbonara varieties. Pizza usually comes from Dominos or Pizza Hut and is eaten with one of the following toppings: meat lovers with barbecue sauce; barbecue chicken with barbecue sauce; margherita with barbecue sauce; super-special with everything possible EXCEPT ANCHOVIES and barbecue sauce; or, if feeling particularly bold, capricciosa (ordered in thick *Godfather* accent) WITHOUT OLIVES AND ANCHOVIES! Despite never having eaten an anchovy, the bogan knows that it hates them more than it hates whoever scrapped the 2011 series filming of *Two And A Half Men* and will loudly tell the pizza maker and anyone else who cares to listen how terrible they are (it does not notice when said pizza maker then forgets to omit the offending Engraulidae).

Mexican — Given its willingness to fork over $9 for a bottle of Mexican beer, it should come as no surprise that the bogan's food tastes have also gone south of the border. To the bogan, Mexican food can be summed up in three words: Old El Paso. With their gloriously overpriced 'dinner kits', Old El Paso provides the bogan with everything it needs to create its very own fiesta (*sans* actual ingredients, that is). Taco or burrito night is one of the highlights of the bogan's culinary week, when it adds taco mix (salt, cumin plus food colouring) to beef mince and serves with iceberg lettuce, sliced tomato, grated cheese and mild salsa (bonus points for serving with Corona/Sol). *Mucho Mexicano!*

African — Just kidding. Africa is not on the bogan's culinary radar. Although it's the second largest land mass on earth and the home of hundreds of different cultural and ethnic groups, most of which have their own unique cuisines, the bogan believes all Africans live off a subsistence diet of plain rice, sand and blowflies. In the unlikely event that someone suggests to the bogan that they eat African, it will joke about Ethiopians fighting over a McDonald's voucher (none of the authors has ever seen a McDonald's voucher).

FINE DINING

Whether for a romantic date or family occasion, or just to break up the nightly monotony of cooking and washing up, dining out is a pleasant way to pass the evening. It provides the opportunity to spend time with friends and family, discuss current events and personal affairs, and enjoy a quality and variety of food and service not usually experienced in the home.

Like the rest of us, the bogan enjoys eating out. Today's bogan eats out much more than it used to and, as we've already discussed, eats at a much wider variety of restaurants than in days gone past. But, as with other pursuits, the bogan does things a little differently from the rest of us, preferring a maxtreme remix on attending a restaurant.

While Europeans have their Michelin star system and Australian gourmands follow the Australian Good Food & Travel Guide's Chef Hats system, the bogan has its own restaurant ranking system: the Maxtreme Masterbelly Food Guide. Being the disciple of the 'doctrine of more' that it is, the bogan's system has five tiers rather than the more conventional three, and uses Xs to score eateries rather than chef's hats or stars. The Maxtreme Masterbelly Food Guide may not be printed (the hungry bogan is in no mood for book reading), but it is as close to a comprehensive overview of bogan eating places as has been compiled. As seen in Table 10.1, the key variables in a bogan's dining decision is a restaurant's degree of connection with celebrities, *Underbelly* and *MasterChef*. The coveted XXXXX is only awarded to a restaurant owned by George or Gary from *MasterChef*. Eateries associated with real or fictional events from *Underbelly* are also highly sought after. Bonus points are awarded for spotting the fat judge from the paper-towel ads somewhere.

Table 10.1 The Maxtreme Masterbelly Food Guide ranking system

X	A restaurant frequented by celebrities
XX	A restaurant owned by a celebrity
XXX	A restaurant featured on *Underbelly* or otherwise connected to a semi-fictional event from *Underbelly*
XXXX	A restaurant featured on *MasterChef*
XXXXX	A restaurant owned or operated by Gary, George or a winning contestant from *MasterChef*

Regardless of where it eats, the bogan will generally behave in the same boorish, obnoxious and disrespectful fashion. It will never make a reservation, and will become angry at the proprietor when told that the offending restaurant requires the bogan to book ahead. To save face in this circumstance the spurned bogan will loudly conclude that 'it's shit anyway'. This anger will quickly turn to glee if told the restaurant is merely full and the bogan needs to queue, for queuing signifies *awesome*. When it enters the restaurant the bogan will invariably try to break the BYO policy, sending its blood pressure soaring once again when told it can't bring in its six-pack of Corona (despite the sign on the window clearly stating BYO WINE ONLY). Once seated the bogan will pretend to read the wine list for ten minutes, its face a mask of mock concentration, before ordering the cheapest bottle of wine on the list or something with 'Penfolds' in the title. When ordering food the bogan will always order far too much and try to pronounce any European dishes in their native tongue (with hilarious results).

During the meal the bogan will be as loud, crude and obnoxious as possible, so that all the other patrons will be forced to hear its conversation about its views on border protection or thoughts on which celebrities' boobs are fake. Having watched *MasterChef*, the bogan now believes it is a food critic and will complain loudly to the waiter that its gazpacho is cold or that its haloumi is too rubbery. Even if the bogan enjoys its meal, it will feign indifference and tell its dinner companions that 'the ambience was lacking in sophistication'. If eating one of the bogan-approved international cuisines, it will make racist observations about the cuisine, country and its people in front of the waiter, assuming he speaks no English when he is really a medical student working at his parents' restaurant.

When the bogan has finished its sixth course and fourth bottle of wine, it will try to order the cheque in Thai, believing its week at a beach resort in Patong has endowed it with fluent Thai. It will become angry when the waiter brings it a live chicken. When the waiter asks the bogan how its meal was, the bogan will bring out its top-shelf material, replying, 'It was terrible ... just kidding!' prompting screeching laughter from its companions and an exasperated look of déjà vu from the waiter. No matter where it eats, the bogan will scrutinise the bill like a forensic accountant going through Bernie Madoff's books, loudly exclaim what a rip-off the place is and then begrudgingly hand over its PlatinumXXX Visa. The bogan will *never* tip. Should one of its companions suggest tipping, it will angrily rant that tipping is 'un-Australian'. Finally, the bogan will return home, jump on the Internet and criticise the restaurant, venting its anger at the cold gazpacho by giving the venue 2/10 for food. It goes to bed happy.

THE BOGAN DIET

In addition to regular physical activity, a healthy, well-balanced diet is vital for maintaining good health and wellbeing. It helps prevent heart disease, stroke and high blood pressure; reduces the risk of cancer, diabetes and heart disease; helps maintain a healthy body weight; and promotes psychological wellbeing and all-round happiness. Generally nutritionists, dieticians and medical bodies recommend eating a diet high in fruit, vegetables, wholegrains and nuts; high in vitamins, minerals and fibre; low in sugar, salt and saturated fats; and containing a moderate and balanced intake of lean meat, poultry, fish and eggs. Omniscient and sagacious creature that it is, the bogan chooses to disregard most of this, dismissing it as a conspiracy by white-coated intellectuals to make it eat things it doesn't like. It should be noted that the bogan will happily recite studies by these same white-coated intellectuals, which it reads in respected medical publications like *mX*, if they endorse the consumption of things it *does* like.

The bogan is much more interested in appearing healthy than actually being healthy, with the male bogan preferring foods that will make it huge and the female bogan opting for foods designed to make it tiny. Both sexes prefer highly processed foods, believing that each stage of processing makes a food one step better. Any food that is of a colour or shape that could plausibly occur in nature fails to catch the bogan's eye, as the bogan knows that nature is only awesome when conquered by the maxtreme consumption of petrol. The bogan occasionally feels guilty about its dietary choices, resulting in it paying too much for a product

Being a conscientious health nut, the bogan's burger will be washed down with a manly diet cola and a Dunhill.

which promised instant wellbeing and inevitably only makes it fatter and unhealthier.

This is a list of some of the key elements of the bogan diet:

Chicken — Chicken is overwhelmingly the modern bogan's meat of choice. Whether cooking at home, eating at a pub or navigating a difficult Asian menu, chicken represents the safe and tested option for the bogan. It is relatively cheap and versatile, has a fairly bland taste, and is used extensively by takeaway restaurants. It also appeals to the femme-bogue due to its mistaken beliefs that all red meat is bad and that chicken will help it lose weight. Male bogans, meanwhile, choose chook due to its mistaken belief that chicken is higher in protein than red meat and will thus help it get huge. Chicken is also the standard staple for the 'parma', which is, in the bogan's opinion, the greatest culinary development since Red Bull was added to Jägermeister.

Beef — Beef is the next most popular meat for the bogan. It is generally consumed in one of two forms: steak or burger. For steak, the size is much more important than the cut and is usually ordered or cooked well done (the bogan will then complain to the waiter that the steak is tough). For burgers, the beef must be 100 per cent ANGUS. McDonald's marketing has convinced the bogan that the Black Angus breed of cattle is superior to the other 800 breeds in existence. More recently, Coles and Angus, Julia and Curtis Stone have also convinced the bogan that beef must be 100 per cent HORMONE FREE.

Lamb — While the lamb roast has long been considered one of the Australian national dishes, lamb long failed to excite the bogan due to its high cost and the bogan's preference for poultry. That was a cause of concern for red-meat group Meat and Livestock Australia, which commissioned a series of advertisements playing on two of the bogan's hottest trigger points: nationalism and celebrities. For the last few years, former AFL footballer and generally angry television personality 'Slammin' Sam Kekovich has appeared on leviathan plasmas around the country in the week before Australia Day telling the bogan that to eat anything other than lamb would be 'un-Australian'. To the bogan, being called un-Australian is akin to being called impotent. For the last six years, sales of lamb have soared leading up to and on 26 January.

Salad — While generally dismissive of salad, calling it 'wussy' and 'rabbit food', since McDonald's started advertising its salad range the bogan has come to view salad as somewhat credible, if still unappetising. The bogan believes eating seven salad leaves drenched in dressing will more than offset the accompanying 1.2 kilogram piece of chicken covered in melted cheese and served with chips, effectively giving it a free pass to eat and drink whatever it wants.

Seafood — The bogan doesn't like seafood. Once, it became ill the day after eating the fisherman's basket while out and subsequently decided that it has a seafood allergy. It has never tried mussels, crab or squid but knows it's allergic to all of these. It doesn't like salmon, but does own three salmon-coloured T-shirts. The bogan is not allergic to fish as long it is battered, deep fried and served with chips. Of the 32 000 known species of fish in the world, the bogan only likes flake (which it thinks is a species). The bogan's seafood allergy also does not include prawns, when cooked on a barbie (it doesn't know how to peel prawns so always buys pre-peeled and deveined). And while it has absolutely no idea how to cook or eat it, the bogan will drop mad cash on lobster if trying to assert its alpha-bogue status at a dinner table.

Vegies — Being the ravenous carnivore that it is, the bogan tends to view vegetables with suspicion and avoids anything directly removed from a tree or plant. It will consent to the odd frozen pea or carrot only when accompanied by a sufficiently large piece of dead animal. The bogan's favourite vegetables are the potato (usually gorged on in chip, fry or wedge form) and the tomato (consumed as tomato sauce or pasta sauce in a jar). While it does not eat them, l'homme-bogue enjoys picking up any phallic-shaped vegetable it sees and making crude penis/fellatio-related jokes to its partner. The bogan will not, under any circumstances, voluntarily eat anything labelled 'vegetarian', which it believes is the domain of 'hippies and fags'. The mere suggestion of eating a vegetarian meal will result in the bogan becoming agitated, a state it will medicate by ordering as many boiled, grilled or fried animals as possible.

Fruit — The bogan may be ignorant, lazy and stupid, but years of public health messages extolling the merits of fruit have left a nagging feeling of guilt in its vacuous skull. Perhaps the strawberry thickshake in its supersized double-quarter-pounder meal wasn't quite enough to keep the doctor away? Then, wandering its local Westfield shopping centre, it spotted other bogans slurping out of brightly coloured, tightly branded cups. Hallelujah! The appeal of Boost Juice to the bogan is manifold: it allows bogans to make a highly conspicuous and tokenistic statement about healthy living (for only $8); it is part of a franchise; and it forces the bogan to queue and then wait with other bogans while its saccharine sludge is prepared. Best of all, bogans can 'boost' their juice by adding extra energy and protein — two of the few things the bogan diet is not deficient in.

The ambience of a nightclub blended into a healthy beverage.

Pasta — Ticking all of its pleasure boxes, pasta is one of the major staples of the bogan diet. It is cheap, easy to cook and has an entire aisle dedicated to it at most supermarkets. To the male bogue it is high in carbohydrates, making it perfect for 'carbo-loading' before it heads to the gym to get ripped and vascular. For the femme-bogue it offers the appearance of gourmet cooking, despite coming out of a jar, and can be cooked in fifteen minutes, ready to be eaten in front of *Today Tonight/Neighbours*.

Rice and noodles — The bogan generally doesn't eat either rice or noodles, thinking both are cheap and for Asians. It will eat instant noodles, but only Maggi chicken flavoured. The bogan is scathing of Asian brands of instant noodles because they cause cancer or something.

Junk food — Junk food is easily the most important element of the bogan diet. Confectionery, chocolate, salted chips and snack food; sweets, lollies, biscuits, ice-cream, fried fast foods — the more stages of processing a food has been through and the more sugar, salt and saturated fat it contains, the better it is in the eyes of the bogan. So important are these foods to the bogan that it will become irritated and angry should it be forced to go more than a few hours without them. In recent years white-coated intellectuals have tried to tell the bogan it should only eat these things in moderation. But the bogan knows only excess. So it has come up with elaborate excuses to justify continuing to eat maxtreme quantities of crap: That gargantuan piece of cake this morning? The bogan is tired and needed the energy hit. That block of chocolate in the afternoon? It is addicted to chocolate, of course. That triple whopper with bacon, cheese and bacon? Well, er ... Hungry Jack's was right there and it's in a hurry! Failing that, the bogan will succumb to societal pressure and go to Subway, where it will order an Italian BMT with double meat, double cheese, the works and mayo, chipotle sauce and ranch dressing. Satisfied with its sacrifice, the bogan will reward itself with a double-chocolate-chip cookie.

Tomato sauce and barbecue sauce — While the bogan doesn't like herbs, spices or condiments, this doesn't mean that it doesn't like flavour. When a food is lacking that indistinguishable something, the bogan reaches for the sauce bottle, covering the unfortunate food item with so much tangy, sweet, saucy goodness that little if any of its original/intended taste remains. It need only adhere to one simple rule: if something was once an animal, immerse it in barbecue sauce; for everything else, drown it with tomato sauce. While the bogan doesn't normally follow rules, this one it sticks to like transplanted hair to Shane Warne's skull. The bogan's undeniable love for barbecue sauce is particularly curious, given that no bogan has any idea what it is (tomato and Worcestershire sauce), but this phenomenon extends to other barbecue products such as barbecue chips (only equally artificial chicken jostles with it for the title of most bogan chip flavour), barbecue shapes and barbecue chicken anything (which is never actually barbecued).

Cereal — Although it is the most important meal of the day, the bogan frequently skips breakfast, preferring a mid-morning bacon and egg thing drowned in (you guessed it) barbecue sauce. On the odd occasion that it does have cereal, the bogan usually opts for one of two cereal products, both manufactured by the same company. Kelloggs understands the bogan and has designed two breakfast cereals scientifically formulated to fleece the bogan of its hard-earned. With more protein, energy and raw machismo than a group of bodybuilders assembling a spice rack, Nutri-Grain promises to turn the alpha-bogue into an iron man and have it pashing hot chicks on *Bondi Rescue* in no time. At the other end of the bathroom scales, the more feminine but no less insidious Special K is a low-fat, high-spin cereal which promises to have the femme-bogue fitting into a size four red dress and looking like Jennifer Hawkins (not Stephen Hawking) before it even puts the milk back in the fridge.

Energy drinks — While the bogan is seemingly unconcerned by the gross lack of most vitamins, minerals and basic nutrition in its diet, it is strangely vigilant in ensuring that it consumes maxtreme levels of energy. For a couple of years now the bogan has been slurping three to four massive cans a day of carbonated, sugary syrup with enough caffeine and other stimulants to kill a stable of horses. Oddly, it doesn't do anything to burn off or use any of this energy, smashing a giant can of Mother or Red Bull before driving to work or sitting down in front of *Border Security*. The exception to this is on a Saturday night, when the bogan will mix an extra four energy drinks with eight Coronas and half a bottle of Jack Daniel's, sending it into a deranged frenzy that ends in a gutter, a tattoo parlour or a jail cell.

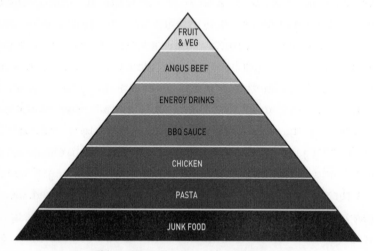

Figure 10.1 The bogan food pyramid

Sugary, carbonated beverages — The bogan love affair with carbonated, sugary beverages is a passionate one. A two-litre bottle of Coca-Cola has long been a permanent fixture in most bogan fridges. But then those pesky white-coated intellectuals/ public health authorities start making some bogans feel slightly guilty at wolfing down the equivalent of four and a half times their daily recommended sugar intake in one sitting. As always, soft-drink producers were able to stay one or two parsecs ahead of the bogan, adding 'diet' to their product names, instantly ensnaring the femme-bogue, who regularly engages in fad diets, fleeting exercise regimens and superstitions with the hope of looking like a celebrity. The male bogan, however, fiercely resists all attempts to get it to drink diet cola. The idea of being on a diet makes it feel faulty, disempowered and feminine. Undeterred, soft-drink producers re-released the same soft drinks with branding as hard as the he-bogue. New black cans, more aggressive fonts and the addition of more xtreme words like 'Max' and 'Zero' proved much more effective in courting the bogan buck.

TO COOK OR NOT TO COOK

The bogan does not like to cook. Cooking requires skill, patience, the ability to multi-task and, above all, the time and willingness to learn. The bogan possesses none of these attributes. The male bogan can operate a barbecue — standing by it, beer in hand, continually turning a sausage or piece of steak until it resembles an amorphous lump of bituminous coal — but in the kitchen it can't cook a piece of toast without starting a small bushfire. The female bogan at least knows a saucepan from a frying pan, but its culinary expertise extends only as far as Dolmio pasta sauce poured over cooked pasta, perhaps garnished with half a block of melted cheese.

Until recently, this did not trouble the bogan. As we've already discussed, it pays little heed to the rules of nutrition and wellbeing. The bogan's lack of culinary expertise represents another reason to eat takeaway, while cooking often gets in the way of prime television viewing like *Today Tonight* and *Two And A Half Men*. It was during the advertisement break of the latter that the bogan changed the channel and spotted something that would change all of this ...

As soon as the bogan saw *MasterChef* (midway through the second series) it was instantly hooked. Adapted from a British program of the same name, *MasterChef* follows a group of amateur cooks who compete on cooking challenges to gain the coveted title of *MasterChef* and go on to wash dishes in the Press Club kitchen (now one of Australia's only XXXXX restaurants). Challenges are overseen and judged by restaurateur and chef Gary Mehigan (the serious, articulate one), chef George Calombaris (the overly enthusiastic, mildly bogan one) and food critic Matt Preston (the fat one). Part of the appeal of the show is that it imitates the format of other successful reality shows like *The Biggest Loser* and *Australian Idol*, moving at a proverbial *escargot*'s pace, jumping back and forth between the 'action' and inane monologues filmed later, during which the contestants provide tedious and mind-numbing commentary of their actions. This is interspersed with theatrical shots of Matt Preston looking thoughtful and hungry, and George Calombaris gesticulating wildly and periodically shouting 'HURRY UP! THERE'S ONLY THREE HOURS LEFT!' while dramatic music builds the suspense like an Ulfrëd Hugecock-directed German pornographic film. Crucially, the show depicts very little actual cooking. The program's broadcaster, Channel Ten, quickly realised that, despite its bluster to the contrary, the bogan doesn't care about how to stuff a spatchcock. So the

Unlike the Beatles, George is the less talented one.

network put all of the technical cooking footage into a special program on Friday night, when the bogan is getting ready to head out to its local glassing barn or watching the footy. All up, *MasterChef* is on air a staggering six nights a week, providing the type of immersive viewing experience the bogan demands. As if this wasn't enough to tickle the bogan's fancy, the evil geniuses in the television world created two spin-off programs to fill the gap between seasons: *Celebrity MasterChef* (*MasterChef* + celebrities = bogan mind melt) and *Junior MasterChef*.

In addition to telling the bogan what to cook, *MasterChef* also tells it what to buy. Through direct advertising, extensive product placements and a barrage of tie-ins and cross-promotions, *MasterChef* has been responsible for redistributing more money in Australia than would have been the case if Robin Hood of Sherwood (and not Twiggy) Forest had designed a mining tax. As the bogan watched Callum prepare a squid for calamari rings with garlic aioli, a giant octopus of another kind prodded and pushed at the bogan's malleable mind and vulnerable wallet, imploring it to buy Coles groceries, Scanpan cookware, Handy Ultra paper towels, Aeroplane jelly, McCormick herbs and spices, Sunbeam kitchen appliances, Sköpe refrigerators, Ariston ovens and range hoods, and Qantas flights. Not to mention *MasterChef*'s own heavily branded cookbooks, cookware, aprons and children's kits.

By the end of season two the bogan had graciously complied and its newly renovated $25 000 German kitchen contained a 74-piece Scanpan saucepan set, a Sunbeam bread maker and ice-cream maker, a cupboard full of Handy Ultra paper towel, every cookbook Gary and George released between them, a *Junior MasterChef* egg kit and a *MasterChef* mandolin slicer.

With a season of *MasterChef* under its burgeoning belt, the bogan now considers itself a regular gourmand. It now orders the Mediterranean parma, 'plates up' its pasta and criticises its wife's chicken casserole for being 'bland' and 'uninspiring'. One night, it decides to try cooking a *MasterChef* recipe itself. Acutely aware of its culinary genius, it skips the easy stuff and goes straight for Chris's stuffed pig's head with beeramasu. But just like it refuses to follow an instruction manual when assembling its new IKEA bookcase, the bogan ignores the recipe and tries its own interpretation — with predictable results. Remembering that it never liked cooking in the first place, the bogan returns to the couch and the comforts of television once again.

While the bogan lacks the skill, patience and desire to learn to cook, *MasterChef* has filled it with a vague wish that it could cook, as well as an unshakeable belief that if it could simply be bothered trying, it would be completely awesome. Fortunately for the bogan and the stability of the space–time continuum, television offers it a simple way to resolve these apparently diametrically opposed desires. Rather than cook itself, the bogan can cook vicariously through celebrity chefs.

While the concept of the television chef has been around almost as long as television itself, only recently have these purveyors of culinary guidance been elevated to true celebrity status. Where the UK has Jamie Oliver and Gordon Ramsay and the US has ... well, the US has Jamie Oliver and Gordon Ramsay too ... the bogan has Curtis. No, not super-fly funk pioneer Curtis Mayfield or golden-era actor Tony Curtis. And definitely not epileptic proto-hipster Ian Curtis. The bogan likes budding celebrity chef and distressingly handsome man Curtis Stone. After honing his chops working alongside renowned chef Marco Pierre in London, Curtis briefly returned to Australia to film the TV show *Surfing the Menu*, featuring two of 'Australia's hunkiest celebrity chefs' cooking up fancy dishes and displaying their chiselled torsos on location at various Australian beaches. Realising that being a TV chef was much more fun than being abused by a Ukrainian sous chef while julienning vegetables for fourteen-hour stints, Curtis moved to the US where he embarked on a successful television career. Curtis's blokey charm, brawny good looks and adequate cooking ability saw him appear on a string of US talk shows including *Oprah* and

Martha Stewart, star in his own series *Take Home Chef*; launch his own range of cookware; write several cookbooks; and be voted one of *People* magazine's Sexiest Men Alive.

Yet the bogan was still relatively unaware of Curtis's existence. An appearance on the *MasterChef* series finale helped, but it wasn't until he started popping up on widescreen 3D TVs around the country during the ad breaks of Channel Ten's Commonwealth Games coverage that Curtis found bogan fame. Needing something to entice the bogan into their supermarkets when *MasterChef* was off air, Coles marketing boffins chose Curtis to be the face of their 'Feed Your Family for under $10' promotion, featuring recipe cards and a series of advertisements in which Curtis helps bogans cook 'his recipes', which allegedly feed a family of four for under $10. In one particularly irritating and offensive advertisement, Curtis helps a bogan woman cook 'his' chicken Madras, after transporting her to a frighteningly realistic depiction of modern India, where attractive Indian women in saris dance and ride elephants, an anonymous Indian man in an apron gives the proverbial thumbs up to Curtis's interpretation of this classic Birmingham dish, an Indian woman ponders marrying her daughter off to Curtis and a group of children cheer when a giant television screen shows a bogan child finishing her plate.

In October 2010 *Choice* magazine awarded the promotion its Shonky award, claiming that Curtis's $7.76 coq au vin would really cost almost $30 when taking into account uncosted pantry items like a bottle of red wine. This forced Coles to drop the 'under $10' part of the promotion, but thankfully Curtis's appeal to the bogan was unharmed. Indeed, Curtis's bogan-baiting skills were enhanced one thousand fold when he was recruited by the one and only Oprah Winfrey to become her very own pet Australian, a move designed to make his appeal to bogans truly global. In early 2011 Coles and Curtis were up to it again, with the brawny chef appearing on televisions and as a cardboard cut-out in stores around the country to advertise the supermarket's 'hormone-free' beef promotion.

Like the 'Feed Your Family' promotion, this came under fire from consumer and industry groups, who claimed that the promotion falsely implied that cows raised on growth-promoting hormones are bad for human consumption and will push up beef prices and hurt farmers.

None of this fazes the bogan, however. Like *MasterChef*, Curtis tells it what to buy and what to cook and this is all right by it. The she-bogue watches the dashing young Curtis and dreams about him poaching its breast while, thanks to Curtis, the he-bogue now knows to tell the waiter not to serve him horny beef.

MORE BEER

Beer has long played a key role in Australian culture. Ever since Captain Cook brought beer and Jessica Watson with him on the *Endeavour*, we have been a nation of beer drinkers. Since it was first brewed towards the end of the nineteenth century, lager has become the beer style of choice, with strong regional brands like VB and XXXX emerging in the different states of Australia. For most of the last century drinkers more or less stuck with these brands, and the world was a happy place. The bogan's forebears were no different, content to smash their state's beer in their backyard or, if they were feeling adventurous, knock back a few VBs, but only after Foster's stopped calling it 'Victoria Bitter'.

Today's bogan, however, has different tastes. Iconic brands like VB and XXXX are no longer enough for it. Even the presence of 4(!) Xs hasn't been enough to satisfy the bogan's tastes. Being the aspirational creature that it is, the bogan's thirst has been increasingly drawn — facilitated by the stern instruction of product marketers — towards premium beers, towards something 'a little bit fancy'. But unlike the adventurous beer drinker quietly nursing a Mountain Goat in the back streets of Richmond or sipping a Schöfferhofer in Surry Hills, the bogan desire for something different is not driven by aesthetic considerations or a quest for variety. The bogan desires premium beer not because it tastes better but because it wants everyone around it to know that it is drinking something premium.

This trend started with Crown Lager. Launched to the public in 1954, the bogan discovered 'Crownies' in the mid-1990s. While it was immediately drawn to the gold label (the bogan's chemical element of choice before platinum), it wasn't until Foster's began marketing Crown as 'Australia's premium beer', and ensuring that celebrities and footy players at awards nights were photographed holding Crown Lager, that bogans around the country decided they need to celebrate their own special occasions with a 'golden microphone' in hand. Foster's has long denied an urban myth that Crown Lager comes from the same barrel as its other lagers; while this may indeed be myth, it is safe to say that it is not the superior taste or finer hops that compels bogans to fork over an extra ten to fifteen dollars for a slab of Crownies over Carlton Draught. The bogan has since moved on to other premium brews, but the Crown brand continues to screw bogans out of their own crowns even today. Aware of the prevalence of bottles of Crown Lager at bogan weddings, twenty-firsts and the Logies, Foster's offers personalised bottles for only $120 a slab. More recently, the company launched a new version of the brand, Crown Ambassador Reserve. Available for only $90 a bottle, the new 'limited edition', 'luxury' brand targets the cashed-up bogan who is eager to make a maxtreme statement about its exclusivity, uniqueness and wealth.

Another word the bogan has come to associate with general awesomeness in beers is 'imported'. This might seem strange given its inherent xenophobia and a cold fear of the unknown, but the bogan has long identified things imported from America and Europe to be synonymous with luxury, celebrities and the seemingly innate need to drop max cash. Ever since it was gifted a 'Beers of the World' pack by its grandmother for Christmas 2004, the bogan has taken to drinking Heineken and Stella Artois in public, believing that the trendy green bottle bestows the appropriate level of international sophistication and European prestige on it.

Unnoticed by the bogan, though, beer producers here casually removed the word 'imported' from the bottles of these beers and replaced it with much smaller print reading 'brewed under licence', as they have paid global brewers to produce beers like Heineken, Beck's, Stella Artois, Carlsberg and Peroni here. The bogan, meanwhile, continues to fork over $50 for a slab of 330 ml bottles that came all the way from Richmond, Camperdown or Milton.

The bogan's penchant for imported beers doesn't stop at European brands. Since Jetstar Asia opened the bogan's eyes to international travel, alcohol distributors have begun stocking brands like Singha, Chang, Bintang and Tiger so that the bogan can reminisce with its footy mates about the time they drank fourteen of these beers each and gang-banged a local prostitute who definitely didn't have a penis. Bogans have also taken to drinking Budweiser and Miller because they come from the land of celebrities, while once a year it will hide its grimace as it pretends to enjoy a pint of Guinness on St Patrick's Day.

The undisputed king of imported beers in the bogan's glassy eyes is Corona. At first glance this may seem to defy boganic logic (if, indeed, there is such a thing): Corona is brewed in Mexico, a country without white people, celebrities (that the bogan has heard of) or many connotations of luxury. Bogans are most likely to associate Mexico with Old El Paso (named after a city in Texas, Mexico). So just why does the bogan pay $60 a slab or $9 a stubby for a bland-tasting beer from a country with no beer-making heritage, along with questionable hygiene standards and drinking water? Why, because it's served with a slice of lemon/lime in it, of course. While a cynic might question whether or not adding citrus fruit to a beer helps mask the fact that it tastes like goat urine, the bogan simply loves the theatre of inserting a piece of lemon/lime into its beer. At the same time, holding a yellow bottle with a piece of fruit protruding from it gives the beverage the appearance and status of a cocktail while being (barely) cheaper than a real cocktail, when buying a drink for a femme-bogue to get into her pants.

Not content with only a proportion of these bogan-derived profits, Australian brewers have recently launched a new range of 'premium' beers with infusions of lime, twists of lemon or notes of orange. Expect to see a bogan paying too much for one of these at a bar near you.

Activity

1. Which of the following is *not* a bogan pizza topping?
   a. Meatlovers with barbecue sauce
   b. Super special with barbecue sauce and NO ANCHOVIES
   c. Barbecue chicken with barbecue sauce
   d. Moroccan lamb with goat's cheese, rocket, preserved lemon and fiery harissa
2. Would a bogan rather eat at a restaurant owned by David Koch, Mick Gatto or George Calombaris?
3. Does the bogan drown a sausage roll with tomato sauce or barbecue sauce?
4. How much would you like to punch Curtis Stone in the chops?
5. What is the largest food group in the bogan food pyramid?
6. After consuming 8 Coronas, 4 Singhas, 2 Stella Artois and 3 Jägerbombs, will the bogan end up:
   a. Safely tucked up in bed?
   b. Sharing a jail cell with a giant Ivorian transsexual named Roger?
   c. In the emergency room of the Alfred?
   d. Out cold on the footpath?

11
THE
INTERNET

The Internet is a global system of millions of connected computer networks which contain private, public, academic, business and government information. These networks are linked by an array of different technologies — from wireless or cable to optical fibre — which carry a variety of services, such as email and the World Wide Web. By visiting dedicated URLs the bogan can view hypertext documents on the web, which it considers to be a series of tubes. An internet can be one small network, as distinct from the Internet, which is the entirety of all of these networks, one of the largest of which is the World Wide Web. The bogan is unaware of any of these distinctions, but simply refers to 'the Internet' in all instances when it is not referring to the Internet as a synonym for Facebook.

The bogan's grasp of the Internet is quite straightforward, even if the way it uses the Internet is not. It can be bisected neatly in the bogan mind into Facebook and Not Facebook.

While the Internet is used by many for research, communication, entertainment and the dissemination of witty quips, the bogan views the Internet as a blank canvas onto which it can spew any and all manner of intellectual, psychological, emotional and bodily fluids in an effort to share with the world that which the world needs most: more bogan.

The history of the Internet

1933–2001

The Internet was invented on a winter's afternoon in 1933 by Richard Jeremiah Facebook. Confounded by his growing inability to masturbate to his depressingly small collection of pin-up girl postcards, he envisioned a way to communicate with other aficionados of the form, in order to share material and greatly further the cause of viewing pornography. He proceeded to set up a telephone-based 'network' between his and his neighbours' homes, consisting of a series of tubes, pulleys and levers. However, he could not conceive of a way to get the postcards to disintegrate and travel across wires. This resulted in him returning to masturbating on his divan. Eighty-eight years later and little has changed.

There were, however, efforts to expand the Internet's horizons in preparation for the bogan onslaught that was still to come. During the 1970s and 1980s two scientists, Al Gore and Richard Wilkins, decided to take Jeremiah's primarily theoretical efforts and apply them to the sharing of celebrity bombshells.

The bogan discovered the Internet on 7 March 1996. That morning it received a call on its decidedly non-cordless landline phone and was told to set up a Lycos mail account so it could be sent a link to rotten.com. On this site the bogan could view such things as severed heads, fresh roadkill and still shots from the kind of pornography it had previously thought only existed in the minds of Austrian fetishists. It was the day everything changed. Two days later, on 9 March 1996, the bogan's computer first crashed due to excessive clicking of pop-up ads promising millions of dollars.

The bogan spent the subsequent five years patiently waiting for sections of a jpeg image of Pamela Anderson to populate the screen of its Pentium-powered home computer, amazed at the reach and scope of this fabulous new technology.

2001–2007

Despite this new-found access to things that it greatly enjoyed, the bogan felt that there was something missing. While it now had access to a Nokia 5110, with which it could send its comrades grammatically incorrect and borderline incoherent messages about things, it needed a better way to do this. More importantly, it knew that the world needed an online forum through which it could learn more about the bogan. In gif format.

Thus MySpace was born. While it was not the first social networking site, it was the first to receive the attention of the bogan, other attempts such as Friendster falling down somewhere between the early adopters and the early bogans. The bogan had once attempted to build a Geocities page but was confounded by its Netscape browser and the need to learn about HTML ('Hate My Life'), and gave up. Bogan monarch Rupert Murdoch identified the boganic value of MySpace and acquired the website for about a half a billion dollars, failing to see the likelihood that bogans, when presented with a different alternative down the road, would abandon it en masse for whatever was the next big thing.

MySpace gave the bogan everything Geocities did, and more. Soon the Internet was full of strangely formatted pages describing people over a shifting hot-pink background, as bogans the world over united in a fluorescent arms race. In an eerie reflection of bogan sartorial habits, bogans on these pages were itching to draw more attention to their list of things that they like (a list, by the by, more ably compiled in 2009), in the strange belief that a colourful page would attract the attention of someone who is yet to see it.

Gradually, the bogan began to realise that while it could now have a web page that could demonstrate how truly awesome it was, via eye-blearing colour, it still lacked the scope that would allow it to broadcast mangled English to a sufficiently wide audience.

A defining characteristic of the early '00s was that companies were actively seeking things bogans wanted the appearance of, in order to create websites to provide those things. One of the results was MSN Messenger. Instant messaging allowed the bogan to take its text-speak and convert it to instant online communication, away from chat rooms where it was posing as a sixteen-year-old hottt girl from Cali, allowing the male bogan to explore its bicurious cyber-sex needs.

As the bogan was spending its evenings communicating with people instantly, it realised it needed something to do while chatting. Again, someone delivered. Napster was a service that took the previously nerd-tastic technology of peer-to-peer file sharing and brought it into the bogan realm by letting the bogan have things for nothing. There wasn't even an interest-free period — the bogan could simply download some software, then begin stealing music at will.

By late 2006 this combination of expressionism, communication and theft led to an era of more and more online bogan activity. Increasingly comfortable with being online, the bogan began looking for new ways to express itself, and savvy companies were looking for ways to access max bogan bucks by letting it do just that.

Thus it was that, one day, a nerd who no bogan would ever have paid attention to changed the bogan's life forever.

2007–present

Since the bogan upgraded from the Internet to the broadband, more has been achievable. The broadband is undeniably the penultimate means of accessing the net. The key Internet development in this era, however, was the move from Web 1.0 to Web 2.0. This signalled a seismic shift in the way the Internet operated and how it applied to day-to-day life. The difference between Bogan 1.0 and Bogan 2.0, however, is less stark, and as a result the greatest shift in modern Internet behaviour has been the introduction of Bogan-Generated Content (BGC).

BGC is the online equivalent of another bogan favourite: talkback radio. Talkback radio allows the elder-bogue to opine furiously about any and all topics that may waft into its attention-deficit brain at any time, all the while receiving the cooing approval of the radio host. With the advent of Web 2.0, the bogan realised that radio was far too slow and allowed the bogan to offer opinions that were far too well thought out. In 2011, this all changed.

While the bogan began spilling its ill-conceived thoughts onto keyboards like so much lukewarm coffee, other, more talented people were conceiving of ways to monetise the bogan need for self-promotion and validation. While there were many alternatives, one in particular has risen up to define the Bogan 2.0 era.

Facebook — while originally aimed at letting intellectuals hook up while in training — was never going to remain free of the bogan taint. Today Facebook is so central to the online bogan's sense of self that it precludes discussion of any other web developments since 2007. Second Life was an attempt to set up a fake reality in computers but the bogan did not react well to it, as it had seen *The Matrix: Reloaded*. In Facebook, however, the bogan found something better: a digital world so real that it would alter its real life to be more real in the fake world.

The book of faces

To suggest that Facebook is important to the bogan is akin to suggesting that it has only a touch of chlamydia. Facebook has rapidly become the alpha and omega of the bogan's universe. It is the first thing a bogan engages with in the morning, and the last thing it gazes upon before it lays its head to rest. Within Facebook's innocent-seeming blue-and-white layout and unassuming fonts lies a panopticon of bogan self-satisfaction, passive aggression, shattered relationships, blurry photos and shame. There is little grammar or syntax.

Facebook is taking BGC to its natural, illogical conclusion. The bogan can now spew its existential angst/awesomeness into the ether for other bogans to feed off and, more importantly, comment on, creating a furious feedback loop of idiotic boganity, as bogans attracting comment will happily continue offering their thoughts up to the void.

To the twenty-first century online bogan, Facebook is more real than reality; it is a world within a world in which the bogan can portray to its 'friends' how truly unique and awesome it is. It is also a means by which the bogan can continually reinforce its own sense of self, and there are many ways it can do this.

'Friends'

Various studies by anthropologists across the developed world have concluded that the average adult person can have, at any given time, about 150 friends, of which between five and ten could be considered close. Upon learning this, the bogan understood it had a target: to achieve more friends than that. This is the guiding principle of the bogan's operation on Facebook. Today there is an equation, developed expressly for the purposes of this book, which accurately indicates the number of Facebook 'friends' the bogan requires to feel good about itself:

$$F_r = n + 1\text{, where } n \text{ is the number}$$
of Facebook friends the bogan currently has.

The bogan will add friends from any social circumstance. Should the bogan speak to someone briefly at a party in Simmo's backyard it will, without fail, add that person as a Facebook friend the next day. A clear measure of whether or not the new acquaintance is a bogan is the rapidity with which they accept that request. If the bogan joins a new workplace it will avidly scour the blue realm, seeking out co-workers in an effort to expand its popularity. The friending frenzy of recent years has even made it easier for bogans to ignore one another after an ill-judged coital encounter that resulted from a night at the glassing barn. Rather than having an awkward conversation regarding exchanging phone numbers, bogans may simply suggest that they find one another on Facebook and promptly forget to look.

As the number of people joining Facebook is increasing at a faster rate than bogans are capable of clicking 'Add as Friend', the potential for bogans to find friends is limited only by the number of other bogans willing to similarly inflate their level of popularity. It can be safely assumed, then, that the potential number of 'friends' a bogan may acquire on Facebook is effectively infinite.

Much as the bogan measures the effectiveness of a political party by the number next to the words 'interest rates' in the Trashmedia (see Chapter 5, Politics), it assesses its own success at life via one simple metric: the number of friends it has accumulated. The more mathematically-minded bogan may contrive to compare its own Facebook army to those of others it knows, but in the end it is the absolute number in the left column that indicates whether or not the bogan is winning Facebook. This has created an unexpected side effect: the de-friending.

As bogans began to add one another to their Facebook pages, they realised that in adding one another they were in effect increasing their rivals' friend counts at the same time. This led to an interesting subset of enterprising bogans intuiting something that many bogan svengalis have known for a long time: the power of scarcity (see Chapter 4, Marketing). These bogans began announcing impending culls of their Facebook collectives, then sitting back and waiting for the validation to roll in as terrified bogans who had lapsed in their interactions came rushing to suggest, in an effort to appear ironically detached LOL, that they were maxcool and should remain in the newly alpha-bogue's list. Of course, this instigator had no intention of removing a single person from its list but realised that, much like at the club or glassing barn, exclusivity counts, and it had mounted a great big digital velvet rope out in front of its profile with nothing more than a passive-aggressive status update. Thus armed with a legion of minions and self-confidence, the bogan can begin its mission to maximise itself publicly.

'Status'

It is the presence of a single word in Facebook's burgeoning glossary that makes this as important to the bogan as it is: status. The bogan craves status with a fervour that is only rivalled by its desire to achieve maxtreme celebrity (although the bogan entirely conflates these two things). Thus, when Facebook asks the bogan about its 'status', the bogan cannot help but respond in a manner that portrays it in the best light, or at least in a manner that achieves the greatest amount of validation from its peers.

The status update function on Facebook began as a meek box in the right-hand column, and only offered the user a drop-down list of mundane options such as 'at work', 'at home' or 'in bed'. As early-adopting Facebook users strove to use this window into their soul as a means of firing witty quips into the intertubes, Facebook responded by opening up that little box to the users' imaginations. It was at about this time that the first bogans discovered Facebook, and that inoffensive box began its climb to the seat of virtual power in the twenty-first century. Today it is the window into the plunging abyss that is the bogan psyche; the means by which the bogan reaches out across the digital ether to rip the Internet's heart from its chest and laugh mockingly as it squirms, slowly dying on the parquetry floor. The bogan now actively lives its life with the constant presence of the status update in the back of its mind, aware that the slightest wrong post could lead to a de-friending — the online equivalent of a shattered pint glass in the face. Or, worse, missing a party invite.

Even efforts by Facebook to provide the bogan with other alternatives for self-expression, such as non-profile pages and Facebook groups, still proffer the small white box into which the bogan pours its heart and soul every day, every hour, every spare minute. The result of this is that bogans have self-organised into several different, easy-to-identify groups of status updaters, which we shall analyse here.

THE PASSIVE-AGGRESSIVE HATER

'Don't you just hate it when someone you THOUGHT cared about you turns out to be a complete dick? Some people are so immature.'

While the Facebogan sees itself as tough and ever ready to rumble, it is, in fact, nonconfrontational. This is not due to the fact that it cares about others' feelings; rather, it is wary of its inability to maintain an argument of any sort when placed under scrutiny. Thus Facebook provides the perfect forum for it to lash out in a manner that will allow it to tell its friends that it totally ripped into the arsehole in question, without having to face repercussions for its actions. An ancillary benefit of this activity is the attention the bogan will receive, as other bogans rush to reinforce the initial vague utterance or simply commiserate with the wronged Facebogan.

THE PITY-SEEKING MISERY HOUND

'X is trying to be strong today. It's really tough ...'

A condition exists called Munchausen's syndrome — sufferers attempt to convince others that they suffer from illnesses they do not have, in order to attract sympathy and basic human connection in a world in which they feel they receive little. A close relative of the Passive-Aggression Facebogan, the Pity-Seeking Facebogan does not suffer from Munchausen's syndrome, however, but simply needs attention and lacks the wit to attract it via regular status updates. The result is that the Misery Hound will plaintively yelp into the void, offering the faintest glimmering of genuine angst coated in a slice of attention-grabbing melancholy.

THE JOKE THIEF

'What does Charles Dickens say in his "Travel Guide to The Orient"? "Great! Expect Asians."'

This particular variety of bogan is renowned amongst its non-digital friends for being jovial, a bit thick and fairly innocuous. On Facebook this harmless bogan becomes a ball of fiery comic genius, and it spends its time trawling Google for the best joke sites from which it can appropriate gems like the one printed above. While this bogan's friends are fully aware of the gulf in wit between its digital and hard-copy self, they happily play along, commenting with regular LOLs and the occasional ROFL, whenever the occasional burst of inspired humour-trawling appears in the Facebook feed.

THE PROUD PARENT

'Little Zavier's first flight of steps lol!'

Since the invention of the still camera, bogan parents have periodically forced their friends and relatives into reliving 'important' moments in their spawns' development. Anything the child does for the first time merits not only recording for posterity but to be wedged in front of others' faces at inopportune moments. It was once thought that the invention of the Camcorder sometime in the sixteenth century would mark the peak of this trend, as bogans began arriving at others' houses and commandeering the television in order to demonstrate their child's skills with the potty. The world was not prepared for the impact of Facebook on this. The bogan can now offer a running day-by-day, blow-by-blow commentary on its litter and which room in the McMansion the offspring has most recently befouled. This confluence of technology allows the bogan to reinforce to itself that its progeny are, indeed, the best progeny going around, so long as other Facebogans are not behaving similarly at the same time. The bogan has won at child rearing. QED.

THE VAIN TRAVELLER

'In Phuket today, lounging with a cocktail and a bucket of vodka! This is the life!!!'

While not limited only to bogans, this behaviour is deeply, deeply annoying. Those close enough to the bogan to know that it is, indeed, in Phuket are already aware that it is in Phuket and likely drinking large buckets of foul-tasting demon drink. The bogan simply wishes to remind people that it is in a better place than others. Other Facebogans will then dutifully respond with comments that are all variations on 'OMG SOO JEALOS!' Thus validated, the globe-trotting originator will go back to its debauchery.

THE SHAMELESS SELF-PROMOTER

'Totally scored a new gig today!!!! Boss fuckin luvs me!!!'

This Facebogan knows that it is ace. It knows that many others also think that it is ace. Yet insufficient people are cognisant of its available doses of pure maxtremity. So, rather than merely telling those near it that it is very good at all things, it will imply that those whom it is sure know that it is good are rewarding it for its goodness. Its boss does not love it, nor did it receive a promotion today.

THE NARRATOR

'Just had a sandwich lol!'

Many other people, most likely, also had a sandwich at about the same time as this Facebogan, yet only the narrator feels the need to share that information with its wider network. The sandwich, of course, is merely an entrée in an ongoing, day-and-night-long saga that is the Narrator's stunted and unfulfilled existence. There will be digressions into what television show it is watching; what television show it will choose to watch next (sometimes putting that out as a polling question — always in the binary); how sleepy it felt when it woke up (very); the fact that it doesn't enjoy Mondays and it loves Fridays (closely linked to the Job Hater); that it is stuck in traffic (the iPhone has been a saviour for the Narrator); is late for work (lol); how many kilometres it ran (actual number is n/2); or that it is going to bed ('night! Xoxo'). This bogan has been hidden from many a Facebook feed. The Narrator is yet to discover Twitter, but cannot be far away.

THE JOB HATER

'Argh, Monday, why do you hate me so? I can't face work yet!'
NARRATOR: 'Don't worry, only five days till the weekend!'
This bogan does not enjoy its job and wants you to know. Unfortunately, it has forgotten that when it was in friend-collection mode it added its boss, who is now privy to its twice-daily exhortations for higher powers to deliver unto it new employment. While not actually seeking work, it is content to paint itself as a wage slave under the thumb of a nefarious bureaucracy at the call centre.

NB: a subset of the Job Hater is the Teacher Job Hater. This Facebogue will routinely complain about the career it chose, studied for years to enter and proclaimed to be something it was passionate about, until it realised that it involved children. At which point its Facebook feed features one of four alternate messages, or variations thereof:

1. 'Fuck, can't face a room full of kids today lol'
2. 'Fuck, is the weekend over ALREADY???!!!'
3. 'OMG I love school holidays'
4. 'Fuck are the holidays over ALREADY???!!!'

THE TOWN CRIER

'OMG Michael Jacksons DEAD RIP'

The Town Crier is the bogan who believes it is at least one hour ahead of the rest of the world when it comes to announcing breaking news stories. The most important stories, of course, are those involving celebrities, particularly if they've just died. However, it will happily spout whatever it saw on news.com.au as a headline, without offering a link to any articles of substance. This bogan does not believe in depth, only events.

THE GROSS COUPLE

'Can't wait to see his special someone tonight. Someone's eating out! ;)'
'Cant wait to see you too babexox'

In the twenty-first century the vast majority of couples over the age of twenty-one cohabitate. With social mores of previous decades rapidly collapsing, couples — bogan and non-bogan alike — can live together without fear of social stigma. Those who do not live together tend to have the benefit of twenty-first century telecommunications to stay in touch. One of the benefits of all of this social change is that couples can regularly communicate and share their private thoughts privately at almost any time. But not this couple. This couple understands just how special their relationship is — more special than everyone else's — and this means that they have a duty to ensure that the world is privy to their love.

PAPARAZZO

The Paparazzo has little to say. It is an *artiste*. It understands that a picture speaks a thousand words, so if it treats every Monday morning as an opportunity to upload several hundred images of Saturday night's session at PJ McTaggerty's, it is something of a bogan novelist. Not that the bogan would tell you, but it believes that the word 'Tolstoy' would not be misplaced. Part of the Paparazzo's technique is an ongoing effort to achieve true *verité* stylings, and there is no way to achieve true photographic verisimilitude other than to include EVERY photo that it took on its iPhone as the night gradually degenerated into a seething mass of Jägermeister, sweat and shame.

THE CHRONIC JOINER

'I just found out which Nandos sauce I am! (Peri Peri — exotic!) — You should find out!'
GUY WHO HAS NEVER NOT COMMENTED: *'I'm sweet herb!'*
This Facebogue has not met a Facebook quiz it does not like. It will join every group ('I like the cool side of the pillow' to which, incidentally, there are at least 400 separate Facebook groups dedicated), sign every petition ('I'll name my son Batman if I get 100,000 members') and, yes, take every quiz presented to it. Moreover, it will require its 'friends' to, at the very least, witness that it is doing this. More often, though, it will insist with a rabid sincerity that all others should do the same. So, whether or not other people care if they favour Team Edward or Team Jacob, or which *True Blood* character they most represent, or what their high score in BeDazzled could be, they must bear witness to the sheer mind-bending multi-tasking of the Chronic Joiner.

HUNGOVER GUY

'So hungover. Jesus I need a McChicken. And nuggets.'
Of a similar mindset to the Paparazzo and the Vain Traveller, the Hungover Guy wants you to know how awesome his night-time excursions are, without being quite as explicit as the others. In fact, there is also a hearty helping of the Misery Hound in the Hungover Guy's behaviour, simultaneously promoting its maxtremity while also seeking nurturing validation from femme-bogues who sympathise, and high-fives from homme-bogues who applaud such behaviour.

THE BOB DYLAN-ALIKE

I don't want to see a ghost,
It's a sight that I fear most
I'd rather have a piece of toast

The Bob-alike is a gentle, artistic soul. It has so much to say yet finds the world so extraordinary, its emotional peaks and valleys so respectively high and deep, that mere words cannot summon the proper emotions. Rather, it will seek the words of the great poets to make the divine human. The lyric must be vague enough that it could apply to any number of readers, thus generating the required responses, but also profound enough that the uninitiated may believe that the Bob Dylan-alike is genuinely soulful. This Bob Dylan is not genuinely soulful.

ASK ME! ASK ME!

'I cant believe that just happened!!!'
'What just happened babe??'

Another offshoot of the Passive-Aggressive Hater and the Misery Hound, the Ask Me! Ask Me! is on a quest for validation and interaction. All of their Facebook status updates are carefully tailored with the specific intention of eliciting the desired response from whomever is on Facebook at the time. Most often the vague, leading statement will revolve around the poster itself in some nebulous way, rather than indicating events outside of the Facebogan's orbit. This is, in fact, a common thread among most Facebogans' online behaviour. Much like the analogue world, the bogan's digital realm extends no further than the places it goes and the people it sees.

THE INSPIRATIONAL QUOTEMEISTER

'If you do what you've always done, you'll get what you've always gotten.'

This quote is actually taken from the inestimable Anthony Robbins — the bogan's Henry Rollins — but you wouldn't know it from reading the status updates of this particular brand of Facebogan.

It will happily appropriate quotations from sources as varied as Anthony Robbins and Anonymous, and faithfully reproduce them in its feed, confident that it has provided its cohort with the life-affirming profundity it needed to get through the day. Like the Shameless Self-Promoter this bogan is often, in person, exactly the kind of bogan who would plaster its walls, fridge and cupboard doors with similar quotes lifted from the grammatically flawed world of the motivational speaker.

CAPTAIN ALL CAPS
'HEY I'M GOING TO THE MUG TONIGHT> WHOSE IN?'
This bogan has little to say at the best of times and is certain that you wish to hear it. It has discovered that, amongst other bogans, the Caps Lock key is the typographical equivalent of going to the races in a lavender polyester suit and white crocodile skin shoes. The suit is no better than anyone else's, but the bogan has figured out a way to stand out from the crowd despite its mediocrity. In the same way, the bogan's unfiltered utterances offer nothing; however, the all-caps conceit automatically has the reader shouting it in their own brain. For the bogan, this is a natural means of communication.

Relationship status

There is, however, one form of Facebook status more important to the Facebogan than the standard status update: the relationship status. When coupled, the bogan is desperate for others to know that it is attached (more extreme versions of this are described above under Gross Couple Facebogans); there are myriad status permutations that the bogan is free to indulge in.

Once the bogan's actual relationship status changes, the most important step is to alter the Facebook relationship status to match. This is an extension of the many attention-seeking status update modifiers catalogued above. Should a relationship end, the bogan will immediately be assaulted with concerned bogans querying 'Are you OK hun xoxox?' even as the commenting bogan

will be secretly thrilled to see the relationship fail. Likewise, a new relationship will be met with similarly grammatically incorrect cries of 'congrats!' In fact, to the bogan, the altering of Facebook status is the single greatest commitment they can offer short of the purchase of a princess-cut 75 carat shiny rock from Tiffany & Co.

Having established that it has status, and status worth sharing, the bogan can move beyond the initial step of telling everyone that it is 'good'. It can use social media for the purpose Mark Zuckerberg had in mind when he invented it: profile pictures.

PROFILE PICS

The bogan considers the profile picture to be an enduring projection of itself. While the status update is vitally important to letting others know that it is great, or attracting the attention that it craves, the update rapidly scrolls down the screen, vanishing into the abyss of forgotten outpourings of bogan existential angst. The profile picture, however, is eternal. It remains atop the bogan's profile and is visible any time the bogan features in any way on someone else's page. If Caps Lock is a cheap suit, the profile picture is the haircut that the bogan will spend an inordinate amount of time primping before it leaves the house in the morning.

Because of this, the bogan knows it must put its best foot forward in the pictorial stakes. It will hone its perfect photo, rapidly collating an album of somewhere between 75 and 2250 photos of itself, and only itself — or the Australian flag — that it may choose from to best represent its current state of mind. Most of these images are taken from the MySpace elevation™, some remaining digital detritus from the mid-'00s. The MySpace elevation™, a form of photography that did not exist until around 1999, simply involves the bogan in question raising the camera in its left hand to an angle that easily obscures any extraneous chins or bellies, while simultaneously enhancing the décolletage (male or female). This may or may not be conducted in the presence of other bogans, but the elevation™ is crucial.

The bogan's obsession with the profile picture actually began before Facebook, unbeknown to the bogan. The proliferation of cheap, small digital cameras, and shortly thereafter camera phones, in the late 1990s made it easy for the bogan to keep their phone with them at all times, and also take the maximum number of photos required to get the right one. It also meant that it could afford to take photos from the MySpace elevation™, as it could make multiple attempts in order to get it right. This appealed to the bogan's inherent sense of self-belief, as without training or proper practice it could convince itself that it had developed professional camera skills by virtue of trial and error alone.

Almost as important as the elevation™ new cameras offer is the facial expression, which no technology can help with. While the bogan's duck-face manoeuvre has been well honed over the millennia, recent overuse has made the bogan reluctant to be too aggressive in its pouting. This pose can be improved further if it is taken while in 'da club'. The bogan feels very much at home in da club, and feels the need to demonstrate this by taking a photo of itself with its phone with one arm raised and several pouting comrades shouldering in. A photo of this calibre will rapidly find its way to the top of the bogan's profile page.

Of course, this applies primarily to younger, unattached bogans. Bogans in serious or semi-serious relationships will routinely place photos of themselves with their significant others as all of their images. The bogan, now attached, wants the world to be entirely clear about the fact that somebody else believes it is terrific enough to sleep with. This extends, naturally, to the institution of bogan marriage. In the twenty-first century there are few legal benefits to marriage, and the bogan has already deftly sidestepped any moral obstacles it faced while spawning out of wedlock. In effect, the bogan gets married for one reason, and for one reason only: to place their wedding snaps online as their Facebook profile page.

Once married, however, the premise of having a be-suited and be-dressed couple standing astride the two respective Facebook profiles can rapidly grow stale. Thus the bogan needs to find a new theme for its precious ciphers. This is why the bogan has children.

At this point the bogan makes a little-understood existential leap: its sense of being is subsumed to the promotion of its child as scion of its own awesomeness. The bogan, no longer cognisant of the difference between itself and its child, begins placing images only of its spawn on its Facebook profile. This states to others on Facebook very clearly that the bogan is such an excellent parent, it is entirely willing to remove itself from the forum it once felt was the single most valuable digital real estate it owned. This is not true. The bogan does not value the raising of its child over all others. If it did, it would spend less time on Facebook. Instead, it carefully cultivates a persona of über-parent.

As a result, bogans who are routinely using their children in place of themselves as their visual representation can take the short leap to using Facebook as a means of promoting their children to others, becoming Proud Parent Facebogans. When this occurs, the book of faces can rapidly morph into the book of faeces, as proud bogan parents regale their minions with tales of their offspring's regular excremental expulsions — their consistency, colour and clarity.

While this is ostensibly a healthy thing for the bogan — as it likely no longer considers its child purely an extension of itself and vice versa, but can conceive of a world where they are unique individuals — it means that Facebook users the world over need to spend more time than appropriate looking at poo.

'IF FACEBOOK START CHARGING TO JOIN, I'M LEAVING!!!'

Facebook has decided to offer the bogan the right to use Facebook for nothing. The bogan is in no way grateful for this, as it never had to pay in the first place, hence it understands 'free Facebook' to be an immutable law of the universe rather than a canny marketing decision. Occasionally bogans worldwide will become agitated by the promotion of a Facebook group or email chain spuriously indicating that Facebook, now flush with hundreds of millions of members, will begin to capitalise by charging a fee for use.

The bogan, naturally, is outraged by this and responds the only way it knows how: by joining the group claiming that it will leave Facebook if this occurs, a demonstration of the awesome people power of the massed bogan consumer. However, the bogan is entirely unaware of the irony inherent in the fact that it used its Facebook status update or Facebook group as a megaphone for broadcasting its ire. The bogan, now so reliant on Facebook as its means of communicating with others, has lost the capacity to leave it. Mark Zuckerberg observes this, strokes his white cat, and smiles.

'CHANGE BACK TO THE OLD LAYOUT OR I'M LEAVING!!!'

The bogan does not like change. Facebook, however, like any growing company, is forced to continually adapt its service offering to ensure its widening market is properly catered to. One of the offshoots of this is that Facebook will periodically tweak the presentation of Facebook and subtly alter the ways its users interact with it and each other; a decision most likely based on the near-infinite amount of data the company collects on user habits. Ergo, it stands to reason that any change to Facebook's layout occurs in an effort to enhance the bogan's user experience.

This matters not to the bogan, who is comfortably ensconced in the nourishing cocoon that was Facebook's old layout and sees no need to go changing what is already a perfectly excellent site. Upon logging in to Facebook, the bogan will spend several seconds staring blankly at the now-unfamiliar series of icons, before a seething rage will enter its soul.

It responds the only way it knows how: by joining the group claiming that it will leave Facebook if the design does not revert. It will furiously make a comment on the wall of that group, effectively reworking the group's thesis statement, *sans* correct grammar and with at least one superfluous apostrophe, then proceed to familiarise itself with the new layout so it can effectively upload photos of the previous night's clubbing and post passive-aggressive status updates about whichever friend it got into a fight with that night. Fifteen minutes later the bogan has forgotten that the layout has changed. However, the Trashmedia — ever alert to a meme — will publish an article that the layout has infuriated users and that Facebook is concerned about a backlash. Facebook is not concerned about a backlash.

In a similar vein, the bogan will hear that Facebook is attempting to lower its privacy thresholds in order to more effectively monetise its ever-growing membership's personal data. The bogan will instantly express outrage on Facebook that this private company to which it gave (and continues to give) its personal information is using that information as a profit-making tool. It will then threaten, in the same Facebook status update, to leave Facebook if things are not remedied. It will not attempt to manually alter the privacy settings available to it.

Addendum: Twitter

The bogan is peripherally aware of Twitter; some bogans have even started accounts and tentatively begun spilling their abbreviated thoughts into the Twitterverse. There is one essential problem, however, with the bogan's Twitter incursion: it views Twitter as exactly parallel to Facebook. That is, it views Twitter as a competition to see who can gain the most 'followers'. The bogan is intrigued by this notion of 'followers', as having a retinue of 'followers' far exceeds the status of having over 1000 'friends'. This raises the prospect that bogans worldwide are carefully collecting armies of disciples to join them on their crusades, but it is more likely that bogans are stupid.

For when the bogan enters Twitter, its first tweet is routinely a variation on the theme of:

'So I'm on Twitter lol but don't have any followers!!! ☹'

Notwithstanding the fact that the bogan is unaware that nobody can read the above missive — because it has no followers — it demonstrates that the bogan is, in fact, unaware that social media is about interacting with others. The bogan believes it is about shouting into the hungry void, and spying on celebs.

Facebook stats

People on Facebook
- More than 10 million active bogans
- 80 per cent of active bogans log on to Facebook in any given day
- Average bogan has 250 friends
- People spend over 700 billion minutes per month on Facebook — of which 1 trillion is bogans

Activity on Facebook
- Average bogan is connected to 180 community pages, groups and events
- Average bogan performs 120 separate acts of Facebook boganity each month

Not Facebook

Armed with this new means of communicating at record pace, the bogan could begin to offer Bogan-Generated Content in volumes previously inconceivable. All it needed was a new forum in which people it did not know could hear what it had to say. Much as the bogan enjoyed being on talkback radio to opine on things and feel simultaneously famous, there needed to be an online equivalent.

The Trashmedia was all too willing to help.

Angry at the Internet

The bogan was once a temperate creature: never quick to strike; always considerate of others' feelings when speaking; a genuine humanist when engaging in discourse on the issues of the day. But that was a long time ago. Today, armed with the indignation fed to it and maintained by the Trashmedia Kraken, the bogan has opinions, and not only wants to share them — it wants to shout down, with righteous fury, all those who would question its clearly thought-out beliefs. Enter the blog.

A weblog is effectively an online diary that a user can maintain. Originally invented during the early 1990s, the abbreviated term 'blog' was applied to it in 1999, and this name stuck as this means of delivering online content took hold of the popular imagination. At first these blogs were simply non-journalists' means of conveying their thoughts to the wider world, as the world waited for Mark Zuckerberg to complete puberty. In 1998 a 'comments' feature was added by Bruce Ableson on Open Diary, quickly followed by LiveJournal in 1999. This was another seminal moment in the history of bogan interaction with the web. While the bogan is highly unlikely to ever write a blog, it is more than happy to wait for someone else to offer an opinion or idea, then disagree vocally with it. Behind the narcotic screen of anonymity the bogan can employ its Caps

Lock key to its heart's content, assaulting a blog's author with a variety of tried-and-true bogan argumentative techniques, which we shall now dissect.

AD HOMINEM

'YOUR CLEARLY A LEFTIST. WHAT WOULD YOU KNOW ABOUT THE HOUSING BUBBLE??'

An ad hominem (Latin: 'to the man') argument must rank among the bogan's favourite means of establishing its general correctness. It is an attempt to invalidate an opponent's argument by linking it to one or several characteristics of the person making the case, either stating or insinuating that these characteristics are flawed.

TU QUOQUE

'YOU CAN'T COMPLAIN ABOUT NEGATIVE GEARING, YOU OWN INVESTMENT PROPERTIES TOO!!1!'

Tu quoque (Latin: 'you too') is more commonly known as the 'appeal to hypocrisy'. The bogan will point out that the person making an argument against something is also a beneficiary of the thing. This has the effect of not refuting the original claim in any way, but it makes the bogan feel most excellent about its ability to identify hypocrites. Hence it wins the argument. Moreover, should the bogan ever discover that the Latin version of this argument is an easy double entendre, this will become an even more common means of dispute escalation by bogans.

POST HOC, ERGO PROPTER HOC

'There are more kids going to public school, and rates of juvenile delinquency are also rising. Clearly, our public schools are leading to civil strife. JULIA SHOULD BLOODY WELL DO SOMETHING!!1!'

'After this, therefore because of this' arguments posit that, effectively, one thing happened, then another thing happened, therefore the first thing caused the second thing. The bogan enjoys making this argument, as it offers the veneer of considered thought and logical progression when, in actual fact, it is simply stringing together two events and inventing causation between the two.

CUM HOC, ERGO PROPTER HOC

Better known as 'correlation does not imply causation', the bogan likes this because it sounds vaguely rude.

ARGUMENTUM AD INFINITUM

'Your betraying your green sympathies again, <insert author's name>, there's no proof of any of this.'
Rinse, repeat.

Otherwise known as argumentum ad nauseaum, in this device the bogan makes the same argument until the opponent gives up. This is the bogan equivalent of almost every argument it has when not sitting at a computer.

IGNORATIO ELENCHI

'You're being rediculous. There is definately a connection between race and criminality. But more importantly, we should consider your time spent as a Labor party apparatchik in 1983 ...'
The ignoratio elenchi, or red herring, is a means of diverting an opponent from the topic of debate. This is less commonly used by bogans as they are often unaware that their original argument is so poor as to require diverting attention away from it.

REDUCTIO AD HITLERUM

'Hitler was a vegetarian'
Coined in the mid-1950s, this is a means of making an argument by association. By linking its opponent to Hitler, one of history's greatest mass murderers, the bogan becomes right.

This is linked to Godwin's Law, a notion put forward by American lawyer and author Mike Godwin. It states: 'As an online discussion grows longer, the probability of a comparison involving

Nazis or Hitler approaches 1', which is to say it becomes more certain. The longer a bogan spends online, the more likely it is to make a reductio ad Hitlerum argument. It reaches this point far earlier than other people.

REDUCTIO AD BOGANIUM
'You're just a fuckin bogan, what would you know???'
The bogan defines itself by what it is and, just as frequently, what it isn't. Often incorrectly. Importantly, it will make a claim about another person while completely lacking in self-awareness, before leaping into another ad hominem argument.

Instant expert
In theory, to the bogan these are iron-clad arguments that result in a smile of smug self-satisfaction as the bogan furiously types its wisdom into the intertubes. In practice, all of these arguments will result in the bogan calling for someone to be sacked.

Once, getting in the paper was an achievement. Today, it requires the loudest voice or, more particularly, the Caps Lock key and a ridiculous point of view. This is not to suggest that the bogan is trolling — trolls tend to make outlandish statements with a view to stirring trouble and igniting controversy. The bogan simply believes outlandish things, in keeping with its profound lack of deep thinking about anything but itself.

As time has gone by, the location of this online vitriol has shifted from amateur blogs to paid ones, usually on Trashmedia news websites. These blogs are where the bogan now goes for its news and information. Thus, as when watching the diving during the Olympics, the bogan can be an expert on anything it chooses.

For many, the phrase 'well, it's on the Internet, so it must be true' is an ironic one. Not for the bogan. Given a means by which it can arm itself with prejudice-confirming information at every turn with almost no effort, the bogan is well placed to follow up its logically inconsistent arguments with factually flawed data and reasoning.

The result has been that online media provide the bogan with a truly phenomenal array of portals from which it can learn things it needs, before spouting back its opinion into an abyss of apathy. The demands of the bogan for sheer quantity of facts that prove things that it 'knows' result in Trashmedia outlets creating more facts for less money. The Trashmedia does this via opinion writing, by which it pays people very little to effectively do in article format what the bogan does in the comments section of that article. Because the information is in an article and not a comment, the bogan can claim it as fact.

Once the article has been written, the bogan will read the opening — and sometimes the closing — paragraph before heading to the comments section to tell the author that they are absolutely correct — or, alternatively, a blight on society because he or she is equivalent to Hitler. Having sought out sufficient articles written by people who agree with it, the bogan is now an expert in all things.

Once it is an expert, it can express its knowledge in one other way: the binary poll.

How effective do you think the ALP policy on
asylum seekers will be at keeping Australia's
borders safe? YES/NO

Do you prefer the Labor or Liberal solution to
climate change? YES/NO

How much of a dick is Mark Latham? YES/NO

Porn

No discussion of Internet usage by bogans is complete without a discussion of pornography. To protect our next book deal we have kept this to a minimum here.

Dating Sites

While the bogan's Internet can easily be defined via the Facebook/ Not Facebook dichotomy, another way the bogan segments its online interactions is this:

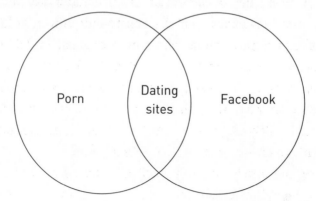

Figure 11.1 Boganic online interaction

The bogan has always longed for max sex. However, it lacks the imagination to conceive of a particularly large variety of ways for its sex to be maxtreme. The Internet changed all that. With exposure to a literally limitless amount of free porn (there is more than one second of porn being uploaded on the web each second), the need to imagine things vanished. As with all things, the bogan is most at home when someone else does the hard work for it.

However, while it may have the capacity for more kinds of sex, the Internet originally did nothing to expand the number of people for the bogan to have sex with. That did not last long. In fact, while dating sites represent the Venn diagram intersection of porn and Facebook, they were actually invented earlier.

Originally, dating sites were merely online extensions of the traditional introduction agency, but that did not last long. As soon as bogans discovered the intertubes, they embraced online dating sites as a means to invest time chatting with other bogans in order to extract fleshy dividends.

More research is needed to fully understand the bogan interactions via dating sites. Our own Michael Jayfox is conducting his third PhD on the subject and will take all precautions to ensure his explanations are sociologically irrefutable and that no one knows his real name or contact details. If he isn't arrested he will publish a serious analysis of the bogan and porn in 2012, titled *Dick Pound and the Bogan Herd* (or something better).

12
PSYCHOLOGY

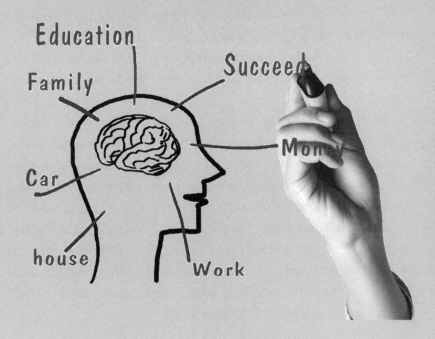

The bogan thinks, therefore it am.

Taking a journey into the bogan mind can be a bewildering experience. The sheer volume of mental tricks and short cuts that the bogan has devised is so daunting that many psychologists prefer to deny that bogan psychology even exists, rather than acknowledge it and delve in. While this denial has no doubt made their lives more comfortable, this book sets out to answer the questions that Ivory Tower Academic Latte Intellectual Arsehole Nobodies (or ITALIANs, for short) are ill equipped to tackle. Let's begin.

The blaming bogan

The process of understanding the bogan's mind has at times been slowed by the ITALIANs' inability to communicate with the bogan. Language difficulties, glassings and allegations of homosexuality have been major stumbling blocks encountered by these researchers but, like anything else, the bogan is adamant that none of this is its fault.

While the non-bogan is generally able to identify the causal relationship between its own behaviour and its results, every negative outcome that the bogan has ever experienced is the result of an evil third party who is hell bent on making the bogan suffer. This lack of personal accountability was incorporated into psychologist Julian Rotter's Social Learning Theory in 1954. Rotter expressed this idea as the locus of control: an individual with an internal locus of control takes responsibility for his or her life, and acts accordingly; an individual with an external locus of control floats along, shirking and blaming all the while.

You can see this in action at your local Harvey Norman store. The bogan sees a gargantuan 3D LCD LED HD television. The bogan wants the gargantuan 3D LCD LED HD television. The bogan leaves the store with the gargantuan 3D LCD LED HD television. This process is made possible by the wonders of interest-free finance, an amazing deal whereby the shiny screen is given to the bogan without the bogan having to pay or plan. Fast forward eighteen months and it becomes clear that the bogan has been betrayed by the corporate vultures over at GE Money. Indeed, the financiers of the gargantuan TV want maxtreme interest repayments from the bogan. How could this be? The bogan wasn't told.

Further investigation reveals that a lifetime of 'getting blind' on rum shots has indeed affected the bogan's vision. It can no longer read any text that is smaller than the large flashing letters that proclaim 'NO REPAYMENTS' on Harvey Norman's max tempo advertisements. Anything smaller or less epileptic than that lettering is hence 'fine print', which the bogan despises. This underhanded fine print legally obliges the bogan to do something it doesn't want to do, and it's someone else's fault. Someone has to pay, and the bogan believes that there's no 'pay' in 'repayment'. At this point the bogan's locus of control is so external that it needs a passport.

This is no time for the bogan to wake up to itself and realise that it has been living foolishly and greedily. A great injustice has been done, so the furious bogan contacts Slater & Gordon, a law firm famous for its 'no win, no fee' pricing model. This way, if Slater & Gordon takes on the case and doesn't win, it's not the bogan's fault and it doesn't have to pay. If, through some phenomenal perversion of logic, the case was to succeed, the bogan is showered in the glory that it so richly deserves. But in this case it's all a rubbish bogan daydream, as there is little chance that Slater & Gordon would bother with a case weaker than Richard Wilkins's one-liners.

Something that will bother with it is the Trashmedia Kraken. After filming the bogan walking along a stormy shoreline, staring balefully out to sea, *Today Tonight* and/or *A Current Affair* will carefully craft a stirring piece of journalism that combines agenda-driven editing of a GE Money spokesperson with touching vision of the bogan's children staring sadly at the corner of the rumpus room where the 458-inch 3D LCD LED HD television used to be. Justice will thus be done.

Patience and the bogan

Julian Rotter, the esteemed psychologist behind the Social Learning Theory, also handed on the torch of boganic illumination to one of his students. In his capacity as a professor at Ohio State University, Rotter taught a young man named Walter Mischel, and it turned out that Walter had an almost psychic connection to the lizard brain of the bogan.

In the late 1960s Mischel conducted what came to be known as the 'marshmallow experiment', which involved taking four-year-old children into a room one at a time and giving them a marshmallow. The experimenter then excused themselves from the room, saying that they had to run an errand. While the child was told that it was free to eat its marshmallow immediately, it was told that if it waited until the experimenter returned, it would receive an additional marshmallow. Alone in the room, the child's mind would wander, with the sweet sugary goodness of the marshmallow ever so tempting.

Some of the kids jammed their marshmallows in their mouths pretty much straightaway; some waited patiently for a few minutes or so before giving in, and some toughed it out until the experimenter returned, eyeballing their future treat serenely. The kids were kept track of for the next fifteen years, and their marshmallow performance was matched up against SAT (university entry) tests at the end of their secondary schooling. As it turned out, the kids who couldn't wait to eat their marshmallow did very poorly on their SAT tests, which measure reading, mathematics and writing ability. Those few minutes spent in a room with a marshmallow at age four turned out to be twice as effective at predicting a person's SAT scores as an IQ test. The most patient third of the children with their marshmallow averaged a score of 652 on the maths component of the SAT, compared with just 528 for the least patient third. What does this tell us? The impulsive, impatient child, regardless of its theoretical intelligence, is almost certain to grow into an impulsive, impatient bogan.

The four-year-old future bogan's refusal to do itself a favour and restrain its urges for its own good is the start of a pattern that marketers help to perpetuate throughout its lifespan. Crazy John's — though never confirmed by psychologists as being truly crazy — has become a giant on the Australian telecommunications landscape thanks to frenetic advertisements that promise the bogan an upmarket new mobile phone without delay, FOR ZERO DOLLARS. Sure, if the bogan waited until it had the money up front it would save on expensive interest repayments, and likely be able to negotiate a better price (or a superior marshmallow). But that is not the way of the bogan.

While the bogan refuses to be patient or modest, it remains convinced that none of the consequences of its actions are its fault. It will expertly team its inability to delay gratification with its trusty external locus of control and create a blame-deflecting fortress that ensures no lessons get learned.

Fight-or-flight response

In 1929 the English cricket team beat Australia 4–1 in The Ashes series. This was humiliating for the bogan's ancestors, who were faced with the choice of running away from the national disgrace or punching any smug Englishman who tried to give the ancestral bogan shit for it. Also in 1929, an American physiologist named

Walter Cannon was studying various animals, including cats, to discover more about how they responded to distressing or threatening situations. Cannon coined the animals' response as the 'fight-or-flight' mechanism, alleging that non-winged animals are capable of becoming airborne if sufficiently fearful. His findings are crucial to understanding the ways of the bogan, who will periodically find itself in conflict as a result of its previously discussed traits of impulsiveness and unaccountability.

Thanks to Cannon's work, we now understand what happens when the bogan senses danger (in the form of a wild animal, brandished pint glass or larger bogan with more tribal tattoos than it). The bogan's mental and emotional state has a major impact on its body, with effects including the excitation of the sympathetic division of the autonomic nervous system. This causes changes in the bogan's muscles, increased release of adrenaline and elevated blood pressure, perspiration and heart rate. The bogan then has to decide: does it try to punch on, or does it flee?

Bogans being bogans, the response is quite predictable. With its need to always be an inappropriate recipient of a 'harden the fuck up' critique from bystanders, the bogan proceeds to fight. It will fight against its immediate threat, it will fight against the rules of whatever establishment it is located in, and it will fight against the faint whimper of common sense emanating from deep within its brain stem. So, when the smarmy Englishman informed the ancestral bogan back in 1929 that Australia and its cricket team were shit, the bogan punched him in the jaw, then kicked him in the groin, then spat on him, then got arrested. This boganic reaction has continued ever since, in response to a bewildering array of minor provocations. During that Ashes series a young batsman named Don scored his first century, and his subsequent centuries over the next nineteen years are believed to have saved the lives of countless people who were prone to enraging the bogan.

The bogan has become so fond of the bodily state of maxtreme fight-readiness that it wants to feel that way even when no

Sorry, this was the best our publisher could come up with.

threats are present. Its gravitation towards massive cans of energy drink allows the bogan to trick its body into believing that it is permanently in a state of psychological arousal, replete with heart palpitations, muscle tension and disorganised speech patterns. Indeed, the bogan has evolved to become so extreme that it no longer has any regular use for the 'flight' component of its inherited instincts. To cope with this, the bogan will intermittently book flights to Phuket, where it can pick fights with other bogans on neutral turf and talk about how it wants to learn Muay Thai. This is known as the 'flight-and-fight' tourism package.

Uncertainty avoidance/ tolerance of ambiguity

If there's one thing for certain about the bogan, it's that it likes certainty. It requires its franchised movies and TV shows to clearly inform it of who the good guy is and who the victor is. Anything more ambiguous bores the bogan, with its attention span entirely unwilling to evaluate for itself, or be patient enough to wait for revelation further down the line.

Generally speaking, the world is kind to the bogan's need for certainty. The Australian media feeds the bogan emphatic seven-second soundbites that keep the bogan certain through even the most confusing of times. *Today Tonight* is also valuable, letting the bogan know who to love and who to hate. *MasterChef* provides 'emotion drums' to help the bogan be certain that something significant is about to happen. But in August and September 2010 this ozone layer of certainty around the bogan broke down.

Generally by dinner time on the evening of a federal election, the bogan is able to loudly proclaim the single, one-sentence reason why the winner won. But 2010 was different — the bogan was torn between lunging into its shallow toolbox of slogans for 'stop the boats', 'our taxpayer dollars' or 'never trust the pollies'. But it didn't know what to do, and became increasingly angry about the lack of a victory that it could either praise or deride. It took more than a fortnight before the bogan could be put out of its misery, and resume viewing the Australian landscape in the pixellated, black-and-white manner which keeps things nice and straightforward.

Eventually the bogan rediscovered its footing, briefly returning to its redhead jokes before abandoning politics in the lead-up to the AFL grand final. While grand finals can have their twists and turns, the bogan knows that a couple of hours later it will be able to experience the certainty of a victorious team being showered in streamers and tickertape. Again, this certainty did not arrive as anticipated, with the game ending in a draw. Bogan confusion manifested itself as pure fury. At the final siren, Collingwood captain Nick Maxwell — who was married while wearing thongs in Byron Bay in 2009 — declared the century-long policy of a grand final replay 'an absolute joke', with numerous players having to reschedule their trips to Bali.

The bogan's distaste for ambiguity doesn't just render it an irritating presence in any room; research has also suggested that intolerance of ambiguity is connected with broader themes. Furnham (1995) noted that open-mindedness, which has been equated with tolerance for ambiguity, may be a predisposition to critical thinking (Facione, Facione & Sanchez, 1994). If presented with the previous sentence, the bogan will become agitated once it encounters the term 'may be'. For certain.

New experiences

While the bogan will tell you that it has an acute understanding of the 'real world', every now and then new information will make its way into the bogan's immediate vicinity. This information can vary immensely in its nature and relevance, which is an important reason why the bogan has developed highly sophisticated psychological mechanisms to ward off anything that it doesn't already know and agree with.

Swiss developmental psychologist Jean Piaget pioneered constructivist theory, which described the mechanisms by which knowledge is internalised by learners. While Piaget's work focused primarily on children, the bogan's general lack of psychological development beyond early adolescence means that the work is highly relevant to understanding the bogan.

According to Piaget, individuals construct new knowledge from their experiences via two processes: accommodation and assimilation. Accommodation involves the individual expanding or adjusting its ideas about the world around it, so that the newly encountered piece of knowledge can fit into the mental landscape. Assimilation, on the other hand, involves incorporating the new piece of knowledge into the individual's pre-existing mental framework without making any alteration to the framework.

Due to the fact that the bogan already knows everything, it will go with the assimilation technique pretty much every time. The prospect that the bogan may have been wrong, or only partially informed, about something induces an intolerable level of terror and/or self-awareness in the bogan, meaning that the accommodation method is to be avoided at all costs. But this is not easy. We live in the information age, and the bogan faces a constant battle to shoehorn an unpredictable deluge of information into the narrow mental trench it elects to reside in.

In a bid to prevent the world around it from presenting too many hard-to-assimilate situations, the bogan keeps its media consumption limited to things it already knows and shows it always agrees with. Particularly important for bogan psychological validation is the Trashmedia Kraken, which, via the well-developed *Today Tonight* and *A Current Affair* tentacles, feeds the bogan a high-kilojoule, low-nutrient syrup of feel-good stories in well-worn templates, and outrage stories about things the bogan already hates. One of the few ways in which a bogan will change its ideas about something is if a celebrity has decided to do it too, but this is because the bogan's greater need is to assimilate any new celebrity details into its larger framework of celebrities always being awesome.

Goal setting

Setting goals is an important and beneficial thing to do. It allows people to focus on what they hope to achieve, providing a sense of direction and purpose. Goal setting is a major component of personal development literature, and personal development literature tends to feature prominently on the boganic bookshelf. One of the bogan's more impressive mind tricks is to convince itself that purchasing yet another self-help book is approximately as good as reading it and implementing its suggestions, because surely nobody but a go-getter would own double-digit quantities of books whose titles proclaim to the bogan that it can achieve anything it wants.

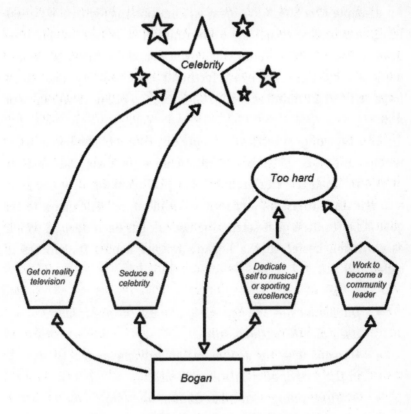

Figure 12.1 Visualise and succeed, bogan style

Management consultant George Doran was amongst the first to crystallise goal setting into something more concrete, proposing that goals should be 'S.M.A.R.T'.

- *Specific* — target a specific area for improvement.
- *Measurable* — quantify or at least suggest an indicator of progress.
- *Assignable* — specify who will do it.
- *Realistic* — state what results can realistically be achieved, given available resources.
- *Time-related* — specify when the result(s) can be achieved.

An example of a S.M.A.R.T. goal is 'I am unhappy with my fitness level, and resolve to get my 5 km running time from 22 minutes down to 20 minutes. To do this, I will run three times per week, doing a 5 km time trial every fortnight. By the third time trial I hope to be at 21 minutes, with 20 minutes to occur 12 weeks from now.'

This type of goal setting is deeply disturbing to the bogan, who is reluctant to consider *how* it will achieve its goals and whether or not its goals are the product of logical thought. The bogan is also reluctant to assign any form of deadline or benchmark to its goal. As a result, a goal-setting framework has been devised which caters much better to the bogan's unique needs. Its process is called D.U.M.B.

- **D**uplicitous — *the bogan's goal must involve it kidding itself about its true nature.*
- **U**nrealistic — *the goal must be maxtreme and/or celeb, in the face of all available evidence.*
- **M**alfunctioning — *it must contain multiple opportunities for the bogan to abandon it.*
- **B**oganic — *at the end of the ordeal, the bogan must be more of a bogan than previously.*

The bogan will commonly articulate a D.U.M.B. goal in a manner such as 'I've decided that I want to maybe run in the Olympics and probably look really fit. A new model of Nike MaxxShoxx shoes has just been released, so I'll buy them and I think they could make me run really fast at the park. I'll train 6 hours a day, probably.'

The psychology of boganic goal setting is largely motivated by the bogan's desire to loudly proclaim its goals to others. The satisfaction that it derives from hearing its own voice verbalising lofty ambitions is considerable, and the nods and squawks of approval from other bogans represents rich reward. There is generally little more than a token attempt to actually achieve the goal, as the goal's impracticality and difficulty soon become apparent, and the bogan does not wish to inconvenience itself in order to achieve. Fortunately, other bogans are unlikely to check to see whether the previously proclaimed goal is on track, because doing such a thing would risk return scrutiny of their own shirked targets.

The sound of bogans proclaiming goals reaches fever pitch in the first seven days of each calendar year, before falling away to a more moderate level, punctuated by the purchase of additional unread self-help books, throughout the remainder of the year.

The clever bogan

The bogan will tell you that it doesn't like intellectuals. Intellectuals are poofs because they think they're better than the bogan, despite the intellectual having an inferior track record in train surfing, Jägerbomb gulping and quoting from *Two And A Half Men*. But despite its hatred of critical or abstract thought, the bogan nonetheless needs to see itself as very intelligent.

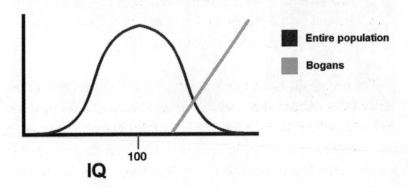

Figure 12.2 Bogan IQ, as estimated by bogans

The lack of life achievements that require high intelligence serves as a considerable obstacle to the bogan being a believer in its own brilliance, and causes the bogan to search for an alternate form of evidence. IQ tests have been popular for over 80 years as a pleasing way to quantify a narrow measure of mental capacity, and the idea of a simple test to substitute for tangible life achievement is immensely appealing to the bogan's ego. The advent of the Internet opened up the world of IQ tests to the bogan, and it now has a clearer idea of its intelligence than ever before.

As soon as Channel Nine does another National IQ test we will update this edition with the latest data. Until then, watching *Who Wants to Be a Millionaire?* is the perfect testing ground for all bogans.

Molly and Plucka prepare for the government's tax forum.

CONCLUSION

At the end of reading this book, you will hopefully have a greater knowledge of all things bogan. Depending on how you rate the modern bogan, you are likely to find yourself in one of two situations: fantasising about becoming a nihilist because civilisation as we know it has reached its nadir; or becoming a rabid anti-bogan activist by registering your interest with a local independent record store. Either path is a journey to betterment. In the unlikely event that you are still a bogan, we can only hope that your addled brain is not impervious to change. In fact, the very purpose of this entire book is to educate, inform and entertain people about the perils of boganity. The ideas presented herein are not meant to be a scathing diatribe on the bogan malaise, despite consistently alluding to its hopeful demise. It is a recognition that, whether or not we like it, the boganic contagion has infested our society, and only by analysing and thinking about it can we find a suitable vaccine. Alexander Fleming, the Scottish immunologist who invented penicillin, also populated his universe with bacteria and viruses in order to discover the world's most effective antibiotic, thereby saving millions of lives over the years. Far from being utilitarian life savers, however, we merely aim to acknowledge and study the effects of the bogan on our everyday lives and attempt to meaningfully exist despite its suffocating impositions. Understanding its myriad behaviours and motivations is therefore paramount to its potential eradication. Or, as in the case of Luke Skywalker's father — you could join the dark side.

Image credits

Pages 5, 9, 11, 14 © iStockphoto; Page 17 © Newspix/Bill Leak; Pages 19, 22, 25 © iStockphoto; Page 20 © Newspix/Marie Nirme; Page 26 © Newspix/News Ltd; Page 28 © Newspix/News Ltd; Page 29 © Newspix/Simon Dean; Page 31 © Newspix/Mark Williams; Page 50 © iStockphoto; Page 53 © Newspix/Tracee Lea; Page 54 © Newspix/Chris Scott; Pages 59, 64 © iStockphoto; Page 66 © Newspix/ John Grainger; Page 73 © Bettmann/Corbis; Page 75 © Bettmann/Corbis; Page 76 © Newspix/Shaney Balcombe; Page 78 © Roger Ressmeyer/Corbis; Page 79 © Newspix/Katrina Tepper; Page 81 © Newspix/Andrew Henshaw; Page 88 © iStockphoto; Page 89 © Newspix/Geoff Ward; Page 91 © Newspix; Page 92 © iStockphoto; Page 104 © Newspix/Damian Shaw; Page 109 © Newspix/Craig Greenhill; Page 114 © Newspix/Tim Clayton; Page 116 © Newspix/Chris Scott; Page 121 © iStockphoto; Page 124 © Newspix/Melanie Russell; Page 133 © Newspix/Tim Marsden; Page 134 © Newspix/Gary Ramage; Page 135 © Newspix/ Colin Murty; Page 137 © Newspix; Page 138 © Newspix/News Ltd (all); Page 139 © Newspix/Adam Knott (Keating), © Newspix/News Ltd (Menzies), © Newspix/ Russell Shakespeare (Waugh); Page 140 © Newspix/Kym Smith (Rudd), © Newspix/News Ltd (Hawke), © Newspix/Bruce Howard (Howard); Page 141 © Newspix/TV screen grab; Page 142 © iStockphoto; Page 146 © Newspix/Michael Perini; Page 151 © Newspix/Adam Ward; Page 159 © Newspix/Chris Scott; Page 169 © Newspix/Jeff Herbert; Page 170 © Newspix/David Caird; Page 173 © Newspix/TV screen grab; Page 176 © Newspix/J. J. Sassine; Page 179 © Newspix/ Igor Saktor; Page 185 © Newspix/Glenn Hampson; Page 189 © Newspix/Brett Costello; Page 190 © iStockphoto; Page 194 © Newspix/Mike Keating; Page 200 © Newspix/News Ltd; Page 211 © Newspix/Cameron Richardson; Page 212 © Newspix/Adam Taylor; Page 215 © iStockphoto; Page 220 © Newspix/Michael Perini; Page 223 © iStockphoto; Page 226 © Newspix/Adam Armstrong; Page 230 © Newspix/media hand-out; Page 232 © Newspix/supplied by Channel Ten; Page 237 © iStockphoto; Page 241 © Newspix/Brad Hunter; Pages 250, 253, 259, 263 © iStockphoto; Page 268 © Newspix/Sam Ruttyn; Page 271 © Newspix/Brad Marsellos; Page 276 © Newspix/Nicki Connolly; Pages 285, 290, 302, 315, 321 © iStockphoto; Page 328 © Newspix/Chris Scott; Page 329 © Newspix/Gary Ramage; Page 330 © Newspix/Chris Scott.